SELLING OUTSOURCING SERVICES IN THE DIGITAL AGE

GRANT S. LANGE

ISBN: 978-0-692-13951-6

This book is dedicated to my father.

He had a true passion for life and was a respected leader and role model both personally and professionally. One of my childhood dreams was to make my father proud of me, and to this day, some 40 years after his tragic death, I aspire to make that dream a reality. Unfortunately, the most important lesson he taught me was how short and precious life truly is. I only wish we had been given more time together.

TABLE OF CONTENTS

INTRODUCTION

Go Digital or Go Home

Fortune 500 companies in all industries are laser-focused on the pace of innovation, the deployment of new and disruptive technologies, and the urgency to digitally transform their business operations and enhance the customer experience. Make no mistake about it, we are experiencing the fastest technological evolution in history and that evolution is built upon four key pillars—cloud, mobile, the Internet of things (IoT), and artificial intelligence (AI). Pat Gelsinger, the CEO of VMware, defines these pillars as, "the four superpowers of technology—cloud is supercomputing power at unlimited scale, mobile is unlimited reach, IoT is unlimited access, and AI is unrivaled intelligence."

"Digitize or Die" has become a frequently utilized tagline and all of the brand name strategy, consulting, and IT services providers have evolved their business models to assist their clients in commencing the digital journey. Success will be predicated upon bringing together customers, content, commerce, and community through a variety of channels that may include: (1) crowdsourcing; (2) mobile; (3) social; (4) everything as a service; (5) the sharing economy; and (6) emerging technologies including robotic process automation (RPA), artificial intelligence (AI), cloud, and augmented reality (AR). At the end of the road, a successful digital environment can be characterized as one that is collaborative, customer-centric, visionary, enabled by technology, driven by data, focused on growth, and most importantly, agile.

Given that legacy outsourcing agreements are generally not built on a foundation of innovation and transformation, you might think the digital journey would have a detrimental impact on the outsourcing industry. However, the opposite has occurred as companies have embraced outsourcing as a mechanism by which they can increase their pace of innovation; support their strategic objectives; reap the benefits of a digital-friendly environment; and still achieve the cost-savings from the pre-digital era. Digital technologies, specifically AI and RPA, are changing the game and unlocking value from traditional outsourcing agreements, the key purpose of which was to maximize cost savings by exploiting labor arbitrage.

The deployment of a digital delivery model will also have a substantial impact on the legacy outsourcing pricing model as consumers generally value physical goods more than their digital counterparts. In an article published by the Journal of Consumer Research in 2018, Ozgun Atasoy and Carey Morewedge attempted to address this phenomenon. After conducting a series of experiments involving movies, novels, textbooks, and photos, they concluded, "Digital goods do not facilitate the same feeling of ownership that physical goods do. Because we cannot touch, and hold, and control digital goods in the way we interact with physical goods, we feel an impaired sense of ownership for digital goods. They never quite feel like they are ours."

While I readily acknowledge a book or movie may be different than personnel deployed to deliver services under an outsourcing agreement, service providers will have to redesign their pricing model to be consistent with the value they bring to bear during the delivery term. By focusing on value delivered versus the number of human full time equivalent (FTE) personnel deployed, service providers will weaken the client perception that once the robots are deployed, the services should be free. Although free may be a bit over-reaching, clients will expect, as reflected in the graph below, to see a substantial reduction in fees over the delivery term and benefit from the value realized from the deployment of automation.

FTE VERSUS RPA FEE STRUCTURE

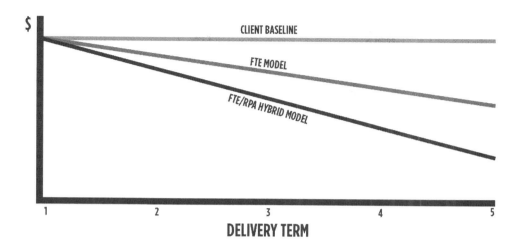

What is Robotic Process Automation?

Simply put, software robots are programmed (the RPA software allows the user to map the end-to-end business process flow in the application) to execute manual, repetitive, and rules-based processes and tasks at a fraction of the cost of their human counterparts. The automation software operates on top of the existing applications and can easily be integrated into a legacy system. Just like a human, the robot navigates through the process and various applications and can access external websites to obtain data or conduct quality checks. The robot population is multiplying—Transparency Market Research reports that the market for RPA is forecast to reach $5B by 2020, a 60 percent annual growth rate.

Historically, the key question regarding automation was whether robots would compete with workers and eliminate their jobs or assist them in delivering value. The answer lies somewhere in the middle as many companies have been able to deploy robots to complete precise and repetitive tasks while allowing their human counterparts time to focus on activities that require the problem-solving capabilities of the human brain. Deploying robots does not guarantee success as Tesla realized when it attempted to automate the final assembly work—parts, seats, and engine installation—in its vehicle production line. Ultimately, defects caused by robots detrimentally impacted the number of cars crossing through the production line. In a message sent via Twitter, Tesla CEO Elon Musk acknowledged, "Yes, excessive automation at Tesla was a mistake...Humans are underrated."

To be clear, the Tesla example is not the norm, as automation in many industries—mining, automotive, construction, garment, and trucking—has resulted in pay cuts for low-skilled machine operators and the complete elimination of certain jobs in the manufacturing process. Conversely, the deployment of automation in other industries has resulted in improved safety and productivity, as well as opportunities for robots to serve in an assistant-like capacity for their human counterparts.

For those of you who fear robots, your interaction with them can be limited. Robots can run unattended on a virtual machine in a data center (back office robots) or can share the same desktop with a human agent (front office robots) who controls where and when the robot is deployed. Front office robots are best used in manual, repetitive, and highly rule-based activities containing decision points that will likely require human intervention, either due to pure judgment calls or the high complexity and volatility of the process inputs. For those reasons, front office robots are best suited for help desks and call centers. Back office robots work in an unattended manner independent of any human interaction and are best used for manual, repetitive, and rule-based back office activities. Irrespective of their location, robots are not picky, can work with legacy systems, cloud, and web-based applications, and are able to read and write any kind of document.

Advantages of RPA include:

1. **Cost:** On average, a robot is a fraction of the cost of its human FTE, which is calculated as the hours worked by one employee on a full-time basis. Consider an instance where a robot can accomplish a task 20 minutes faster than a human. Over an 8-hour day, that yields 160 minutes of free time for the FTE to focus on other value-added work. Because robots never get tired or hungry, they can run 24x7 if necessary. Processing costs can be reduced significantly (anywhere from 30 to 80 percent) and the return on investment timeline is measured in months versus years.

2. **Speed:** RPA can yield a 40 percent reduction in average handling/ cycle time and a corresponding increase and focus on customer outcomes.

3. **Accuracy:** All human error is eliminated. If a transaction does not fit within the rules or parameters for which it has been programmed, the robot sets aside the transaction for human intervention. Quality is job one and service levels are set at the upper limits and achieved on a recurring basis.

4. **Scalability:** A robotic workforce never gets tired, can scale with minimal impact and predictability, and can be trained concurrently. When volumes increase, quality remains constant.

5. **Analytics:** Real-time performance data on volume and exceptions will facilitate optimization of systems and processes and yield continuous improvement.

6. **Customer Satisfaction:** The robots focus on the rules while the humans focus on the customer-centric portion of the process.

7. **Training:** The typical costs associated with turnover are reduced and institutional knowledge does not leave the building via attrition.

8. **Employee Satisfaction:** Employee morale will increase given the focus on customer-facing and value-added activities.

9. **Compliance:** Each action the robot takes is monitored and recorded so audit and compliance requirements are more efficient and cost-effective. There is also a reduced risk of theft or misuse of information.

What is the Internet of Things?

The Internet of things is the network of physical devices including vehicles, home appliances, thermostats, lighting, media, and security systems, and other items that are embedded with electronics, software, sensors, actuators, and connectivity which permits them to connect and exchange data. This connectivity allows for the direct integration of physical devices into computer-based systems, resulting in convenience, efficiency improvements, cost-savings, and reduced levels of engagement with humans. Gartner estimates that the number of IoT devices (excluding smartphones, tablets, and computers) will exceed 30 billion by 2020. From a business process outsourcing perspective, the deployment of IoT-enabled devices will yield real-time and customer-rich data that service providers can utilize to drive innovation and optimize the delivery environment.

What is the Cloud?

Cloud computing is the on-demand delivery of computing power, database storage, applications, and other IT resources delivered through a cloud services platform over the Internet with pay-as-you-go pricing. The cloud services provider owns and maintains the network-connected hardware that is required for these services. The benefits of cloud computing include: a significant reduction in capital expenses (there is no need to invest in data centers and servers) and operating expenses (you only pay for the computing resources you actually consume); the optimization of infrastructure capacity; the ability to scale up or down with limited notice; access to unlimited computing power with the click of a button; freedom from managing infrastructure; the ability to deploy applications globally with lower latency (the delay before a transfer of data begins following an instruction for its transfer); and a renewed focus on customers and quality.

At a macro-level, cloud computing yields unparalleled control, flexibility and management. There are three main models for cloud computing, each of which represents a different component of the cloud computing stack. The first, Infrastructure as a Service (IaaS) provides access to networking features, hardware, and data storage space. The second, Platform as a Service (PaaS), provides a platform and the underlying infrastructure—including hardware and operating systems upon which applications can be developed, deployed, and managed. Finally, Software as a Service (SaaS), provides the user with applications that are run and managed by the cloud provider. With SaaS, the provider maintains the software and the underlying servers and operating systems upon which it is deployed, allowing the user to focus on how it will use the application.

You may be wondering how the evolution and deployment of cloud computing will impact the terms and conditions that will govern service delivery. Before the evolution of cloud computing, the service provider would generally provide the outsourced service directly from one of its data centers and would have direct control over the environment—physical security, authentication, authorization, patch management, anti-virus and malware management, auditing, disaster recovery, confidentiality, security incidents, and network management—from which the services would be delivered. In the current environment, clients are generally contracting directly with the largest cloud providers—Amazon Web Services, Microsoft, Google, and Oracle—for the delivery of their cloud computing services and the service provider is not a party to that agreement. Even if the service provider is contracting for cloud services on behalf of the client, the client's data will reside in data centers over which the service provider has no physical control. While the service provider may have responsibility for the management and optimization of the client's cloud services, it is important to be mindful of the service provider's level of control over the data center when negotiating disaster recovery, audit, security, and availability terms and conditions. As we will discuss later, neither party to an outsourcing agreement should be held accountable for risks outside of its control and that core contracting principle certainly applies in this area.

What is Artificial Intelligence?

In lay-person terms, AI refers to anything a computer can do that formerly would have been considered a job for a human. Like RPA, AI can function in a stand-alone capacity or assist its human counterparts in making better and more informed decisions. Think of AI as intelligent software with human-like capabilities, some of which include: identifying images, recognizing handwriting, completing half-written words in text messages, answering questions through your smart phone or smart speaker, plotting the most expeditious driving or walking route, recognizing familiar faces at your office building or front door, completing your playlist, presenting ads for products that are consistent with your buying habits, powering autonomous vehicles, predicting the outcome of a legal dispute, or prescribing the appropriate treatment protocol for a cancer patient.

Early efforts to advance AI were constrained by programmers' inability to write code that considered all of the possibilities in the human decision making or problem-solving process; however, machine learning techniques eliminated the need to manage those endless possibilities by using statistical analysis to make predictions. The only limitation on machine learning techniques was harnessing the vast amounts of data and processing power required to make more accurate predictions. With endless streams of application data and unlimited processing power readily available from the largest cloud providers, machine-learning algorithms, particularly a type known as neural networks, can be easily established. This level of accessibility has put AI at the top of every company's technology wish list. Research firm IDC predicts that by 2021, organizations will spend $52.5 billion annually on AI related products. The return on that investment will come primarily from the value and efficiencies realized—matching products to customers or treatment protocols to patients— in the accuracy of the predictions. PwC estimates that AI could contribute up to $15.7 trillion to the global economy in 2030. Like its RPA counterpart, the AI market will grow exponentially in the coming years.

Think of a neural network as a human-brain-inspired computer that is able to learn without being programmed with any rules or logical relationships. For example, programmers start by identifying and feeding a large body of data into a neural network to train it to recognize certain images. Once the network has digested the data, the programmers feed in a new set of data that may or not be consistent with the images contained in the initial data set. The objective is for the neural network to be able to distinguish between those images which are consistent with the initial data set and those which are not. While recognizing images is an example of a simple neural network, imagine harnessing that same intellectual horsepower to determine treatment protocols for cancer patients that will yield the highest survival rates. Ultimately, the success of a neural network can be gauged by the quality and accuracy of the predictions it makes.

From a more traditional outsourcing perspective, AI can be deployed to function as a virtual IT help-desk which can answer calls, respond to email, and remediate a substantial portion of support tickets without any human intervention. Like its RPA counterparts, AI will dictate a substantial change in the FTE-based legacy outsourcing delivery model.

What Exactly Has Changed? Can't We Just Add a Short Appendix?

At its core, a legacy outsourcing agreement consists of two key components, a monthly managed services fee which is based upon the number of FTEs that will be deployed to deliver the base services (which will be clearly defined in the statement of work) and a service level matrix which contains the quality and performance targets that are expected to be achieved and against which the service provider will be measured during the delivery term. Over time, the monthly managed service fee will gradually decrease as the service provider achieves greater productivity and the service level targets will gradually increase based upon the continuous improvement provisions contained in the service level methodology. The size of the base services team is dependent upon the projected transaction volume (expressed in terms of incidents, tickets, or calls) that they will be responsible for handling. To the extent that the projected transaction volume should increase or decrease beyond a contractually-stipulated dead-band (generally plus or minus 10 percent of the baseline transaction volume), the price will automatically adjust based upon a variable fee structure stipulated in the agreement.

The legacy outsourcing model is predicated upon pushing the limits of labor arbitrage (utilizing an offshore, less expensive, highly skilled, educated, and English-speaking workforce) to the maximum extent possible. The introduction of RPA and AI will yield a hybrid workforce where humans and robots work jointly to deliver value. While the robots and humans can certainly co-exist peacefully, the underlying terms and conditions contained in a legacy outsourcing agreement do not contemplate the deployment of robots or neural networks into the delivery model. To that end, the terms and conditions in those agreements must be amended to accommodate a hybrid workforce and adding a brief appendix will not suffice as the changes required are significant. To facilitate making the necessary changes, the following questions should be asked:

1. Will there be an assumption that automation will achieve the anticipated benefit? No matter what?

2. If all human error is eliminated with the deployment of RPA, is it legitimate to expect that all service levels will be set at 100 percent?

3. Is there any substantive impact on the delivery model and price if a material business event (acquisition or divestiture) occurs?

4. Why pay for a human when a robot can get the job done in a much more timely, quality, and cost-effective manner?

5. If the robots can work 30 percent faster than their human counterparts, will those savings be reflected on a dollar-for-dollar basis in the pricing model?

6. Given that the humans will focus on customer satisfaction, is it safe to assume that the service provider will place more fees at risk tied to the achievement of customer satisfaction service levels?

7. Will there be a transition period during which there will be redundancy between the robots and their human peers?

8. Will the savings or productivity targets be guaranteed?

9. Will the choice of method (extent and type of automation) by which any guaranteed productivity is achieved over the delivery term reside solely with the service provider?

10. Given that the robots can easily scale to accommodate increases in volume, will the agreement stipulate that service quality will remain constant over the delivery term?

11. Will there be any limitations placed upon the composition of the service provider's delivery team—x percent robots versus y percent humans?

12. Why should the client wait for an annual delivery review when the benefits from new technologies can be immediately recognized?

13. Will the deployment of RPA automatically yield an improvement in service levels?

14.   What about exception cases that require human intervention?

15.   Will availability, reporting, and monitoring improve?

16.   Will there be a focus on speed to resolution and accuracy without a corresponding increase in price?

17.   How will the deployment of AI and RPA impact the allocation of blame and the consequences of failure?

18.   What happens if the robots go rogue and provide an answer that is sub-optimal?

19.   What if the robots destroy data or fail to comply with protocols that results in breaches of confidential and personal information, security violations, and facility and audit deficiencies?

20.   What type of oversight will exist for the RPA and which party will be liable if the robots are at fault for a breach?

21.   What if the robots lock the humans out of the system? Are we losing control? Is the Terminator coming?

22.   Which party owns the software, algorithms, and process automations?

23.   What about competitor use of the algorithms?

24.   Will the focus be on best-in-class/industry process automatons that are utilized by many or a strong desire for IP ownership?

25.   Should the process automations be owned by the Service Provider so they can be aggregated and fine-tuned to leverage best practices and maximize efficiency?

26.   Is there any competitive advantage to the client owning the process automations?

27. What about third party IP that may be embedded in the automations?

28. Do transition, termination rights and termination assistance provisions change as a result of deploying RPA or AI?

29. Given the pace at which the robots can learn, is a lengthy transition period necessary?

30. Do the robots continue to function during a force majeure event? Are there any instances in which they don't show up for work on time? Are they impacted by business continuity events?

31. What about the notification period for a termination event?

32. What impact will RPA have on termination fees?

33. Will termination fees specifically include the cost associated with configuring and implementing the robots?

34. What about the duration of termination assistance services?

35. What happens to the RPA software and all underlying tools after an expiration or termination event?

36. Does the deployment of RPA or AI impact compliance with laws and regulatory requirements?

37. Will the client maintain responsibility for the build specifications, maintenance, and management of the robots?

38. Is the scope of the benchmarking provision broad enough (Does it include the method of service delivery or is it simply focused on price?) to trigger a benchmarking condition which would facilitate or even dictate the deployment of RPA, AI, or other generally available emerging technologies?

39. Will the benchmarking provision extend beyond a pricing exercise and include service level achievement and the method (FTE versus RPA) by which the services are being delivered?

40. Given the rapid pace at which technology is evolving, will the frequency of benchmarking exercises be accelerated?

41. Can the benchmarking effort include the pace at which the service provider is deploying new technologies in relation to the other engagements in the sample?

42. Who will absorb the on-going cost associated with implementing RPA or AI and eliminating service provider personnel?

43. Is there some form of termination for convenience if the FTE count drops below a certain threshold? Should a similar standard apply for the robots?

44. What about wind-down and demobilization costs for the displaced individuals?

45. What about labor laws and a timeline for redeployment?

46. Does the pricing model need to be amended to accommodate a shift from FTE-based to transaction and outcome-based pricing?

47. Do the continuous improvement provisions need to include RPA and other new and emerging technologies including Artificial Intelligence and Cloud?

As the demand for AI and RPA increases, service providers will be forced to adapt their staffing, pricing, delivery, and contracting models. From a contract and pricing perspective, the client expectation is that an RPA/FTE hybrid workforce will yield lower fees, greater productivity, and higher service levels over the agreement term.

Selling Outsourcing Services in the Digital Age

The deployment, RPA, AI, and other emerging technologies will require service providers to do the following:

- Target capital investments, acquisition plans, and organizational changes to reflect that the limits of labor arbitrage have been reached in many geographies and an extensive off-shore delivery network may no longer be a competitive advantage.
- Deploy new technologies as they become generally available in the marketplace and focus on innovation—better, faster, and cheaper—over the delivery term.
- Adjust the size, skillset, and geographic location of the delivery workforce.
- Deliver a more robust set of services to mitigate the commodity-like nature of a robot and achieve market differentiation.
- Acknowledge and accept higher service levels and productivity targets over the delivery term.
- Change the FTE-based pricing model to one which is a transaction or outcome-based.
- Amend contractual provisions to reflect the robotic component of the workforce.
- Re-train its personnel to focus on higher value transactions and more frequent customer engagement.
- Combat the client expectation that, "once robots do everything, the services should be free," by commanding a price that is consistent with the value proposition it brings to bear over the delivery term.
- Break the link between the number of FTEs deployed and price.

The deployment of RPA, AI, and other emerging technologies will require clients to do the following:

- Structure its outsourcing engagements to be transaction or outcome based (per ticket, per server. per invoice, per claim processed, or per pizza sold).
- Seek terms for outsourcing engagements that are as short as possible with the ability to terminate, pivot, or lift and shift scope with limited financial impact.

- Strive for a menu-driven pay-as-you-go model than can easily accommodate significant increases or decreases in volume.
- Focus on innovation and the rapid deployment of technology as a key buyer value when selecting an outsourcing services provider.
- Expect significant cost savings (robots are much cheaper and more efficient than their human counterparts) with guaranteed increases in productivity and service levels.
- Demand a preference for automation—why pay for a human when a robot can accomplish the same task in a more timely, quality, and cost-effective manner?
- Rely less on customization and more on best-in-class automation.
- Focus less on IP ownership so long as a perpetual license is granted that extends beyond any termination or expiration event.

To succeed in the digital outsourcing age, service providers will have to innovate, transform, and digitize to maintain their existing delivery footprint. Even with those changes, the core principle and foundation upon which a legacy outsourcing agreement is based—delivering the outsourced application, infrastructure, or business process in a timely, quality, and cost-effective manner—remains unchanged. To that end, a focus on basic blocking and tackling—a narrowly tailored statement of work that is free from ambiguity, clarity on the roles and responsibilities of the parties, a robust list of any assumptions or dependencies upon which the service provider's delivery is conditioned, change control and governance processes that are strictly followed, and acceptance criteria that are objective, measurable, and verifiable—is still mandatory.

When the first version of this book was published in 2015, innovation was certainly a key buyer value but the value proposition being asserted by service providers in this area was difficult to measure. The advancements in RPA and AI and their general availability in the marketplace and integration into the delivery model have certainly facilitated that objective. Commitments tied to the deployment of RPA and AI are easy to measure and innovation obligations will be much more substantive and measurable in the outsourcing agreement of the future. Simply agreeing to place 12 percent of fees at risk tied to the achievement of critical service levels and guaranteeing conservative productivity targets on an annual basis will no longer be sufficient; an on-going and robust commitment to innovation will be required as we enter the next evolution of outsourcing.

This book will reinforce the requirement for basic blocking and tackling but will also focus on fine-tuning and amending a typical legacy outsourcing agreement to account for the deployment of digital technologies, specifically RPA and artificial intelligence. With that said, let's focus on preparing for success as we commence the negotiation process.

Preparing for Success or the Consequences of Failure

Preparing for the consequences of failure is not the best way for a strategic supplier and trusted advisor to kick off a multiyear outsourcing relationship with a client. And yet, it is a familiar storyline. When negotiating the terms and conditions for an outsourcing agreement, it is typical for days, weeks, and months to pass of deal shaping, downward pricing pressure, multiple down-selections, decision gates, and checkpoints, and contentious and parallel negotiations with multiple vendors. During this period, significant financial resources are wasted, and service commencement and business case benefit realization dates are deferred. The net effect is that the current sales cycle and procurement approach for large outsourcing engagements is inefficient across time, quality, and cost parameters, and an industry shift is inevitable.

Irrespective of the role you play and the party you represent at the negotiation table, I challenge you to think about your most recent outsourcing services negotiation. Was the focus on failure—hashing out the terms and conditions that define the rights and obligations of the respective parties upon termination of the agreement, establishing indemnity obligations and liability limits related to damages claims, negotiating the percentage of fees at risk and defining how many critical service level defaults yield a termination right, or establishing the procedures for and implications of an unfavorable benchmarking report? Or, was your negotiation geared toward success—focused on those terms and conditions and components of the agreement that facilitate timely, quality, and cost-effective delivery, collaboration, joint ownership, and partnership between the parties? Although the answer may be both failure and success, it is easy to conclude that too much time was devoted to focusing on the consequences of failure and the allocation of blame, and not nearly enough time was spent focusing on collaboration, partnership, and success.

The irony of this ongoing dynamic is that for each contentious and heavily negotiated term and condition, a market-relevant standard exists that could easily be the departure point for negotiation. If the parties could simply acknowledge that standard, the negotiation could focus on tempering and fine-tuning those terms and conditions, service level constructs, and fee structures in a way that would yield an acceptable level of risk and reward for the parties and that would be commensurate with the underlying buyer values. Have you ever been a party to a negotiation that starts with extreme positions, is followed by minor concessions occurring over weeks or months, and concludes with a compromise position? If you have been in this situation, it is obvious that the compromise position is, for the most part, the recognized industry standard for the issue under negotiation and, frankly, the likely landing point anticipated by the parties when they began the process. It certainly raises the question: Why waste time with a series of minor concessions when you could have put your best foot forward? Wouldn't it be much more productive to immediately move to the compromise position, or at least within its relative range, and then identify a mutually agreeable option that is commensurate with the underlying nature of the solution and that meets the interests of the parties? For the golfers out there, compare this approach to surrounding the hole and then determining the line and pace necessary to sink the putt.

If the market standard is so widely recognized by clients, their counsel, third-party advisors, and service providers, then why is this glaring inefficiency and corresponding waste allowed to continue in perpetuity? The answer may be that there is no incentive for a course correction. As I like to say, it is that simple and that complex. Clients may be immature or inexperienced in outsourcing or may have read countless stories about the importance of selecting the right outsourcing vendor. These clients blindly follow their legal counsel and third-party advisor out of fear that they would select a vendor and agree on non-market-relevant terms that would yield suboptimal delivery results. Counsel and third-party advisors are constantly seeking to move the market with more favorable terms and conditions for their clients and have more risk shifted squarely onto the shoulders of the clients' service providers. As for the service providers, I am unclear about their motivation for perpetuating the status quo, because they feel most of the pain in the form of increased business development costs and detrimentally impacted relationships. Maybe they are unwilling to put their best foot forward or equate doing so with some competitive disadvantage they would encounter in the negotiation process. Or maybe they feel compelled to, "play the game" because that is what they are expected to do. Thus, you see the challenge—how do you incentivize people to correct their course when they believe their pace and speed are optimal?

External counsel and third-party advisors are the catalysts for this cycle by introducing contract templates that are not balanced, that are heavily skewed in favor of the client, that are not commensurate with the market, and that do not yield an acceptable level of risk and reward for both parties to the transaction. And let's not forget about the typically open-ended time and materials billing construct under which external counsel and third-party advisors may be engaged. Although it seems as if the service providers would be the primary proponents of accepting a course change, namely, focusing on delivery capabilities and price as their competitive differentiators, that is not the case. Rather, they embrace the madness out of fear of disqualification and perpetuate these inefficiencies by accepting more risk in an effort to unseat incumbent service providers, defeat their competition, and capture market share.

Unfortunately, this dynamic can put clients in a difficult position, because they are faced with a tightrope-like balancing act on multiple fronts—undermining their relationship with their counsel and third-party advisor, or detrimentally impacting the relationship with the service provider with whom they are about to embark on a multiple-year relationship. This dynamic can also manifest itself when a client's counsel and third-party advisor are procuring an outsourcing solution that is not consistent with the client's current delivery environment and user expectations. Assuming an agreement is ultimately executed between the parties, the result is suboptimal. Relationships have been damaged, the best suited vendor has not necessarily been selected, collaboration and innovation have become an afterthought, and timely, quality, and cost-effective delivery has been compromised.

INTRODUCTION

This book is intended to ask difficult questions, to challenge the status quo, and to provide an alternative mechanism to achieve timely contract execution that can be adopted by clients, counsel, third-party advisors, and service providers. At the center of this alternative construct is acknowledgment by all parties that an accepted industry standard exists for each term in a typical outsourcing agreement. All parties to the transaction must focus on putting their best foot forward and agree that the industry standard is the starting point and departure point from a negotiation perspective. This acknowledgment drastically decreases the contract execution cycle time, because many of the multiple redline and iterative processes typically associated with an outsourcing negotiation are eliminated. This acknowledgment could take many forms, either as an industry-standard agreement or a template created by counsel, third-party advisors, and service providers that embodies the same terms. While I understand that this approach is difficult given the competing interests I previously mentioned, a change is inevitable. So, why not now?

To be clear, this acknowledgment does not mean that the negotiation is completed and we can move on to the signing ceremony. Every outsourcing transaction is different, and the underlying client buyer values, the scope of the solution procured, the extent of automation to be deployed, and the service provider delivery capabilities dictate the ultimate shape of the out-sourcing agreement. Instead, attention shifts to tempering the terms and conditions according to the underlying solution and focusing on those components of the agreement that are most critical but typically turn into afterthoughts. These components include developing a narrowly tailored statement of work that clarifies the roles and responsibilities of the parties, defining objective, measurable, and verifiable acceptance criteria and service levels, establishing a robust governance process, and documenting all key assumptions and dependencies, especially in a multivendor delivery environment. The focus on buyer values is critical. It is not uncommon for the clients' stated buyer values to be inconsistent with the negotiation approach and the terms and conditions promulgated by their counsel and third-party advisor. From my perspective, the most consistent buyer values include a vendor that can be trusted, that delivers a low-risk and quality solution, that has global delivery capability, that has a strong reference base, that can deliver on its value proposition, that focuses on innovation and continuous improvement during the delivery term, and that yields predictable results.

To reiterate, I am not suggesting that every outsourcing engagement is the same; that could not be further from the truth, given the broad scope of services outsourced in the marketplace. However, there is a core set of service-type-agnostic terms and conditions that are consistent and do not require extensive negotiation in each agreement. With this approach, the starting point focuses on tempering and fine-tuning the terms and conditions in the agreement to be commensurate with the underlying nature of the solution provided. With this shift in focus, the parties can focus on what really counts—those terms and conditions and key components of the agreement that yield timely, quality, and cost-effective delivery.

Building a Trusted Advisor Foundation

It would seem that negotiating terms and conditions governing delivery in a complex and strategic long-term outsourcing program would establish the foundation for a trusted advisor relationship between the two parties, thereby enhancing the probability of success and creating opportunities for collaboration and partnership. In practice, that is rarely the case. The most heavily negotiated terms and conditions typically set the stage for how the parties address and allocate the consequences of failure. Those items that support collaboration and partnership often seem to be afterthoughts. This failure-first sequence will have a detrimental impact upon timely, quality, and cost-effective delivery.

Ironically, during the sales cycle, discussions between the buyer and decisionmaker about the solution and underlying contractual agreement often go smoothly. The focus of these conversations is typically on how the depth and breadth of the service provider's delivery capabilities help the client achieve its mission and vision, advance the client's strategic agenda, and realize a significant return on the client's investment. In return, the service provider expects to build a robust pipeline of opportunities, enhance its reference base, expand its delivery footprint, deliver on its value proposition, and develop a long-term trusted advisor relationship.

When the service provider comes out of the initial sales meetings, the service provider's confidence is usually high, which helps foster the belief that any ensuing price and terms and conditions negotiation will go smoothly. The focus of any dialogue up to that point centers on collaboration and value creation, and not on low price and risk deflection. Unfortunately, that optimism may fade quickly. The participants at the negotiation table are typically limited to procurement staff, legal counsel, and third-party advisors. It becomes clear that the courting process has ended, and it is time to hash out the terms and conditions of the prenuptial agreement. As many of you know, when this process begins, it may become very emotionally charged and—depending on the reasonableness of the parties and their desire to strictly adhere to their positions—continue this way for some time before reaching closure.

The unfortunate mindset that perpetuates this behavior is that many clients view their service provider's role in an outsourcing engagement as all encompassing. If you compare this role to building a ship, clients take the approach: "You go and build it. You are the experts, and we will see you at sea trials." What clients may not realize is that irrespective of the underlying service and the level of automation that will be deployed, you cannot outsource responsibility. Clients and their respective IT and other supporting organizations still own the delivery and the service, and they must work in partnership with their service provider to achieve success.

Let's Look at the Statistics

If you question the contention that most negotiations and subsequent contracts focus on allocating failure rather than promoting collaboration, consider an annual study conducted by the International Association for Contract and Commercial Management in which feedback was solicited from more than 500 international companies about which terms and conditions they negotiate most frequently. Since 2002, when this study was launched, the results have remained unchanged for the top 10 most frequently negotiated terms. Although there has been slight movement over the years, the overwhelming majority of the most heavily negotiated terms and conditions are squarely centered on the allocation of blame and the consequences of failure. They are as follows:

Term
1. Limitation on liability
2. Indemnity
3. Intellectual property ownership
4. Price
5. Termination
6. Warranty

7.   Confidential information/data protection
8.   Delivery/acceptance
9.   Payment
10.   Liquidated damages

There may be differences, depending on the client and service provider, the nature of the underlying services provided, the geographic region, and the applicable law. It is abundantly clear, however, that most clients—or, at least their procurement, legal counsel, and third-party advisors—view the terms and conditions in the contract as the mechanism by which blame is allocated when a delivery failure arises. While this approach may seem like the most viable option, given the scope and complexity of the underlying engagement and the significant risk associated with failure, it certainly does not lay a strong foundation for success. Irrespective of that complexity and risk inherent in delivery, there is clearly a dichotomy. C-suite executives and true economic buyers communicate a message about collaboration, partnering for success, and the ease of doing business with their organization. At odds with this message are the methods and tactics promulgated by their procurement and legal organizations in the execution of the underlying contractual agreement.

This book reviews each of the key terms and conditions of a complex outsourcing agreement and addresses how those terms must be drafted to contemplate the deployment of a hybrid—robots and FTEs—workforce over the delivery term. Rather than focusing on the extreme positions that may be initially taken by the parties and the multiple redline iterations that inevitably ensue during the evaluation and negotiation process, the book focuses on parties putting that best foot forward. To that end, it will provide the market-relevant and industry standard approach on each term that can serve as the baseline for the agreement or that, where appropriate, can be tempered based on the nature of the underlying solution. The book also discusses the key components of an outsourcing agreement that drive success, namely, the statement of work; any assumptions or dependencies upon which delivery is conditioned; clarity about the roles and responsibilities of the parties, especially in a multivendor environment; objective, measurable, and verifiable acceptance criteria for deliverables and milestone achievement; a well-documented governance process; and a change order process that is understood and strictly followed.

INTRODUCTION

This approach is a radical departure from the current model of starting from a newly introduced template and negotiating a 500-plus page outsourcing agreement. Although this approach may represent a change from the status quo, it is built on a foundation of efficiency and legitimacy, and it is commensurate with the evolving market for outsourcing services that is screaming for speed to value. To that end, this approach is grounded in the following key tenets:

1. The current process by which outsourcing agreements are negotiated is not efficient from a time, quality, or cost perspective.

2. The overwhelming focus of the negotiation process is on the consequences of failure and the allocation of blame when there is a performance deficiency.

3. There is an established industry standard for each of the most contentious and heavily negotiated terms and conditions.

4. Both parties to the transaction must put their best foot forward and use this standard as the departure point for the negotiation process.

5. There will still be plenty of opportunity to fine-tune and temper each term and condition to be commensurate with the underlying nature of the solution provided.

6. The scale must be tipped such that there is a much greater focus on collaboration on those components of the agreement that drive timely, quality, and cost-effective delivery, including the following: a narrowly tailored statement of work that is free of ambiguity and that clearly sets the expectations of both parties; clear service levels that are objective, measurable, and verifiable; a strong governance process; absolute clarity about roles and responsibilities; and a robust set of assumptions and dependencies, especially in a multivendor delivery environment.

7. There is no value in having each party take an extreme position from which they each agree to minor concessions over an extended

period of time and, ultimately, compromise when they both knew their likely landing spot from Day 1—the market-relevant standard on that particular issue.

8. Caving in to a position asserted by the other party after months of saying "no" is extremely frustrating, and erodes trust and credibility.

9. Constantly asserting what other vendors may agree or have agreed to lacks context and is irrelevant. Stop playing games and focus on market relevancy.

10. There is no purpose in unnecessarily extending the sales cycle and creating tension between the two parties. It will serve only to detrimentally impact a relationship that has yet to officially begin.

11. An outsourcing relationship requires collaboration and partnership between the parties to achieve success.

Finding the Right Balance

Let's be clear: The scope of outsourcing services that the largest IT service providers deliver is large and the deployment of automation will exacerbate the complexity of the delivery model. These services require diverse teams with deep functional and institutional expertise for delivery, may span multiple years, traverse multiple geographies, and are mission critical to the client organization. Given those parameters, it is prudent to develop terms and conditions that define the following: the rights and obligations of the parties in a situation of nonperformance or some other occurrence that dictate how a dispute is resolved; the allocation of any related liability; or the termination of the underlying agreement. However, although preparing for the consequences of failure is always a critical component of the negotiation process, it should be balanced with those terms and conditions that focus on collaboration and are a foundation for a strong partnership between the parties that is necessary to achieve timely, quality, and cost-effective delivery.

Clients select an outsourcing vendor based upon its service quality, its brand awareness, and its broad reference base for delivering similar solutions in a timely, quality, and cost-effective manner. Those solutions are competitively priced in relation to the prices of the other vendors in the marketplace and commensurate with the underlying nature of the service provided. Conversely, through successful service delivery, the most successful IT service providers continue to expand their delivery acumen and develop quality, predictable, and repeatable solutions, focus on continuous improvement, fine-tune staff capabilities and functional expertise, and, most importantly, strive to achieve a trusted advisor relationship with their clients. Given this dynamic, the largest IT service providers should put their best foot forward and take the initiative with their clients by promulgating an agenda that focuses on achieving a better balance during the negotiation process. Narrowly tailored statements of work, objective and measurable acceptance criteria, detailed governance models, clarity on roles and responsibilities, a comprehensive set of assumptions and dependencies, and a clear change order process should not be afterthoughts, given the size and complexity of the engagements being delivered. In my experience, afterthoughts are what they have become.

Prudence dictates that the parties prepare for the consequences of failure; failing to do so would be negligent, to say the least. But a focus on partnership and collaboration is much more commensurate with the mission, the vision, and the trusted advisor relationships that every IT service provider strives to achieve with its clients. Finding the right balance serves both parties well and facilitates the key underlying interest of both parties—successful delivery.

If you can embrace these key tenets and are ready to challenge the status quo, then I encourage you to read on. Go ahead if you dare—take a chance and put your best foot forward. You might be surprised at the results.

SECTION 1

LET'S COVER
THE BASICS

CHAPTER 1

HOW ARE SERVICES REALLY SOLD?

Before we can dive into a review of terms and conditions, we need to be mindful of how outsourcing services are really sold and the importance of relationships in the sales process. This understanding is critical because overestimating the value of relationships can have a significant impact on the negotiation process and the likelihood of "getting ink"—achieving contract execution—when the dust settles.

Just How Important Are Relationships?

The impact of relationships on the award process should never be underestimated. Whether pursuit teams craft a capture strategy or evaluate the likelihood of success in a competitive procurement for outsourcing services, relationships do play a critical role in the selection process. Given that dynamic, pursuit teams spend countless hours enhancing existing relationships and cultivating new ones with any client representative they believe can influence the final award decision. The strength and substance of those relationships are likely to be clearly documented in a relationship map that is scrutinized throughout the sales process.

Ultimately, the level of reliability of that relationship map can be the difference between success and failure. Strongly perceived relationships may yield overconfidence, which can be very dangerous in a competitive environment with similarly qualified vendors. Weakly perceived or limited relationships may yield a decision to abandon the opportunity completely and focus business development resources elsewhere, to offer an overly aggressive price, or to accept unfavorable delivery terms and conditions to compensate for any such weakness and to avoid disqualification.

Relationships and the Evaluation Process

The evaluation criteria used by existing and prospective clients vary according to the size and complexity of the opportunity, but may include the following:

- functional and industry expertise of the vendor
- proposed technical approach (including the deployment of automation and other emerging technologies) that is the foundation for the delivery of services
- quality and experience of the team to be deployed for delivery
- vendor's expertise in delivering similarly situated solutions in the client's industry
- level of executive involvement in the proposed solution
- level of relationships and trust between the parties
- vendor's acceptance of prescribed terms and conditions that govern delivery
- client's perception about the delivery capabilities of the vendor
- vendor's prior delivery history within the client's IT landscape
- vendor's financial viability and ability to scale on a global basis
- price

Although the level of trust and the strength of relationships between the parties are typically not stand-alone criteria, they definitely factor into the award decision. Make no mistake about it: Clients who undertake large, complex, and mission-critical outsourcing engagements demand predictable results that manifest themselves through timely, quality, and cost-effective delivery. The stakes are too high and failure is not an option, given the potential impact on the viability of the underlying business and the customers, suppliers, and employees these systems support.

Do Strong Relationships Guarantee Success?

When developing the strategy for a new sales opportunity, you must carefully assess the strength of relationships across all hierarchical levels within the client's organization—from the C-suite and likely decision-maker, to every member of the evaluation team, to all the way down to procurement. To help facilitate that process, a red-yellow-green encoded relationship map is likely to be used to highlight the strength and substance (saying "hello" in the hallway or at a social event versus being a trusted advisor) of those relationships and, most important, how those individuals may influence the decision-making process.

Most sales executives believe that their client relationships are ironclad and will be the driving force when decision-making time rolls around. Whereas relationships are extremely important, they must be augmented with a strong track record of delivering sustainable results. A trusted advisor relationship with a client gives you some credit in the bank, a seat at the table, the ability to have an open and candid conversation, the luxury of being considered for opportunities that may not exactly fit in your sweet spot, a first look at new opportunities, and insight into the client's agenda and priorities. This relationship, however, is by no means a guarantee of success. This position was confirmed recently at a sales conference when a senior executive at one of the world's largest suppliers of building materials was asked what factors most influenced his leadership team when evaluating consulting, technology, and outsourcing providers for mission-critical programs in his organization. His answer was: "Trust matters, but it's the deal that counts."

Relationships Versus Best Value

Assume a vendor has well-established brand awareness in the market, a strong reference base, and a history of quality and timely delivery in the marketplace, but lacks any substantive relationships in the account it wishes to penetrate. Given those parameters, is it possible to capture a competitive opportunity? The answer depends on the nature of the services provided, and where those services are in what I refer to as the relationship/best-value continuum, which is displayed below. As you see, when it comes to outsourcing services, the value of relationships is minimal and should not be relied upon too heavily when a service provider is engaged in a competitive outsourcing procurement. I have served as the lead negotiator on competitive outsourcing engagements where the sales leadership team was absolutely convinced that the strength of the team's relationships and prior delivery history would somehow materialize in the form of a white knight who would sweep in, exempt the team from the wrath of the external counsel and the third-party advisor, and direct the award to us. Unfortunately, that help never arrived. My best advice: Keep your overconfidence in check and focus on your ability to innovate, especially when you are engaged in a highly competitive procurement for outsourcing services.

RELATIONSHIP/BEST-VALUE CONTINUUM

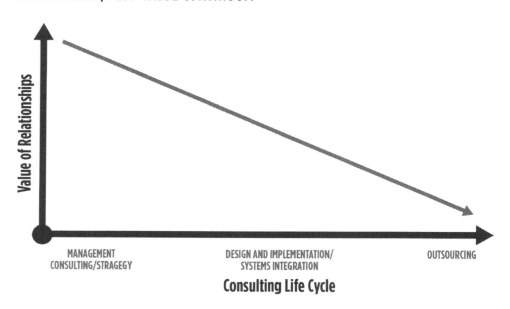

Value of Relationships

| MANAGEMENT | DESIGN AND IMPLEMENTATION/ | OUTSOURCING |
| CONSULTING/STRAGEGY | SYSTEMS INTEGRATION | |

Consulting Life Cycle

Corporate Strategy Versus Outsourcing Services

For management consulting and corporate strategy services delivered directly to the C-suite, relationships still rule the day and trump best value time after time. For these types of services, it is common for a partner or director in one of the top strategy firms to build a relationship with and become a trusted advisor to the board of directors, CEO, or executive management team, and provide all strategy services until there is a change in leadership.

These services are typically contracted directly with the CEO or board on a noncompetitive basis, can be sizable in amount, are typically outside the purview of anyone in the procurement organization, have extensive senior executive involvement and a corresponding lower-leverage model throughout delivery, are not subject to extensive price negotiation, are, in some cases, a line item in the annual budget, and are generally exclusively provided by one party.

The bottom line is that the strategy provider's relationships render it sacrosanct in the procurement process and price reasonableness. A former colleague once boasted that as a director for one of the major strategy firms, he had developed a long-standing trusted advisor relationship with the CEO of a financial services company, where he and his team were the exclusive providers of strategy services. For a specific engagement that he was positioning with the CEO, my colleague looked the CEO directly in the eye and said: "The cost for the engagement will be $1 million. And that is my cost; my team is free." This is an extreme example, but it epitomizes the delivery of high-end strategy services that are still sold primarily on a relationship basis and are exempt from the much more rigid procurement process associated with more competitive opportunities across the consulting life cycle.

While that approach might be viable in the C-suite with a long-standing client who has a good sense of humor and with whom you have a trusted advisor relationship, its application is extremely limited. What if that former colleague attempted a similar approach with a client's counsel, procurement leadership, and third-party advisor on a competitive applications outsourcing engagement where he was unable to differentiate his services and lacked any substantive relationships within the client's buying community? Well, he probably would have a very short meeting and plenty of time to play golf in the afternoon. Clearly, as you progress farther across the consulting life cycle and leave the strategy realm, best value becomes much more important, vendors become more prevalent, competition is fierce, services are more commodity-like, and procurement and legal become much more engaged in the buying process.

Selling Outsourcing Services With Limited C-Suite Relationships

If you have or can develop a trusted advisor relationship with C-suite leadership, that relationship should be leveraged to the fullest when pursuing downstream outsourcing opportunities. If you lack such a relationship, target your business development efforts toward functional leadership that may be a few layers removed from the C-suite. Those leaders have both strategic and tactical agendas to pursue, have an ample budget, and are likely to engage third-party providers in an outsourcing capacity to help them achieve their objectives.

The bottom line is that despite the strength of any C-suite relationships, best value should be a key component of every outsourcing sales strategy. If you overlook best value based upon the perceived strength of some C-suite or other relationship, you likely have an acute case of overconfidence and a successful outcome will be tenuous at best. If you think about the relationship/best-value continuum, best value becomes much more important the farther you move away from corporate strategy in the consulting life cycle. Just to be clear, relationships in the client organization most certainly help in selling outsourcing services as well, but their relative weight diminishes as the services become more like commodities.

Relationships in Action

Let's look at an example that highlights the impact relationships may have in a competitive procurement for IT services. Assume that a leading IT services provider maintains a great relationship with the IT leadership in a *Fortune* 500 financial services company, and the CIO is contemplating the award for outsourcing the maintenance and development for their full suite of financial and human resources applications. The services provider has a reputation for delivering similarly situated solutions in a timely, quality, and cost-effective manner, and its brand awareness and reference base is very strong. The provider is one of two competitors that have made it through the down-selection process for this large and strategic program. Both vendors have similarly situated technical solutions, delivery timelines, and equal capabilities in staff and industry expertise. However, one of the two vendors is 15 percent lower on price. After confirming that both vendors have submitted a proposal and corresponding price for the exact scope of services that are specified in the request for proposal (RFP), the client is now forced to address the value of the relationship and the level of price sensitivity it has for the services contemplated.

Relationships Versus Price Sensitivity—It's Decision Time

Although a 15 percent premium may not be a big deal on a $100,000 management consulting engagement, this kind of global applications outsourcing engagement may span multiple years, is mission-critical to the organization, and requires a significant investment. When faced with this situation, most clients choose the vendor with whom they feel most comfortable, from whom they can receive predictable results manifested in timely, quality, and cost-effective delivery, and with whom they have a strong relationship. But at what point does the price variance become too high to justify an award that will cost 15 percent more during the delivery term?

If the lower-cost vendor has a less technically viable solution and there are questions about the vendor's ability to deliver the services and meet the service levels, then, maybe, 15 percent is not a big deal and not worth the risk of failure in choosing the wrong vendor. But that is not the case here, as these vendors are similarly situated in capability and likelihood of success. So, it is decision time— what is the value of the relationship? How strong of a technical solution, reference base, reputation for quality delivery, and long-standing relationship does it take to justify an award to a higher-priced vendor? Is it 5 percent? Is it 10 percent?

What Does the Fed Say?

There is no firm answer, but there is a reference point in the public sector. The Federal Acquisition Regulations (FAR) govern the procurement of goods and services by the U.S. government and provide for a "best-value" approach in the selection process. "Best value" is defined in Section 2.101 of the FAR as "the expected outcome of an acquisition that, in the government's estimation, provides the greatest overall benefit in response to the requirement." While the FAR guidelines do not state a specific one that would allow for an award to other than the lowest-price offeror, a 2010 General Accounting Office (GAO) study of best-value contract awards by Defense Department agencies reflected a 5 percent price premium as the average variance that would justify making an award to a higher-price vendor based upon best value. Once the price premium increased above 5 percent, the probability of win decreased significantly. When making a contract award to other than the lowest priced offeror, the government is required to carefully document how the perceived benefits of the higher-price proposal merit the additional cost. Given the multiple service provider options available and a continued focus on reducing IT costs wherever possible, a 5 percent to 7 percent gap, at most, would be the benchmark in a typical commercial outsourcing opportunity. Even that variance can be difficult to justify, given the commodity-like nature of the underlying services delivered and the level of influence that procurement and third party advisors may play in the award process.

So What's the Final Word on Relationships?

There will always be exceptions to this general rule, but the bottom line is that procurements for the delivery of services outside of the management consulting and corporate strategy realm are extremely competitive, and relationships do not guarantee success. Given this dynamic, it is critical to carefully pick delivery sweet spots and to deliver in a manner both commensurate with the nature of the services provided and competitive with the other vendors in the market. Strong relationships are always important and are a key foundational component for a successful services provider; however, the inherent value of those relationships is mitigated as commoditization and price sensitivity become more important in the decision-making process.

CHAPTER 2

WHAT ABOUT MY FRIENDS IN PROCUREMENT?

Procurement continues to play a critical role in the evaluation and selection process for outsourcing services, particularly when selling to *Fortune* 500 companies. To that end, procurement representatives engaged in the negotiation process should be treated as legitimate stakeholders and their level of influence should not be understated.

The Evolution of the *Fortune* 500 Procurement Organization

Over the past few years, there has been a fundamental change in the way *Fortune* 500 companies procure consulting services. The net effect of the change is that *Fortune* 500 clients, regardless of industry or geography, have become much more sophisticated buyers of management consulting, technology, and outsourcing services. This new level of sophistication has broad implications for the negotiation teams who are at the center of this transformation. In this Chapter, we focus on the evolution of corporate procurement organizations and the resulting environment that a service provider is likely to encounter during the sales and negotiation process.

Historically, selling services to *Fortune* 500 entities was straightforward. A service provider would identify a potential consulting opportunity, propose its service offering to the prospective client, agree on the scope of work and corresponding price, execute a contract, and begin service delivery. Procurement organizations were extremely decentralized, functional and geographic leaders had complete autonomy over their external consulting budgets, and service providers were routinely engaged at different points in the corporate hierarchy and across multiple business units in the organization. Given this level of procurement decentralization, coordination of third-party consulting expenditures was nominal, at best. Multiple agreements, many with conflicting pricing structures and delivery terms and conditions, could prevail at any one time. Because of the significant size of the third-party consulting expenditures in many *Fortune* 500 companies, in some cases in excess of $100 million annually, this process was clearly inefficient and yielded an extremely suboptimized procurement and performance management process.

To combat this trend, *Fortune* 500 companies across all industries and geographies have undertaken efforts to centralize and streamline their procurement processes, particularly as it relates to the utilization of external consultants. To that end, they have instituted a much more sophisticated buying methodology and have migrated toward a very centralized procurement process under which global master services agreements are executed with a select group of preferred vendors. Through this process, the typical *Fortune* 500 company strives to optimize its global consulting spend and to share best practices among operating entities through:

- streamlining the vendor base
- comprehensive use of master services agreements and identification of "preferred" vendors
- institution of a more rigorous and disciplined buying process with aggressive negotiating tactics in pricing, and terms and conditions
- implementation of a vendor performance management system

Sitting squarely at the intersection of this new strategy is corporate procurement. The bottom line is that the relative influence and power of corporate procurement organizations have grown significantly in recent years, and these organizations have been empowered—through chief procurement officers reporting directly to the CFO or CEO—to aggressively pursue their agendas. Given this ever-present market dynamic, prudence requires that sales teams develop a strategy by which corporate procurement organizations are leveraged to help facilitate business development and footprint expansion. To this end, it is critical that procurement understands your value proposition, your global scale, your full consulting life-cycle delivery capabilities, and your ability to help clients achieve predictable results in a timely and quality manner under terms and conditions commensurate with the nature of the services provided and priced competitively with the client's other preferred vendors.

Procurement's Underlying Interests

If procurement fails to reach these conclusions and, in particular, if it believes that a particular service provider is not cost-competitive, then business development, footprint expansion, and the negotiation process will be a steep, ugly, uphill battle. I was recently engaged in a competitive applications outsourcing procurement. Procurement's role was to continually provide red-laden heat maps that reflected the extreme variances between the rates my organization had proposed and procurement's perspective on market-relevant rates for similarly situated services. Although the rates that we were benchmarked against were not legitimate, procurement's continued reinforcement throughout the sales cycle that the rates were not competitive turned that perception into a reality that was too powerful to overcome. As a result, an award to a lower-cost, India-based outsourcing services provider came shortly thereafter. To avoid disqualification as a result of a flawed benchmarking exercise and to work effectively with *Fortune* 500 corporate procurement organizations, it is important to understand what they want, what motivates them, and what they are trying to achieve. The agenda of the typical *Fortune* 500 procurement organization are not that much of a mystery. Specifically, these organizations want:

- Optimization of global consulting spend and sharing of best practices across their organizations.
- Fewer and more strategic preferred vendors with broad delivery capabilities.
- Vendors with "skin in the game."
- Aggressive pricing (OK, as cheap as they can get), with volume and other discounts in exchange for the "preferred" vendor label.
- Pricing structure commensurate with the nature of services provided and competitive with the other preferred vendors— separate rate schedules for management consulting, systems integration, and outsourcing engagements.
- Vendors that deliver best value—timely, high-quality, and cost-effective delivery.
- Competition among vendors for commodity-like services.
- Increase in compliance and reduction in "maverick spending."
- Efficiency gains (reduced cycle time), cost savings, and control over the buying process through implementing e-procurement solutions.

- Performance management systems in which vendors are evaluated across quality, time, and cost parameters, and stripped of the "preferred" label if they fail to meet performance standards.
- Business and legal terms and conditions that yield an acceptable level of risk and reward.

While procurement wants to achieve each of the aforementioned agenda items, never underestimate the importance of aggressive pricing. All these agenda items are important, but procurement organizations are motivated by and recognized and rewarded for obtaining cost reductions from their vendor community—hard stop. Think about it: Who doesn't want to go back to their boss, most likely the CFO, and wave a flag that says they were able to negotiate an additional 5 percent discount from one of their largest preferred vendors? Even though 5 percent may seem nominal, the savings can become significant, given the annual transaction volume being generated with large IT service providers.

Can I Just Ignore Them and Pursue My Alternative?

Most business development or delivery executives want to avoid procurement during the sales and delivery process. This might have been a viable approach ten years ago, but this is no longer true, given the overarching influence procurement has in the buying process. Until recently, many brand-name strategy providers chose to pursue their alternative, avoidance, when building relationships with and aligning their sales strategy with procurement. That is to say, they leveraged their relationships and sold directly to the C-suite. This alternative was viable when third-party consulting and technology spend were below the radar. However, the recent trend is to focus on centralization and to leverage global purchasing power, with a corresponding reduction in selling, general and administrative (SG&A) expense that is being sponsored by those same C-suite executives who embodied the alternative strategy. The new mantra has become: "the relationship matters, but it is the deal that counts."

Given this dynamic, it is much more prudent for you to craft and pursue a sales and delivery strategy that aligns with procurement's strategic agenda and focuses on attaining preferred vendor status, being accountable for delivering on your value proposition, and partnering with procurement for success. To that end, it is imperative to include procurement in your power map and manage those relationships in a manner consistent with other key stakeholders that may influence the buying decision.

The current trend is no passing fad, and the bottom line is that procurement, while considered by many to be the Evil Empire, can be a valuable ally when you are selling outsourcing services to *Fortune* 500 companies. Irrespective of your strong brand awareness, trusted advisor relationships, and successful delivery history, it is imperative to build upon existing relationships and establish new ones with client procurement organizations, because they can serve as your ally across their buying community. The current procurement landscape gives them significant influence in the buying process, and it is, therefore, critical that they understand the depth and breadth of the capabilities that the service provider brings to bear as well as its value proposition.

Just How Much Influence Are We Talking About?

The short answer is: a lot. When it comes to compliance and control, *Fortune* 500 procurement organizations have implemented stringent policies on engaging third-party service providers, and these policies are endorsed deep into the Csuite. These policies typically include provisions such as the following: approval thresholds that escalate, depending on the dollar materiality or complexity of the engagement; the number of bids that must be solicited before an award decision can be made; and limitations on change orders, and the penalty for noncompliance can be significant. These policies place procurement right in the middle of the contracting process for third-party providers and give them broad enforcement powers both during the selection process and the delivery term.

As for gauging delivery quality and instituting penalties for poor performance, the trend in *Fortune* 500 entities is to implement a structured process by which delivery success is evaluated across time, quality, and cost parameters, and is reviewed quarterly with the vendor. By using such an approach, procurement can measure the quality, timeliness, and cost-effectiveness of delivery, and gauge the effectiveness of its service providers based on a consistent set of objective, measurable, and verifiable criteria. Ultimately, such data can be used to remove a service provider from the preferred vendor program, to exclude it from a new opportunity, to terminate its agreement, or justify the basis for a new sole-source award.

What About the Pricing Discussion?

Procurement organizations are measured by and want to be recognized for optimizing third-party consulting expenditures. They pursue these objectives by putting extreme downward pricing pressure on their vendors to attain favorable pricing, particularly in those areas where they believe that the services provided resemble commodities. As we all know, they can be relentless in seeking additional price concessions from their service providers. Their rationale may be motivated by their belief that they can obtain a similarly situated service at a more favorable price from an alternative service provider or that they have an internal mandate to achieve cost savings. And the current economic climate and continued focus on reducing IT spending has only made *Fortune* 500 procurement organizations even more aggressive in the negotiation process. They now look for significant across-the-board discounts, irrespective of the brand awareness, reference base, and reputation for timely, quality, and cost-effective delivery by their vendors. In many instances, these requests may come well after the initial agreement has been executed and service delivery has begun.

With respect to outsourcing services, the market has changed drastically in recent years. There used to be a significant gap in delivery acumen between the most highly regarded Tier-1 service providers—Accenture, IBM, and Capgemini—and their India-based pure play competitors. However, that gap has narrowed to where most clients believe that they can obtain the same quality and predictable results from either source. In the past 10 years, the largest Indian pure play providers—TCS, Cognizant, Infosys, Wipro, and HCL—have increased their global market share and geographic delivery scope and enhanced their delivery acumen. The term "pure play" really no longer applies as they have expanded their service offerings across the consulting lifecycle. This commodity-based view of the outsourcing marketplace has resulted in price becoming one of, if not the most important, criteria in the evaluation and selection process.

While each request and solution is different, the following principles can reinforce the legitimacy of your initial pricing submission and can serve as the foundation for responding to any such request:

- Make sure that the client is paying premium prices for premium services and that the prices the client is paying for commodity services are competitive with other vendors in the marketplace.
- Don't assume strong relationships will justify an award to a higher priced service provider.
- Be mindful of the client's ability to make an award to other than the lowest priced service provider. Once a relatively small price premium threshold is crossed, the client's ability to do so will be limited.
- **Be smart:** If you agree to a price concession, it questions the integrity of the initial price submission. Always be cognizant of the fact that if your client does not trust you, then you might as well pack up and call it a day.
- If you decide to give additional incentives, concessions, or discounts, make sure you are getting something in return—a volume commitment, preferred vendor status; access to the C-suite or to certain procurements historically reserved for other competitors; exclusive marketing rights to a particular entity or region; more favorable payment terms; changes in roles, responsibilities, or scope; or the elimination of high-risk terms and conditions. But make sure you get something in return, and consider all possible options if you pursue this course of action.
- When you have given all that you want to give and believe that your rates are competitive with those of other vendors in the market for similarly situated services and reflect the level of risk associated with delivery, then remain calm. Hold your ground, focus on your value proposition, make it clear that low price does not equal best value, consider your options and alternatives, and be prepared to say "no."

The Master Services Agreement: Friend or Foe?

A key component of the more sophisticated buying methodology has been the migration to a model under which global master services agreements are executed with a select group of preferred vendors. The master agreement typically contains the terms and conditions as well as the rates that govern delivery for all services across the consulting life cycle. Through this master agreement process, *Fortune* 500 procurement organizations hope to make progress in achieving three items on their agenda:

- Identifying a preferred vendor community that delivers in a timely, quality, and cost-effective manner.
- Developing competition among vendors for similar services.
- Securing business terms and conditions that yield an acceptable and predictable level of risk and reward for their organization.

Many sales and delivery executives have expressed some concern about the migration to the master agreement process because they see it as inhibiting the sales process. A viable option is taking the opposite approach and strongly supporting the execution of a master services agreement with every client with whom you are currently engaged and for which you have growth aspirations. The biggest challenge that many services providers face in this area is negotiating a master agreement that contains terms and conditions that can be tempered or flexed so the terms are commensurate with the underlying nature of the services provided—consulting, systems integration, or outsourcing. Thinking about future opportunities can be challenging because the master agreement is the starting point in most relationships, and its focus is on the initial opportunity contemplated between the parties. This agreement also drives the process, substance, and options being developed from the perspective of both terms and conditions, and rates.

Given this dynamic, it is critical to focus not only on the initial underlying opportunity but also on the development of a sustainable agreement with a rate structure and governing terms that can span the full consulting life cycle. I cannot tell you how many times I have been engaged to take a master agreement that was executed for the delivery of management consulting or systems integration services, and amend it or create an addendum to include outsourcing services under its umbrella. What may sound like an easy exercise is challenging, because clients seek to maintain a firm grasp on the consulting-like terms in the master agreement, whereas the services provider seeks to introduce terms specific to outsourcing services. To avoid this dynamic, take the time to execute a robust master agreement that can span the full consulting life cycle.

Although the master agreement negotiation process may be cumbersome, the benefits received upon contract execution are significant. The master agreement is a free hunting license and communication mechanism, so use it accordingly—

walk the halls, talk to procurement and potential buyers, conduct brown bag sessions, provide sales collateral, promote your capabilities on the procurement intranet website, and participate in other activities that educate the buying community and facilitate footprint expansion. In addition, a robust master agreement can accelerate the sales cycle, given that the delivery terms and conditions, and the rate structure, have been previously negotiated. Of primary importance is that the master agreement gives you a reason to meet with your clients and stay relevant, even if there are no immediate opportunities on the horizon. Finally, it can facilitate expansion into other service delivery areas over the consulting life cycle. Holding a master agreement comes with good visibility and can contribute to building brand awareness, an internal reference base, and a reputation for quality delivery across the organization.

What Does the Landscape Look Like Going Forward?

Gone forever are the days of decentralized procurement, multiple engagements with disparate terms and conditions and pricing structures, limited performance management, and purely relationship-based selling. Both procurement executives and clients are seeking innovative solutions and options from prospective service providers that embody a better, faster, and cheaper approach. In addition, both clients and procurement organizations are looking for alternatives to some of the entrenched providers and stagnant solutions that they have been subjected to for many years.

As we have discussed, the corporate procurement organization has changed drastically. It is now centralized, more sophisticated, and very influential in the buying process. It is focused on streamlining its vendor base, executing master services agreements that govern delivery globally, and anointing a limited number of preferred vendors across a set of discrete service lines. All of this has been done to optimize and leverage the global consulting spend, and to hold preferred vendors accountable for timely, quality, and cost-effective delivery.

Given the staying power and level of influence wielded by procurement, my recommendation is that you build on existing relationships and establish new ones with client procurement organizations in the same manner and with the same rigor as you would with your ultimate client. These organizations can be your allies across their buying community. Take the time to make sure that they understand your value proposition, your ability to deliver in a timely, quality, and cost-effective manner, and the depth and breadth of the capabilities that your organization brings to the marketplace. At minimum, such relationships give the service provider insight into the RFP process, enhance its competitive positioning with new buyers that seek counsel from procurement about vendor capabilities, and help enhance brand awareness.

The current economic climate, extreme downward pricing pressure, and desire for consistency in operations will most likely enhance procurement's power base and level of influence. Given this trend and for the aforementioned reasons, embracing the concept that procurement can be your friend and ally as you navigate through your respective client community is highly recommended. Ultimately, this approach can yield footprint expansion, insight into a previously noninclusive RFP process, enhanced marketing opportunities, new master services agreements with preferred vendor status, introductions to new buyers, and, most important, generation of net new sales. When you are developing account plans and strategy, remember that procurement can be your friend and engage them accordingly.

CHAPTER 3

A PRIMER ON NEGOTIATION

Approaching the Negotiation Process

I am always asked if there is a "silver bullet" to being a successful negotiator. Unfortunately, there is no answer to this question. At a basic level, negotiation is a task of influence—trying to get someone to do or to stop doing something. Whether or not you realize it, you are in active negotiations with people around you throughout the day. Ultimately, your ability to be an effective negotiator in both your personal and professional lives depends on a number of variables, including your social style and how you deal with conflict.

I will leave it to you to determine your social style, your personality type, and your style of approaching conflict. What I will say is that while your social style may be so heavily ingrained in who you are as a person that it cannot change, how you approach conflict can be successfully tempered at the negotiation table. I speak from experience as an extremely competitive individual who has learned to temper his approach to conflict by keeping his competitive arousal in check and focusing on collaboration to be more effective at the negotiation table. Regardless of your social style and conflict mode, to be a successful negotiator, you need three things:

1. A strong mental and situational awareness that yields the ability to spot the "game" that unfolds during the negotiation process;

2. A process utilized in each negotiation that you are engaged in and the skill to use that process in a disciplined manner;

3. The ability and willingness to have difficult conversations.

Your situational awareness (No. 1) and your affinity for difficult conversations (No. 3) must be perfected over time. As I will discuss shortly, preparation for any negotiation is absolutely critical. Failure to do so is likely to yield failure. As it relates to preparation, I strictly adhere to the approach which New York Giants head coach Tom Coughlin shared during a press conference before Super Bowl XLVI—humble enough to prepare, confident enough to perform. As you prepare, be mindful of the fact that the actual negotiation may not flow as smoothly as it did when you role-played with your colleagues at the office. As long as you can spot the game and utilize the process suggested in No. 2, then you will be properly prepared for success. As it relates to utilizing a disciplined process, prepare for the negotiation as you might for a boxing match. In the words of the great philosopher and pugilist Mike Tyson, remember: "Everyone has a plan till they get punched in the mouth."

Keeping Your Competitive Arousal in Check

The other key component you need to be a successful negotiator is the ability to keep your competitive arousal in check. As an attorney, I have no problem saying that most attorneys are extremely competitive and are trained to see conflicts in terms of right and wrong. So you can only imagine the level of intensity and competitiveness that results when two attorneys from opposing sides negotiate delivery terms and conditions for an outsourcing agreement. Generally, if you let the attorneys run the show, it will be chaos. Even more so than their procurement colleagues, they are laser-focused on the allocation of blame and the consequences of any failure during service delivery. In their perceived role as the defenders of their respective clients, the attorneys very quickly take a position that they are unwilling to yield.

In almost every outsourcing negotiation in which I have been engaged, the client and the client's counsel provide their standard terms and conditions for review and comment by the service provider. Given the likely unbalanced allocation of risk and reward in the standard terms, the service provider's counsel reviews the terms and conditions, redlines them extensively, and sends them back to the client. Upon receipt, the client reviews the changes and deletes most of them using another color in the "Track Changes" function in Microsoft Word. The process usually continues for multiple iterations until a call or meeting is scheduled to formally negotiate any outstanding issues. If you have ever been a party to one of these calls or meetings, battle lines are drawn quickly. It is not too long before an impasse is reached, as neither party is willing to retrench from the party position. I do not want to indict all attorneys as members of the deal-prevention force. Some of them can find a reasonable middle ground that yields an acceptable level of risk and reward, given the nature of services being provided. But those attorneys are clearly the exception to the rule.

Attorneys who can see the vast gulf between right and wrong, and understand the commercial aspects of the pending transaction should be sought out for outsourcing negotiations. The Advanced Commercial Mediation Institute conducted a survey in which commercial mediators were asked if the disputing parties were more focused on winning or on obtaining a good deal. The responses revealed that the disputing parties were much more likely to focus on winning when their attorneys were heavily involved and influential at the beginning of the dispute. In a *Harvard Business Review* article from May 2008, Deepak Malhotra, Gillian Ku, and J. Keith Murnighan suggested that this win at all costs type of decision-making was driven by an "adrenaline fueled emotional state," called competitive arousal.

We can probably all think of a time when we were victims of our competitive arousal and made a decision in the heat of battle that, in retrospect, looked foolish. Sometimes, we want to win at all costs, even if the decision-making process lacks any sound judgment and is solely based on competitive arousal. To mitigate this win at all cost dynamic, it is critical that the business leadership understand the legal issues, so they can stay in control of the negotiation and bring the attorneys to the table only when absolutely necessary. Similarly, once they have been invited to the party, the attorneys need to understand the nature of the services being contemplated in the transaction and the amount of risk inherent in delivery. By taking this approach, the level of competitive arousal can be kept in check, and reaching agreement on key terms and conditions can be achieved.

Let us assume that we have reined in our competitive arousal, our attorneys are in the bullpen, and we are now about to begin the negotiation process. The key question is: How do we reach an agreement that yields an acceptable level of risk and reward for both parties to the transaction? My answer has been the same for many years and has served me well in the marketplace. Frankly, it is not overly complex and has four key principles and seven elements. If you can master the

"4x7," then you are well on your path to becoming a very successful negotiator. The four principles are as follows:

1. Temper your approach based upon the amount of risk inherent in delivery.

2. Temper your approach based upon the geographic region in which you are engaged.

3. Temper your approach based upon the person sitting across from you at the negotiation table.

4. Remember that conflicts are created, conducted, and sustained by human beings and can be resolved by human beings.

Principle 4 is a recent addition to the list (a list that I had not changed in 15 years, so this was a big deal). The addition came from a 2010 speech by former Senate Majority Leader George Mitchell, who was named as a special envoy to the Middle East. After being introduced into this most critical and challenging role, Mitchell stated that "conflicts are created, conducted, and sustained by human beings and can be resolved by human beings." This statement, while obvious, made me pause and think about some of the most challenging negotiations I have ever experienced in my professional career and how I could have resolved them much more effectively by knowing this simple rule. I have, therefore, adopted this exact quote as my fourth key negotiation principle. I am in no way comparing negotiating outsourcing terms and conditions to negotiating peace in the Middle East, but keeping the scope of the negotiation in which you are engaged in perspective is something you should think about when drawing the battle lines around potential "deal-breaker" provisions.

In addition to these four core principles, it is important to remember that every negotiation has seven elements. The seven element approach to a principled negotiation stems from the book *Getting to Yes* written by Roger Fisher and William Ury of the Harvard Negotiation Project. The seven elements are interests, options, legitimacy, alternatives, commitment, communication, and relationship. The key to success is your ability to identify these elements and their connectivity, and, most important, to understand how they evolve during a negotiation. In addition, as we discussed above, it is absolutely critical that you take the requisite time to prepare for any negotiation and carefully consider how the seven elements can impact the negotiation. If you have not prepared properly, you might as well cancel the meeting because the result will not be optimal. On this issue, I will restate New York Giants coach Tom Coughlin's approach: humble enough to prepare, confident enough to perform. With respect to this approach, I simply say: Learn it, know it, and live it.

Ultimately, these seven elements dictate your likelihood of success in any competitive procurement for outsourcing services as well as the ultimate words within the four corners of the agreement. The interconnectivity between the elements is demonstrated in the basic negotiation equation, a desired output of which is to reach an agreement that satisfies the mutual interests of the parties. If an option is identified that fulfills those interests, then a clear path forward exists; if not, then the parties may have to pursue their alternatives, more commonly known as their best alternative to a negotiated agreement (BATNA). As I like to say, negotiation is that simple and that complex. Those seven elements are as follows:

1. **Interests:** What are the needs, concerns, goals, hopes, and fears that are motivating the other party to negotiate?

2. **Options:** What approaches can be identified that meet the mutual interests of the parties?

3. **Legitimacy:** What criteria exist—industry practices, expert opinions, laws, rules or regulations, or precedent—to measure if the options being considered or agreement reached is fair and sensible?

4. **Alternatives:** What unilateral steps can either party take—how can their interests be satisfied elsewhere—if the parties are unable to reach an agreement?

5. **Commitment:** Is the other party prepared to reach an agreement and is the party empowered to do so?

6. **Communication:** Are the parties listening to each other, engaging in collaborative dialogue, and remaining unconditionally constructive?

7. **Relationship:** Do I care about maintaining an ongoing relationship with the party across the table?

Many legal professionals are unable to follow the four core principles and to spot the seven elements. These professionals are too focused on adhering to some predefined standard template and the template's positions, or they are unable to consider other options that still meet their client's underlying interests. The focus on and the benchmark for success should be an agreement that does the following:

- satisfies the interests of the parties
- minimizes waste and reflects the best of many options
- under which neither party feels taken advantage of
- is better than your best alternative, or BATNA
- embodies a commitment among the parties
- is grounded in open communication
- reinforces the underlying relationship between the parties

Your ability to spot the seven elements will greatly assist in executing an agreement that meets these objectives. A macro-level view of the seven elements is as follows:

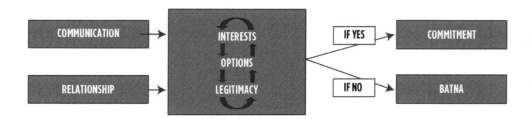

Many large IT service providers also strive to achieve a corporate standard in the negotiation process and fail to temper their quality assurance, risk management, and approval thresholds based upon the amount of risk inherent in delivery. In essence, they treat all transactions the same, which results in a very inefficient risk management process. You can read lots of books and attend plenty of trainings on successful negotiation techniques and tactics. However, I assure you that if you accept the fact that no two outsourcing services transactions are the same and do everything you can to strictly adhere to the four core principles and maintain a laser-focus on the seven elements, you will make great strides in the art of negotiation.

Now let us review some of the core negotiation principles in practice. What exactly does it mean to temper your negotiation stance based upon the amount of risk inherent in delivery? As we previously discussed, a number of factors should be considered in determining the amount of such risk. A thorough understanding of these risk criteria helps clarify the risk profile associated with an opportunity, and that, in turn, drives the stance to be taken in the negotiation process. A sampling of the risk criteria are as follows:

CLIENT RELATIONSHIP AND BACKGROUND

- Strategic importance of the client within the service provider portfolio
- Historical relationship with the client and current delivery footprint
- Size of the client entity and industry
- Competitive landscape
- Strength of relationships
- Client buyer values and selection criteria

SOLUTION

- Experience delivering similarly situated solutions in a timely, quality, and cost-effective manner
- Geographic scope of the solution
- Complexity of the underlying solution
- Organizational readiness for the amount of change required for success
- Complexity of the IT architecture and the state of the service or process to be outsourced
- Client's outsourcing experience and maturity
- Staffing capabilities required for delivery

CLIENT COMMITMENT TO PROGRAM

- Client commitment to the project and governance process
- Hierarchical level of the client executive sponsor

- Technical expertise of the client team and ability to meet delivery dependencies
- Client decision-making ability
- Depth of the client third party ecosystem

CONTRACT/PRICE/TIMELINE

- Project timeline
- Contract type
- Terms and conditions
- Narrowly tailored statement of work with clear roles and responsibilities
- Price sensitivity
- Client financial strength

According to the second principle, it is important to temper your approach based upon the geographic region in which you are engaged. What works well in New York or San Francisco does not necessarily work well in the United Kingdom, Germany, Japan, or the Middle East. Before jumping into the negotiation process in a foreign country, it is important to understand not only the local laws but also the impact that culture may have on the negotiation process. Is the style quiet and less flamboyant, requiring some level of deference, as you might find in Japan, or louder and more aggressive, as you might find in France or the United Kingdom? I am not a cultural expert, but I have negotiated terms and conditions in a number of countries and can absolutely tell you to conduct adequate cultural due diligence and to seek the advice of local colleagues before jumping into the process. Once you are there in the country, remember to temper your approach accordingly, both in terms of style and prevailing law.

Finally, remember to temper your style and approach based upon the person sitting across from you at the negotiation table. While you can study countless books on negotiation tactics, I urge you to make every attempt to understand the style, personality, motivation, and interests of the person with whom you will be negotiating; ultimately, your success hinges upon your ability to work with him or her to reach an agreement with an acceptable level of risk and reward for both parties to the transaction. To that end, I would like to introduce you to the "Harley Principle." I have been riding Harley-Davidson motorcycles for the past

15 years, and it is a great passion of mine. I have a VROD and a Screaming Eagle Springer, and love the feeling of rolling down the road with the wind in my face on a beautiful summer day. If I enter the office of a procurement executive or attorney with whom I will be negotiating and see anything Harley-Davidson or motorcycle related, I always ask about it, and the conversation quickly shifts to a passion we both share.

Finding this common interest lets us to identify with each other in a manner beyond the pricing, terms and conditions, and adversarial negotiation process that we are about to undertake. While I am not suggesting that a common passion for Harley-Davidson motorcycles results in an easy negotiation process, it allows me to develop some level of affiliation with the person with whom I am engaged. Though I have no scientific evidence, I can absolutely tell you that my negotiations with motorcycle enthusiasts over the years have been very successful. So make an effort to affiliate with the party with whom you will be negotiating beyond the terms and conditions in the agreement; it definitely makes a difference. Now, let us dive into the following Chapters and focus on what drives success and the key terms and conditions in an outsourcing agreement.

SECTION 2

FOCUS ON COLLABORATION AND PARTNERSHIP

CHAPTER 4

HOW WILL WE MEASURE SUCCESS?

The consistent ranking of the Top 10 most heavily negotiated terms in the International Association for Contract & Commercial Management (IACCM) survey reinforces the notion of an uneven allocation of time and focus on those terms and conditions that allocate blame and address the consequences of failure at the expense of those that facilitate collaboration and partnership and enhance the likelihood of timely, quality, and cost-effective delivery. Given the maturity and evolution of the outsourcing industry, I would have expected that the composition of this list should have evolved from being so heavily focused on the consequences of failure. While the complexity of the current delivery environment may legitimately require that the 10 key terms identified in the IACCM survey will always reside at the top of the list, it is important to be aware of how success is measured throughout the delivery term—both for the services provider and the client.

In addition to the roster of service levels, clients are using other metrics to gauge delivery effectiveness. They include the following:

- technical and functional expertise of the delivery team
- level of automation to be deployed over the delivery term
- ability to partner effectively with other client vendors, manage scope, and adhere to the change order process
- ability to jointly manage the program timeline and make decisions in a manner that facilitates achieving key milestones
- quality of the deliverables developed, and their conformity with the contractually agreed-on acceptance criteria
- level of knowledge transfer embedded into the client user community

- level of innovation used by the services provider for the tools, techniques, methodologies, and bank of intellectual capital brought to delivery
- ability to achieve the value proposition and ROI articulated in the initial business case
- focus on cost controls and efficiency

Clearly, understanding a multi-faceted evaluation model of this type and its underlying performance metrics is important because it is the primary measuring stick clients use to gauge delivery quality and, ultimately, measure success. These performance metrics are not in any way focused on the consequences of failure but rather on partnership, collaboration, joint ownership, and success. If both parties have the same underlying interest in achieving project success, the question arises: Why spend so much time and effort preparing for failure?

Successful delivery helps to ensure longevity throughout the community of client buyers and to build and to sustain a trusted advisor relationship, Therefore, it is essential to have a more balanced focus during the negotiation process, favoring those terms and conditions and structural components of the agreement that promote collaboration and the likelihood of success. Those critical components are often an afterthought in the negotiation process but are the root cause of failure and disputes in most cases. These components include:

- a narrowly tailored statement of work that is free from ambiguity and that clearly sets the expectations of both parties
- legitimate service levels consistent with the client's delivery expectations and, like all acceptance criteria, are objective, measurable, and verifiable
- a strong governance process with a mutual incentive to escalate issues and concerns early and often
- absolute clarity on roles and responsibilities
- a robust set of assumptions and dependencies that the service provider's performance is conditioned on, especially in a multivendor delivery environment

If you can get these things right—basic blocking and tackling, in my opinion—then you are well positioned for delivery success.

CHAPTER 5

DON'T EVEN THINK ABOUT STARTING WITHOUT A NARROWLY TAILORED STATEMENT OF WORK

It is critical that the solution in the service provider's proposal be translated into a statement of work that is narrowly tailored, free from ambiguity, clear about both parties' roles and responsibilities required for delivery as well as any assumptions or dependencies that delivery is conditioned on and commensurate with the price proposed. The importance of this exercise cannot be overemphasized, and it is in the best interests of both parties to execute a statement of work that meets these requirements. The quickest path to a dispute in an outsourcing engagement is the lack of clarity on the delivery scope, and the roles, responsibilities, and expectations of the parties. Taking the requisite amount of time to overachieve in this exercise will pay significant dividends downstream.

For a statement of work, an objective third party should be able to review it and clearly articulate the respective roles and responsibilities of the parties. I am a strong proponent of the four corners rule and, therefore, firmly believe that the statement of work must stand on its own and must clearly set the expectations of the parties. Both parties need to be crystal clear about when the delivery obligations of the services provider start and when they are completed. To aid in this endeavor, I ask myself one question: Could my mom review this document and tell me exactly what is being delivered and how success will be measured between the parties? If my answer is "yes," then I feel confident that the statement of work can stand on its own and easily dispense with any disputes about scope.

Selling Outsourcing Services in the Digital Age

It would seem that the statement of work would be a critical component of the outsourcing agreement, receiving plenty of scrutiny in the negotiation process. To the contrary—I assure you that it becomes an afterthought, and the parties scramble to complete it prior to contract execution. And it is very frequently a lack of clarity or ambiguity in the statement of work, or the interpretation of it, that is the root cause of disputes that arise during the course of delivery.

With a large number of stakeholders and moving parts, it is critical that everyone understand exactly what the outsourcing vendor is delivering, to what extent it may be relying upon the client or another vendor in its ecosystem, and when delivery on key milestones is complete—in essence, when can the vendor raise its hand and claim completion? The statement of work should also contain a series of milestones that can be translated into a payment schedule.

Keep in mind that the primary reason projects fail is *scope creep*, or deviations from the agreed-upon scope in the statement of work. According to the Standish Group, only 37 percent of IT projects are completed successfully; 42 percent go over budget, are not completed on time, or do not deliver what they are supposed to; and 21 percent flat-out fail. One of the primary reasons identified as contributing to this dynamic was a failure by the parties to properly define scope. Given that statistic, a narrowly tailored statement of work is an absolute necessity, especially in a multivendor environment.

Although you might think that executing a statement of work that meets the criteria I identified would be easy, think again. All parties agree that a statement of work is necessary, but there is always disagreement about the scope, the dependencies that the service provider's delivery is conditioned on, and the level of specificity required in delineating the roles and responsibilities of the parties.

For roles and responsibilities, it is a common practice to include a Responsibility Assignment, or RACI, matrix in the agreement to clearly articulate the levels of responsibility for each function described in the statement of work. A RACI matrix may identify the party responsible for and assigned to do the work; the party who is accountable, makes the final decision, and maintains ultimate ownership; the party who contributes to or is consulted before a decision or action is taken; and the party who is informed that a decision or action has been taken. Ultimately, the inclusion of a RACI matrix can be valuable in that it ensures that key functions are not overlooked; that each function is properly staffed; that both parties clearly understand their delivery roles and responsibilities; that no one resource is overburdened; and that in the event of a turnover or a change in priorities, resources can be redeployed as necessary. Ultimately, a review of the RACI can determine if there are enough individuals assigned to deliver the service; if, optimally, there is a single node of accountability for each function; if the number of resources contributing to the function will facilitate or inhibit timely decision-making; and who must be informed when a decision is made or an action is taken.

While this may seem like a prudent practice to follow, many of the third-party advisory firms are not proponents of it. They are concerned that it results in the service provider seeking relief when the client or other vendors in the delivery ecosystem do not meet their obligations. They prefer the notion of an all-encompassing statement of work—if it is included in the statement of work, then it is included in the supplier's delivery obligations. If it is not included, it is not a part of the supplier's delivery obligations. Although this approach seems logical, it can become challenging if any ambiguity exists in the statement of work or if complying with the delivery obligation, completing the deliverable, or achieving the milestone requires the involvement of the client or third-party providers.

To compensate for a statement of work that might not be 100 percent accurate, third party advisory firms are strong proponents of the inclusion of a sweeps provision in the agreement. We will discuss the mechanics of a sweeps provision later. However, given the complexity of some outsourcing engagements and the level of staff being displaced, it may be difficult to identify every function and component of the outsourced service that will transition to the new delivery environment. To address this issue, a sweeps provision was developed. The purpose behind this provision is to "sweep" into the delivery obligations of the service provider those functions or services not included in the statement of work agreed upon by the parties. These functions and services, instead, are implied in the nature of the outsourced service insofar as they are inherent in or a necessary component of the proper performance or provision of the services. The failure to include these implied services in the statement of work may result if the functions were not disclosed or were unknown during the due diligence process. As you can imagine, the size of the broom and the number of additional obligations swept up can have a material impact on the services provider's delivery obligations and financial performance.

I cannot stress enough the importance of the statement of work. It sets the expectations of the parties and is the first document reviewed by an arbitrator or court if a dispute should arise during delivery. Every member of the delivery team should carefully review the delivery obligations of the service provider and have a clear understanding where those obligations start and stop, and how they are interconnected with the roles and responsibilities of the client and of any other vendor in the delivery ecosystem. If the delivery scope changes, if the other parties are not meeting their delivery obligations or their other responsibilities, it is of paramount importance that a change order be executed or that the deficiency be immediately escalated through the governance process. When in doubt, take advantage of the governance process and escalate the issue for resolution.

CHAPTER 6

ASSUMPTIONS AND DEPENDENCIES: DON'T ABSORB RISKS YOU DON'T CONTROL

When negotiating an outsourcing agreement, it is an absolute necessity to have a clear set of assumptions that address a variety of intervening factors and a set of dependencies on which the timely and quality delivery of the service provider is conditioned. Do not let anyone convince you to the contrary—no matter what. Having these assumptions is absolutely critical in a multivendor delivery environment. While documenting assumptions and dependencies also seems to be benign and a best practice, it, like clarity on responsibilities, is not a preferred approach of third-party advisors and legal counsel. They view assumptions in particular as an escape hatch where outsourcing service providers can obtain relief from service-level credits or other client remedies, including termination triggers, in the event of a performance deficiency. They expect that all assumptions are addressed and resolved in the due diligence process, and either eliminated completely or embodied in the statement of work or elsewhere in the agreement.

A lengthy list of dependencies is also not a desired approach for third-party advisors or counsel, because they provide relief to a service provider for circumstances beyond its control. However, in a multivendor delivery environment, where multiple parties may be handling incidents against a time clock tied to service-level credits, these dependencies become an integral part of an outsourcing agreement. It is not legitimate for any party to absorb a risk they do not control. If a dependency is not met by the client or third party, the service provider can seek appropriate relief through a savings clause.

We will discuss savings clauses in much more detail later, but the net effect is that they excuse a service provider's performance, including its obligations to meet service levels, if that performance is prevented by the client not performing any of its obligations under the agreement or by the acts or omissions of a third-party provider. A savings clause requires that the service provider notify the client as soon as it becomes aware of the deficiency, that it demonstrate via a root cause analysis that the deficiency was caused by the client or third-party vendor, that it use commercially reasonable efforts to mitigate the impact of the deficiency, and that it use commercially reasonable efforts to meet the obligation as stated in the agreement. Examples of dependencies upon which the achievement of increases in productivity or service level targets are conditioned include the client providing its timely consent for the service provider to deploy automation in its IT environment and maintaining responsibility for any change management or compliance obligations associated with the automation.

I am not suggesting that a lengthy list of assumptions and dependencies be always mandated, but such a list should be developed where a service provider is absorbing delivery risks beyond its control. If the assumptions and dependencies are not met, then the agreement must specify the recourse for a failure. That remedy could include: that the service provider be temporarily relieved of its delivery obligations and any associated service-level credits or other penalties; that any milestone dates be adjusted accordingly; or that the client pay the cost associated with the service provider deploying additional resources (if the dependency was focused on the client's commitment of resources) that yield compliance with any such assumptions or meet a dependency.

Often, assumptions and dependencies are also afterthoughts when negotiating an outsourcing agreement. It may be reasonable to address assumptions during due diligence and embed their impact into a statement of work and the corresponding price, but a list of dependencies should never be overlooked. In a typical client ecosystem, multiple vendors are delivering outsourcing services, the scope of which are interconnected and can detrimentally impact the timely and quality delivery of their peers. Although many vendors agree to eliminate delivery dependencies completely and take their chances with the savings clause, relief may be unlikely, unless its provisions are strictly followed.

ASSUMPTIONS AND DEPENDENCIES: DON'T ABSORB RISKS YOU DON'T CONTROL

Adherence to the savings clause requirements does not yield automatic relief. Do not accept a risk outside your control; clearly document your delivery dependencies and immediately escalate and seek relief for any performance deficiency caused by the client or a third party.

CHAPTER 7

WHAT SHALL WE DO WHEN FACED WITH A DISPUTE?

Given the size, scope, cost, and complexity of most outsourcing engagements, transition timelines are tight, scheduling delays are not easily absorbed, and little tolerance for performance deficiencies exists. Outsourcing a key business process, such as procurement or human resources, multiple bundles of mission-critical applications, or a key infrastructure component such as desktop management or the service desk, may have a significant impact on the organization. Therefore, it is critical that the client's leadership participate in an oversight or steering committee to monitor performance quality, to manage relationships, and to assist in the facilitation of any disputes or other challenges that may arise throughout the vendor ecosystem. This level of engagement is critical for delivery success and reinforces the proposition that you cannot outsource responsibility.

In a multivendor delivery ecosystem, oversight over the various vendors and the protocols that should be followed where their services are interconnected must be carefully orchestrated. The net effect of this approach is that each vendor must cooperate with its peers in the ecosystem and put the client's interests first when solving broader issues beyond their specific delivery scope. Taking into account that the vendors may be fierce competitors in the marketplace, achieving a high level of cooperation is much easier said than done. All vendors must be equally motivated to act when faced with exigent circumstances and not feel compelled to sit on the sidelines out of concern that they will be held accountable for the deficiency or will not be compensated for their efforts.

WHAT SHALL WE DO WHEN FACED WITH A DISPUTE?

The method by which order is maintained in a multi-vendor ecosystem is typically contained in the governance provisions of the agreement. Specifically, a robust governance process is a critical component of an outsourcing agreement because it will specify how key project-level decisions are made and how disputes and other ordinary-course delivery issues that arise between the parties are escalated for resolution. We will discuss the key components of a governance program later, but suffice it to say that strict compliance with the governance process is an absolute necessity in a multi-vendor environment to avoid a bunch of finger-pointing among vendors if an overarching deficiency arises.

The governance process may not seem to be that important, but it does serve as the contractually stipulated entry point—the trial court, if you will—before the parties can pursue more formal relief via arbitration or litigation. For a governance process to be effective, the parties must be willing to exercise their rights under it immediately upon recognizing that a dispute or performance issue exists.

The governance process for the review and acceptance of milestones or other critical deliverables, and any subsequent warranty claims, is usually stipulated in the acceptance and warranty provisions of the agreement. Typically, if a deliverable was tendered for acceptance and failed to meet the acceptance criteria, the service provider would have a contractually stipulated timeline in which it would repair the deliverable at its cost and tender it again for acceptance. What many governance provisions lack is defining the process to be followed if the re-tendered deliverable is still deemed to be nonconforming by the client. Will the service provider be given another opportunity to repair the deliverable and re-tender again for acceptance? What if a dispute should arise about the level of conformity? Will the client be able to pursue its termination rights? Will the client be entitled to a refund or some other remedy? Will an objective third party be identified who can review the deliverable and render a binding decision on its conformity with the acceptance criteria? Even though there is no right answer, be sure to think through the various options when crafting a governance model in this area.

With regard to project-level decisions, it is advised to include a framework in the agreement that identifies the specific individuals who are empowered to make binding decisions and prioritize issues based upon their level of importance and time sensitivity. The framework should also specify the timeline for both routine and fast-track decisions under which the client must respond to maintain forward momentum in the transition schedule or delivery timeline.

In addition, a key component of any governance process is a dispute resolution framework that identifies the escalation process followed by the parties before initiating any formal arbitration or adjudication. Including a robust dispute resolution process in an outsourcing agreement is a necessity, because it escalates problem issues to the appropriate hierarchical level within the client and service provider organization, and specifies a number of days during which they can resolve the dispute before it makes a transition to the next level in the process.

CHAPTER 8

LET'S BE OPEN TO CHANGE

Let's keep in mind the study completed by the Standish Group. One of the primary reasons IT projects do not succeed is the parties' failure to properly define scope. Given that statistic, a narrowly tailored statement of work is an absolute necessity, especially in a multivendor environment. Assuming that we have been disciplined in the development of the statement of work, some change is likely to occur during the delivery term. Because of such routine changes, it is critical that the parties define a change order process that addresses any client requests that deviate from what is articulated in the SOW. A well-documented change order process goes hand in hand with the governance model and should address the scope, pricing, and approval process for change order requests as well as a time line that can accommodate routine as well as fast-track change requests.

We will review a market-relevant change order provision later, but at its heart, a *change order* is a document executed by both parties to the agreement that changes the method, manner, performance, specifications, or terms and conditions of the statement of work initially agreed upon by the parties. An efficient change order process is one under which both parties to the transaction are clear that there will be no deviations in scope unless a written change order has been executed by the parties. No exceptions to this rule are allowed, irrespective of the exigency of the circumstances. An efficient change order process is also one that places time constraints on the request, response, review, negotiation, and acceptance processes.

CHAPTER 9

AM I GOOD ENOUGH FOR ACCEPTANCE?

For each of the stipulated milestones or critical deliverables in an outsourcing engagement, a set of *objective, measurable, and verifiable* acceptance criteria must be identified, even if the output is nothing but paper-based deliverables. All acceptance criteria must meet this standard and be free from any ambiguity. This approach is critical because those criteria are the baseline against which deliverables are accepted and the viability of a warranty claim is measured. As soon as the criteria become subjective, immeasurable, and unverifiable, both parties have different expectations about delivery, and a dispute is likely to ensue. When developing these criteria, it should be assumed that an independent third party is responsible for reviewing the completion of a milestone to determine conformity with these criteria. If there is some dispute about acceptance of a particular deliverable or achievement of a milestone, the governance model should address escalation and resolution.

It is important to remember that scope creep results when statements of work are not narrowly tailored and the acceptance criteria—the measuring stick used to gauge deliverable quality—are vague and ambiguous. This same dynamic is true about service levels. They must be clearly defined and objective, measurable, and verifiable. So when you think that the statement of work, acceptance criteria, and service levels are clearly defined, take one more look from the perspective of an objective third party unfamiliar with the scope of services rendered, but, nonetheless, might be asked to render a decision in adjudicating a dispute between the parties in the future.

SECTION 3

LET'S DISSECT AN OUTSOURCING AGREEMENT

CHAPTER 10

THE AGREEMENT FRAMEWORK

Once we get past the preamble, background, objectives, and provisions that address definitions, the incorporation of the various schedules, and references, it is important to address the overarching framework for the agreement, how it will govern the currently contemplated as well as future engagements, and other general parameters of the agreement, including the order of precedence, the requirement for any local agreements, the provision of services through affiliates, and a parental guarantee, if applicable.

While it may seem innocuous in nature, the objectives section of the agreement should not be overlooked. As we have discussed, an agreement which contains terms that are free from ambiguity, narrowly tailored, and objective, measurable, and verifiable is optimal. I am a strong proponent of the four corners rule, namely that the words contained in the agreement reflect the intent of the parties and should be clearly understood by an objective reviewer. Ambiguity must be avoided at all costs.

To the extent there is a formal dispute resulting from an ambiguous term in the agreement, it is common for an arbiter or court to look at extrinsic evidence—any correspondence from the contract negotiation—that will assist in determining the actual intent of the parties. While an agreement free from ambiguity should be the overarching intent of the parties, it may be difficult to achieve.

To ensure clarity as to the intent of the parties, clients and their counsel will include a set of business goals and objectives for the agreement against which any ambiguous terms should be construed in the event of a dispute. By including such a provision, the likelihood that an arbitrator or court would look to any extrinsic evidence to clarify the intent of the parties would be mitigated. This section of the agreement should therefore reflect the legitimate expectations and objectives of both parties and should be balanced and consistent with the scope of the underlying services.

When negotiating an agreement for outsourcing services, it is a common practice to execute a master agreement under which one or more service agreements could be executed by the parties. Each service agreement would potentially encompass a different stream of services, including application outsourcing, infrastructure outsourcing which may consist of data center, security, service desk, workplace, or network services, or business process outsourcing which may consist of finance and accounting, health administration, insurance, marketing, human resources, procurement, or supply chain services, or systems integration services. In addition, the parties should articulate what, if any, service types would be excluded from delivery under the terms of the master agreement. Finally, neither party to an outsourcing agreement has a crystal ball and can predict the impact changes in technology may have on the delivery or pricing model or the governing terms and conditions. Despite the evolution of RPA and AI, the future is still unknown. The best advice I can provide is to execute an agreement with a governance model that provides for flexibility based upon underlying changes in technology or law.

The challenge usually encountered in this area is that the master agreement is typically negotiated in reference to a specific sales opportunity for a specific service line. Because the parties are so heavily focused on negotiating terms and conditions commensurate with that service agreement, they do not take the requisite time to determine if any deviations in the master agreement would be appropriate—a menu-driven approach, if you will—for future opportunities of a different services type. An example would be agreeing to a liability limitation for a systems integration engagement; such a limit would typically be expressed as a multiple of the amount of fees paid under the statement of work from which the claim arose. However, this liability construct would not apply to an outsourcing engagement under which the liability limitation would be expressed as the amount of fees paid by the client over the prior rolling 12-month period. Given this dynamic, this is one area where I would say that the parties need to slow down and prepare for these future contingencies.

It is much easier to establish terms for future opportunities while the master agreement is being executed instead of trying to execute an addendum for a different service stream type post-execution. While many master agreement terms are service-type-agnostic, a number of terms vary, depending upon the underlying nature of the services provided, and should be modified accordingly. As you are going through this exercise, it is also important to make sure that the agreement contains clear definitions of the different types of services that the service provider may deliver over the term of the agreement. Establishing these clear boundaries allows for the easy identification of work type, which should facilitate a much easier path through the menu options for the affected terms. A sample provision that addresses different types of service offerings is as follows:

The following service area descriptions will apply irrespective of engagement size, duration, and delivery geography.

- **Business Process Outsourcing:** An outsourcing engagement under which Service Provider assumes management, operational, and delivery responsibility for a cross-industry business process service including human resources, finance and accounting, learning, procurement, or supply chain or an industry-specific service including credit services, health administration, insurance, network, pharmaceutical, or utilities.

- **Management Consulting:** Strategic, functional, and industry-focused consulting engagements, including business process management, change management, risk management and enterprise resilience, supply chain management, customer/channel strategy, talent and organization performance, mergers and acquisitions, corporate or business unit strategy and operations management, and IT strategy and transformation.

- **Systems Integration and Technology Consulting Services:** Application development and systems integration and technology services engagements including the design, build, test, and deployment phases as well as program management and process improvement services for all commercial off-the-shelf and custom-developed applications.

Formally instituting this level of clarity while the master agreement is being negotiated is much easier than doing so after the fact, because the client typically seeks to adhere to the provisions in the master agreement, and the service provider seeks to deviate in similar fashion. And let us not forget that both parties may seek to reopen any terms and conditions from the master agreement whose final result they did not like; so it can become a cherry-picking contest as well. The key here is to create a menu option in the body of the master agreement only for those terms that are not generic and for which a legitimate deviation exists for different service offerings across the consulting life cycle. Liability and termination are two good examples where a menu option would apply. Terms like invoicing and payment, acceptance provisions, taxes, and insurance are more generic and for which a deviation is not legitimate. I have attempted the "wait and we will deal with it later" approach on many occasions, and it has not been a pleasant experience. It yields more time with attorneys and the likelihood of a dispute. A menu-driven approach, as referenced above, serves the parties well over the master agreement's term.

As we have discussed, the overarching objective is to have a contractual structure that can flex during the delivery term to accommodate new opportunities. While the structure itself is usually not overly controversial, acknowledging legitimate deviations for specific terms and conditions as well as any excluded services is a necessity. A sample provision that addresses the agreement framework is as follows:

> The Parties intend for this Master Services Agreement to establish the contractual framework pursuant to which Client and Service Provider may enter into one or more service agreements that describe specific products and services to be provided by Service Provider to the Client for information technology outsourcing services consisting of application development and maintenance, data center, security, managed network and end user computing and service desk services and Systems Integration services, and any additional terms and conditions that will apply to the provision and receipt of such products and services.

For the avoidance of doubt, this Master Agreement may not be used for Management Consulting or Business Process Outsourcing services.

Another typical and much more controversial provision in the framework section of the agreement addresses the due diligence parameters, whereby the services provider develops its solution and pricing construct for the applicable service agreement. In a typical outsourcing sales cycle, the service providers competing for the project effort are typically given the opportunity to conduct due diligence on the services to be initially outsourced from the client or transitioned from another service provider.

While this is a reasonable requirement—you typically would not buy a car without taking a look under the hood—a recent practice is for clients to provide historical incident volumes and a set of stated and aspirational service levels in lieu of any formal due diligence process. Under this construct, the prospective service providers are not provided with any historical evidence of achievement of service levels. They are also not given the benefit of any other data they would typically receive during a more robust due diligence process that could span anywhere from two to four weeks, depending on the complexity of the services. Irrespective of those glaring limitations and the complete lack of data, clients expect that the service providers competing for their business will, nonetheless, tender a managed service price over a five-year delivery term. From my perspective, this approach is not grounded in legitimacy and seems to set the stage for failure. If neither the client nor its existing service provider had been able to attain the stated service levels, then how is it reasonable to expect that a new vendor can achieve the same?

I encourage you not to accept the likely client response, namely that the robots will save the day. This non-due-diligence approach is also typically coupled with provisions that do not allow for any adjustments to price or service levels after delivery begins. Any contracting approach which is predicated upon stated or aspirational service levels, limited due diligence, and guaranteed productivity targets is likely to become more widespread with the deployment of automation. Given the client expectation that automation eliminates all human error, that increases in volume can be easily accommodated with no impact on quality, and that the workday has been expanded to 24 hours, stated or aspirational service levels in the 99.999 percent range and significant productivity guarantees will become table stakes in competitive outsourcing procurements.

In my opinion, this construct is nothing more than playing pin the tail on the donkey with mission-critical applications or infrastructure needed to run the client's business. The risk in this approach can be mitigated by providing for an expedited due diligence process, instituting presumptive service levels, delineating a baseline period when the actual service levels are set, and by establishing a price adjustment mechanism if volumes increase beyond a certain threshold.

Most importantly, the assumption that the robots will save the day is not legitimate given the on-going role that their human counterparts play in initiating incidents and tickets, remediating incidents that require exception processing, adhering to changes in business processes, allowing the robots to be deployed in their IT environment, supporting the process automations, and accepting and complying with change. Even if the human component of the service is executed flawlessly, this limited due diligence approach is still negligent, at best. When contemplating the out-sourcing of a key process or bundle of applications, why would a client not provide every opportunity for its potential vendors to conduct a thorough due diligence review and to query key client personnel, all under the guise of receiving a set of competing proposals grounded in legitimacy and yielding predictable results? This construct—no due diligence, zero price adjustment, limited data, stated and aspirational service levels, and assumption the robots will fill the gaps—goes a step beyond preparing for the consequences of failure; it pretty much guarantees that result.

The due diligence process may include the following:

- interviews with key client personnel and existing service providers
- reviews of existing contractual agreements
- analysis of tickets or incident volumes, including the severity, frequency, and nature of the incidents in the prior 12 months
- performance levels achieved by the client or the existing service provider
- technology sets and tools used by the client
- skill levels of employees currently providing the service

- average time required to resolve incidents
- total head count currently supporting the service
- complexity of the current change request process
- complexity of any documentation requirements
- upgrade frequency for various tools and technologies
- audit frequency and corresponding level of effort

Each data point obtained in the due diligence process assists the services provider in establishing its price—either a fixed monthly managed service fee or an estimated price derived from a time and materials rate card—and evaluating potential options with respect to the terms and conditions that govern delivery. When the potential vendors have had the opportunity to conduct their due diligence, then it is legitimate to hold them accountable for their proposed managed service fee and not allow for any adjustments, except when the vendor has relied on a misrepresentation or incomplete or inaccurate data in establishing its team roster and price and that reliance materially and adversely impacts the service provider's ability to deliver the services under the terms of the agreement.

An example that embodies this approach is as follows:

Service Provider acknowledges and agrees that it will be solely responsible, at no charge to client, for conducting any due diligence activities, including obtaining and evaluating any information and data necessary to provide the Services in accordance with the Agreement and any Service Agreements executed thereunder. Service Provider acknowledges and agrees that it will conduct to its satisfaction the appropriate level of due diligence activities and corresponding validation and verification activities on client (including on any applicable Equipment, Software, systems, third-party contracts or personnel) operations so that it can properly perform the Services described in each Service Agreement in accordance with the terms of such Service Agreement and this Master Services Agreement.

Client will provide Service Provider with the information, cooperation and assistance as reasonably requested in relation to such due diligence activities. Service Provider acknowledges and agrees that there will not be any opportunity or provisions that will allow for any adjustments (to the applicable Charges, Performance Standards or Services description) to the applicable Service Agreement or to the terms of this Master Agreement after the applicable Service Agreement Effective Date due to Service Provider's failure to conduct adequate due diligence, except as may be agreed upon by the client in its sole discretion or as provided in this provision.

In the event that either Party determines, after the applicable Service Agreement Effective Date, that Service Provider has reasonably relied upon a misrepresentation made by client in writing prior to such Service Agreement Effective Date, or there is incomplete due diligence information as specified in the applicable Service Agreement, and the reliance on such misrepresentation or identified incomplete diligence information has had or will have a material adverse impact on Service Provider's ability to provide the Services in accordance with the terms and conditions of the Agreement, the Parties will adjust such terms and conditions in accordance with the Change Control Procedure.

While this provision allows only for a price or other adjustment in certain circumstances, it is legitimate because it gives the vendor the opportunity to conduct any necessary due diligence from which it can develop its proposal. As long as the services provider has the opportunity to conduct a robust due diligence process, as previously described, I would say that it is reasonable to hold it to its managed service fee, unless there are extreme changes in incidents or ticket volume that could not have been foreseen at the time of contract execution.

The other key components of the agreement framework section of the master agreement are likely to include an order of precedence provision to address any conflicts between the master agreement, the service agreement, and any other appendices, attachments, or other documents incorporated by reference into the master agreement. In this area, I propose using a construct under which the buck stops with the terms and conditions in the master agreement, unless they are explicitly excluded or modified in a service agreement, as follows:

The terms of this Master Services Agreement will be deemed to be incorporated into each Service Agreement and the terms and conditions set forth in this Master Agreement will govern Service Provider's provision of Services under each Service Agreement, except for provisions in this Master Services Agreement that are specifically excluded from or modified in a Service Agreement, which, in order to be effective, will require the Service Agreement to include a reference to the applicable Section of this Master Agreement being excluded or modified. Any exceptions to this Master Agreement agreed upon in writing by client and Service Provider pursuant to a particular Service Agreement will apply only for purposes of that Service Agreement, and will not be deemed to in any way amend, modify, cancel or waive the provisions of this Master Services Agreement with respect to any other Service Agreement.

The other key components of this section may include a provision which requires a parental guarantee, if necessary, a provision which authorizes the service provider to utilize affiliates in its provision of the services, a provision which allows for the execution of local country agreements if the service provider will be delivering services to service recipients outside the United States, and a provision which addresses securing any consents required for the delivery and receipt of the services. The objective of executing the local agreements is to comply with the applicable laws in a particular country; to mitigate the tax or regulatory liabilities of the parties; or to mitigate foreign currency exposure because doing so would facilitate invoicing in local currency between the service provider affiliate and the client affiliate in that location. Other than in those key areas, the local agreement typically has the same terms and conditions as those in the master agreement.

Given the comingling of equipment, software, services, resources, or materials that occurs in an outsourcing engagement, it is highly likely that both the service provider and the client will need to obtain consents—a series of licenses, waivers, permits, authorizations, clearances, or approvals—that will be required for the successful delivery and receipt of the services. Each party will be responsible for obtaining certain consents, providing any assistance to the other party as may be necessary to secure the consent, complying with the requirements of any consent, and paying any costs or fees required—license, transfer, upgrade, or termination—for the necessary consents.

Finally, this section includes provisions that address the term of the master agreement. Generally, these provisions establish a three to five year initial master agreement term, the term of any service agreements executed thereunder, and the ability of the client to extend the term of the master agreement or any service agreement, with the applicable notice periods required for doing so. While I do not expect the term of the master agreement to be shortened with the deployment of automation, it is probable that the term and structure of any underlying service agreements (Application, Infrastructure, or Business Process Outsourcing) will change. From a structural perspective, the service agreements will likely be priced on a transaction or outcome basis (per invoice, per transaction, per widget) versus the current managed service base team capacity model. In addition, the term of the service agreement will likely be variable as clients will seek the ability to terminate certain components of the services, lift and shift scope to other vendors, or repatriate the services with limited notice and no financial impact. To the extent the delivery team is heavily composed of robots and the underlying software, algorithms, and process automations are owned by the client, this level of flexibility is not unreasonable as the impact to the service provider from a reduction in scope should be minimal.

CHAPTER 11

LET'S MAKE IT MINE

Before the run phase of an outsourcing engagement can begin, an orderly transition must occur in a manner that facilitates the appropriate level of knowledge transfer, that does not disrupt or cause any detrimental impact on the client's business or IT operations, and that does not result in any service degradation. Like executing a statement of work for the overarching service itself, a discrete transition plan needs to be developed that clearly articulates the transition phases and timeline, any transition milestones or deliverables, as well as any critical deliverables that must be accepted by the client before the transition is completed and the run phase of the engagement can begin. In addition, the transition plan should clearly articulate the roles and responsibilities of the parties as well as the specific activities, quality gates, and corresponding acceptance criteria that must be met before the service provider can navigate through the transition phases. Finally, given the time sensitivity typically associated with the transition phase, there must be an accelerated acceptance window—no more than three days. During that time, the client must review transition deliverables, evaluate them in light of the acceptance criteria, and either accept them and allow the service provider to move to the next transition phase or provide the basis for any rejection.

It is critical to carefully review the activities that must be completed before the service provider can move from one transition phase to the next. As with any acceptance criteria, make sure the completion criteria are objective, measurable, and verifiable. If not, the service provider could remain in the transition phases much longer than anticipated. Also, it may be appropriate to let some of the phases to be conducted concurrently rather than sequentially.

Selling Outsourcing Services in the Digital Age

The transition is a critical phase of an outsourcing engagement and should not be overlooked. Because many service providers provide a transition at no cost, they cannot recoup any of that investment if they cannot successfully navigate through the transition into the run phase of the program. Therefore, do not accept the approach taken by some third-party advisors that the transition is the service provider's responsibility, with limited input from the client. The parties must work in partnership to successfully navigate through the transition and, ultimately, deliver the service in accordance with the service levels.

The deployment of automation will have a significant impact on both the scope and term of transition. The primary objectives for transition are to allow for the orderly handover of the outsourced service to the new service provider and to allow the service provider to demonstrate it can deliver the service in a manner consistent with the agreed upon service levels. As we will discuss, the typical transition process consists of multiple phases including planning, knowledge acquisition, knowledge transfer, and stabilization. Each of these phases allows the service provider personnel the ability to undergo the appropriate level of training and knowledge transfer required to deliver the outsourced services. The transition term may span sixteen weeks or longer during which the FTEs conduct interviews, develop process and procedures manuals, shadow the personnel that are currently providing the service, and establish a level of operational readiness and efficiency.

Consider a newly outsourced service where the delivery team is composed primarily of robots and the level of human involvement in service delivery is minimal. Is a lengthy transition period necessary? Do the robots require months to learn and demonstrate their level of operational readiness? In this scenario, the end-to-end business process flow will be configured in the automation software and the robots can be deployed immediately in the legacy environment. No extensive knowledge transfer period is required and all human error is eliminated. Ultimately, the transition plan will vary significantly, depending on the scope of the services transitioned and the composition of the workforce that will be responsible for delivery. To the extent that certain components of the service will be fully automated, an expedited transition period is possible. When negotiating the transition term, the level of exception processing that will require human intervention should also be considered.

Irrespective of the composition of the delivery team, it is important to clarify the activities that must be completed before the service provider can move to the next phase or quality gate in the transition plan. A transition is not something that can be completed in isolation by the service provider; it is critical that the client identify a transition manager who serves as the primary point of accountability for the transition, who reviews and accepts transition deliverables in a timely manner, who monitors the client's adherence to and performance of its responsibilities as specified in the transition plan, and who consents to the deployment of automation within the client's IT environment. In addition, the client transition manager will be responsible for overseeing any change management and compliance obligations associated with the processes being automated.

From a contractual and negotiation perspective, the key transition components to be addressed include transition delays as well as termination rights that are triggered if the service provider breaches a material obligation related to transition, is unable to obtain acceptance for a transition deliverable or achieve a transition milestone, or exceeds the transition milestone credit cap. Although the penalty for failure may be high—up to and including termination for cause—I believe that it is appropriate, given the importance of a timely and quality transition. To the extent that the service provider cannot successfully navigate through transition, then the client should have a variety of options at its disposal, up to and including termination.

For client delays, there should be a day-for-day extension of the affected transition milestones. There should also be a notice period and a limitation on the length of the delay. If the client seeks a delay longer than 15 days, then provisions should be made for the impacted service provider's staff. Either they are removed from the transition effort, they are redeployed to another active engagement with the same client, or the client can hold the transition staff but reimburse the service provider for its time and expenses in accordance with the rates identified in the applicable service agreement.

If there are no client-imposed delays, it is important to identify what, if any, credit accrues for any critical deliverables that are not accepted by the client on or before the transition milestone date. To be clear, not all transition deliverables and milestones are designated as "critical" in the agreement. For those labeled as critical, the parties need to agree on the amount and recurrence of the credit. A sample provision that embodies this construct is as follows:

> Each Service Agreement or Statement of Work executed thereunder will delineate the Transition Deliverables and Transition Milestones that must be completed and achieved by the Service Provider. Certain Transition Deliverables and Milestones will be designated as "critical" in the applicable Service Agreement. For each Critical Transition Deliverable and Critical Transition Milestone, the applicable Service Agreement will set forth a credit that will be paid by Service Provider if any Critical Transition Deliverables or Milestones are not accepted by the client, due to the fault of Service Provider, on or before the applicable Transition Milestone Date.

> The Service Provider will incur a Transition Milestone Credit on the Transition Milestone Date if the applicable Critical Transition Deliverable or Critical Transition Milestone is not accepted by the client on such date and on a recurring basis thereafter until it achieves Acceptance of the applicable Critical Transition Deliverable or Critical Transition Milestone in accordance with the applicable Service Agreement.

This provision includes the concept of a recurring milestone credit until the deliverable is accepted or the milestone is achieved. The notion of a credit associated with transition deliverables is consistent with the market. The more appropriate question addresses the amount of the recurring credit, any limitation placed on the accrual of credits, and what remedy the client pursues if that limitation is exceeded. We will discuss service levels and fees at risk related to service level achievement later in this book. However, I believe that it is reasonable to place a limitation on transition milestone and deliverables credits in a manner consistent with the amount of fees at risk for service level defaults. Therefore, if the service provider is placing 12 percent of its monthly managed service fees at risk, tied to the successful achievement of the identified service levels, then it is not unreasonable for it to place 12 percent of its transition fees at risk, tied to the successful delivery of the critical transition deliverables and achievement of any critical transition milestones, which we will discuss next. This construct is captured as follows:

In the event of a Critical Deliverable Default, then in addition to any other remedies available to client under the Agreement, at law or in equity, client may elect to recover for such failure the applicable Critical Deliverable Credit. Service Provider will continue to pay the applicable Critical Deliverable Credit following the Critical Deliverable Milestone Date until the Critical Deliverable has been accepted by client. Service Provider will take all necessary actions, including assigning additional Service Provider Resources, after failing to achieve Acceptance by the Critical Deliverable Milestone Date to achieve Acceptance of the Critical Deliverable.

The Critical Deliverables that are applicable to the Service Agreement are set forth in the following table. Critical Deliverable Credits will be allocated to each Statement of Work, proportionally, in accordance with the total Transition Charges specified in each Statement of Work under this Service Agreement. With respect to a Statement of Work, the amount of any allocated Critical Deliverable Credits and the Transition Milestone Credits under such Statement of Work will not exceed 12 percent of the Transition Charges under such Statement of Work. Critical Deliverables that are applicable to a particular Statement of Work will be set forth in such Statement of Work.

CRITICAL DELIVERABLES:

CRITICAL DELIVERABLE NAME	CRITICAL DELIVERABLE COMPLETION/ MILESTONE DATE	CRITICAL DELIVERABLE CREDIT
Policies and Procedures Manual initial draft—Transition sections	30 days after Service Agreement Effective Date	**Initial credit:** $10,000 **Recurring credit:** $5,000 per week
Policies and Procedures Manual initial draft Remaining sections	45 days after Service Agreement Effective Date	**Initial credit:** $10,000 **Recurring credit:** $5,000 per week
Final Policies and Procedures Manual	60 days after Acceptance of initial draft	**Initial credit:** $25,000 **Recurring credit:** $10,000 per week

In addition to the critical transition deliverables, it is typical for the service provider to place a portion of its transition fees at risk in the form of critical transition milestone credits if the service provider cannot successfully navigate through the transition quality gates in a timely manner. These critical transition milestone credits, along with the critical deliverable credits, should not exceed 12 percent of the total transition fees under the engagement.

A typical transition plan contains a variety of phases and corresponding quality gates, each having a set of discrete activities and deliverables that must be completed and accepted before the service provider can move to the next phase in the process. Those phases vary but at a macro level should include the following: (1) a planning phase in which the parties refine and finalize the transition plan; (2) a knowledge acquisition phase in which the service provider documents and learns all of the processes associated with the scope of services to be transitioned; (3) a knowledge transfer phase in which the service provider establishes its level of knowledge and demonstrates its delivery capabilities; and (4) the ever-important stabilization phase in which the service provider demonstrates its knowledge base over a contractually stipulated period—30 days—and its ability to deliver the services in accordance with the service requirements and service levels.

Specific activities in each phase are as follows:

1. **Planning Phase:** technical requirements; staffing, training, and implementation plans for all applicable methods, tools, and processes; finalize the transition period processes in the policies and procedures manual; readiness planning for each location where the services will be provided, and finalize the transition plan.

2. **Knowledge Acquisition:** conduct subject matter expert interviews; document knowledge of the scope of services and supported business processes; develop run books that allow the service provider to manage and troubleshoot the underlying applications or system; execute the training, access, and mobilization plans; identify high-risk areas; and confirm operational readiness.

3. **Knowledge Transfer:** service provider personnel shadow client personnel to expand on the depth and breadth of their knowledge base; service provider receives live incidents, tickets, and

maintenance requests for resolution, with client support as necessary; and service provider demonstrates its use of the incident management system and knowledge base required for operational readiness for the run phase of the engagement.

4. **Stabilization:** complete the policies and procedures manual; measure and report on service level performance, confirm that the service provider can provide the services and operate in a manner commensurate with the terms and conditions of the agreement.

The best advice I can give on specific activities in each phase and corresponding quality gates is to make sure that the deliverables are objective, measurable, and verifiable. A transition is intended to occur in a defined time period and is priced accordingly; thus, it is critical to make sure that the service provider's ability to navigate through the transition phases is not inhibited by the client's subjective perception that the service provider is not ready to graduate into the run phase of the engagement. While I am not suggesting that the service provider should advance unless it is absolutely ready, objective measures of operational readiness, both for humans and robots, should be the benchmark for making any such determination. As previously discussed, the other implication here is that certain quality gates are deemed critical transition milestones to which transition milestone credits will apply. Although the transition milestone credits are capped accordingly, the service provider does not want to be stuck in a transition indefinitely because crossing the cap is likely to yield a no-cost termination right for the client. I am a proponent of this termination trigger because if the service provider cannot advance through the quality gates—assuming it has objective acceptance standards—then the client should be able to exit the agreement accordingly and the service provider may want to consider another line of work.

An example of the critical transition milestone credit construct is as follows:

NUMBER	CRITICAL TRANSITION DELIVERABLE OR CRITICAL TRANSITION MILESTONE	TRANSITION MILESTONE DATE	ACCEPTANCE CRITERIA	TRANSITION MILESTONE CREDIT
1	Final Transition Plan	60 days after SOW Effective Date	The Acceptance Criteria will include meeting the requirements specified in the Transition Schedule.	**Initial Penalty:** $20,000 **Recurring Penalty:** $5000 (Every 2 weeks after initial penalty)
2	Transition Quality Gate #2 – Knowledge Acquisition	As per agreed Transition Plan	The Acceptance Criteria will include meeting the requirements specified in the Transition Schedule.	**Initial Penalty:** 2% of SOW transition value **Recurring Penalty:** 1% of SOW Transition value (Every 2 weeks after initial penalty)
3	Transition Quality Gate #4 – Stabilization	As per agreed Transition Plan	The Acceptance Criteria will include meeting the requirements specified in the Transition Schedule.	**Initial Penalty:** 5% of SOW transition value **Second Penalty:** 3% of SOW Transition value

We have now identified our critical transition deliverables and critical transition milestones and any related fees at risk, agreed on a transition plan, and established objective acceptance criteria that allow the service provider to move through the approval stage gates. Then we must ask what happens if the service provider cannot successfully proceed through the transition. Although the premise of this book is not to spend too much time preparing for the consequences of failure, prudence dictates that we must address this scenario.

As stated previously, I believe the market-relevant approach is that the client should be able to terminate the individual service agreement (and any related, but not all, service agreements) without cost or penalty and without the payment of any termination charges if the service provider does the following: (1) commits a material breach with respect to the transition and fails to cure such breach within 30 days after its receipt of notice of the failure; (2) fails to achieve acceptance of a critical transition deliverable or critical transition milestone within 30 days of the transition milestone date; or (3) exceeds the transition milestone credits limit specified (in the previous example, 12 percent of the total transition fees) in the applicable service agreement.

The transition is the precursor to the run phase of an outsourcing engagement. It must not be overlooked and should be treated similarly to a stand-alone engagement. There should be a clear transition plan that sets forth the roles and responsibilities of the parties, the amount of automation to be deployed at the commencement of service delivery, as well as the phases and stage gates and corresponding acceptance criteria that must be met to progress accordingly. The transition requires working closely with the client or a third-party vendor to acquire the knowledge necessary to deliver the services and achieve the service levels. Given the consequences of failure, its importance must not be overlooked in the negotiation process.

CHAPTER 12

LET'S SWEEP IT UP

Like in any other consulting engagement, you would expect that the scope of services in an outsourcing engagement should be straightforward—the service provider should deliver its obligations as delineated in the statement of work. As discussed previously, the statement of work should be narrowly tailored, free from ambiguity, and clearly define the roles and responsibilities of the parties and the delivery obligations of the service provider. Unfortunately, achieving that level of clarity is not that clear cut. Along the way, someone created the concept of a sweeps provision. It sweeps additional delivery obligations to the service provider, even if they were not included in the statement of work and the service provider had not foreseen these additional services when developing its managed service fixed price.

In essence, a sweeps provision is intended to be a catch-all for a statement of work that might not be 100 percent complete. Given the complexity of some outsourcing engagements, the potential unknown processes, or "below the radar" outputs, delivered in the current environment, and the level of staff displacement, it may be difficult to identify every function and component of the outsourced service that will be transitioned into the new delivery environment. The purpose of a sweeps provision is to "sweep" into the delivery obligations of the outsourcing provider—with no corresponding increase in price—functions or services that were, in good faith, excluded from the statement of work agreed upon by the parties. These functions and services, however were implied in the outsourced service because they are inherent in or a necessary component of the proper performance or provision of the services. Exclusions of this type may occur if the functions were not disclosed or were unknown during the due diligence process.

The key to successfully developing a sweeps provision is to carefully manage the size of the broom and the amount of additional delivery obligations swept into the supplier's delivery obligations, because they could have a material impact on the service provider's financial performance and ability to meet the service levels. When viewed though a market-relevant lens, the broom should be the size of a handheld dustpan and capable of sweeping in no more than a de minimis amount (no more than 5 percent) of additional delivery obligations to the service provider. The challenge is that clients and their counsel have latched on to the concept of a sweeps or implied services provision, and want to use a commercial-size broom with a much greater sweeping capacity. To avoid any disputes regarding broom size, the focus should be on taking the requisite amount of time in the due diligence process to develop a thorough statement of work. I have encountered a few instances where the parties agree to use the words, "like for like" to describe the scope of the outsourced service. These three words, while innocuous in nature, will yield a broom of monumental proportion. My guidance is to never, under any circumstance, use this language as it will absolutely result in a dispute.

The level of automation to be deployed over the delivery term will also have an impact on the implications of a sweeps provision. Under the legacy FTE model, if a necessary and inherent function was excluded from the statement of work, the impact could be significant depending upon the number of service provider personnel required to perform the excluded function over the delivery term. Many disputes have arisen regarding the necessary or inherent nature of the excluded function. Disputes of this type may be mitigated if the excluded function or process can be easily programmed into the end-to-end business process flow in the automation software. To the extent that the robots can complete the underlying task over the course of their extended workday, there would be no cost impact to the service provider. While taking the time to document a complete statement of work remains an absolute requirement, the impact of failing to include some underlying function or component of the outsourced service may be mitigated if the gap can be easily remediated by the robots.

A sample services description in an applications outsourcing agreement that acknowledges potential gaps in the statement of work but seeks to limit the size of the broom is as follows:

Description of the Services

General

Commencing on each applicable Service Agreement Effective Date and continuing throughout the applicable Service Agreement Term, Service Provider will provide to the Client the following Functions, which may evolve or be supplemented, enhanced, modified or replaced in accordance with the Agreement (collectively, the "Services"):

the Functions described in this Master Services Agreement;

the Functions described in the applicable Service Agreement; and

the Functions that were performed by the applicable employees, independent contractors, contractors, and service providers of client who were (a) transferred to Service Provider, (b) displaced or (c) whose Functions were displaced, in each case, as a result of the applicable Service Agreement, even if such Functions are not specifically described in the applicable Service Agreement, provided that such Functions (i) relate to the Functions described in the applicable Service Agreement and (ii) with respect to application maintenance and support services, relate to Applications within the scope of the applicable Service Agreement. Nothing in this Section is intended to cause an explicit client Function under a Service Agreement to become a Service Provider Function.

Implied Services

If any Functions not specifically described in the Agreement are inherent in, and necessary and required for, the proper performance and provision of the Services in accordance with the requirements of the Agreement, such Functions will be deemed to be implied by and included within the scope of the Services (and provided to the Service Recipients at no additional charge) to the same extent and in the same manner as if expressly described in the Agreement.

It is important to know that any implied services swept in under a sweeps provision do not impact the managed service fixed price of the vendor; so always be mindful of the depth and breadth of the broom.

CHAPTER 13

WHAT ABOUT VARIANCES IN VOLUME?

The other key concept that should be addressed when evaluating delivery scope and price is variances in volume related to the services. For example, in an applications outsourcing agreement, the monthly managed service price would, typically, be established based on incident and ticket volume. There are many options to be considered when determining how underlying changes in volume impact the monthly managed service price. Clients, their counsel, and third-party advisors may prefer a construct in which the monthly managed service price remains firm, irrespective of any underlying changes in volume. A more legitimate and market relevant approach, however, is to establish a dead band that, when exceeded, would result in a corresponding increase or decrease in the monthly managed service price, based on a construct—a variable fee structure consisting of additional resource charges (ARCs) and reduced resource credits (RRCs)—agreed on at the time of contract execution. It is also important to know the actual recipients of the services and to have a price adjustment mechanism if the number of service recipients varies beyond some contractually stipulated threshold. In addition, a price adjustment mechanism should be agreed upon to account for variances in volume or service recipients resulting from acquisitions or divestitures.

Utilizing an ARC/RRC adjustment mechanism is optimal in a managed service environment as it provides a structure by which the monthly managed service price is automatically adjusted based upon underlying changes in volume. The inclusion of an ARC/RRC mechanism is in the best interests of both parties as it yields a level of efficiency and predictability to account for volume changes that materialize once service delivery has commenced. In order to establish the

WHAT ABOUT VARIANCES IN VOLUME?

ARC/RRC variable fee structure, the parties must first agree upon a resource unit baseline. The resource unit baseline is generally established based upon historical or projected transaction volume (incidents/tickets/calls) that is translated into the number of FTEs that will comprise the delivery team.

To the extent that the actual volume remains constant or fluctuates within a contractually-stipulated dead-band range of plus or minus 10 percent during the delivery term, there is no corresponding change in the monthly managed service price as changes within the dead-band threshold are considered normal variation. However, if the actual transaction volume exceeds the dead-band threshold for three consecutive months, an ARC or RRC fee adjustment will be applied to the monthly managed service price in accordance with the agreed-upon rate per resource unit. The three month threshold is recommended as it is indicative of a sustained change in volume versus normal variation. The ARC/RRC adjustment mechanism can flex to accommodate a 30 percent increase or decrease in volume. To the extent that the actual volume exceeds that flex threshold, then the agreement will generally stipulate that the parties re-visit the resource unit baseline and re-negotiate the monthly managed service fee structure under the agreement.

The deployment of automation will have a significant impact on the pricing and delivery implications of variances in volume during the delivery term. Under the traditional ARC/RRC construct described above, the agreement will specify a dead-band range in which increases or decreases in transaction volume will not have an impact on the monthly managed service price. The dead-band concept is predicated on the concept that the service provider can accommodate a marginal increase in volume without having to deploy additional personnel to the delivery team. The workload associated with the additional and temporary increase in volume could likely be satisfied with some nominal overtime. Once the dead-band is exceeded on a sustained basis, the volume becomes overwhelming for the delivery team and service levels begin to suffer. In this scenario, it would not be legitimate for the service provider to incur service level credits for a risk—additional and unforeseen transaction volume—outside of its control.

Unlike their human counterparts, the robots do not become overwhelmed with additional transaction volume and can work well into the night without getting tired, requiring breaks, or sacrificing the quality of their work product. Given the robots can easily scale to accommodate sustained increases in volume, the dead-band range and variable fee structure may become a much less contentious component of the negotiation process. Of course, this will be predicated on the amount of automation deployed and the extent of exception processing that requires human intervention.

There are a number of other areas related to the scope and price that clients, their counsel, and advisors are seeking to achieve. The perspective they have taken that is embodied in their contractual templates is that once the managed service price is established, it should not adjust under any circumstances, unless, of course, there is a decrease in service volume. I understand the concept of not wanting to deviate from a fixed-price agreement, but it is not legitimate to maintain this perspective when there have been material changes in the volume of tickets or incidents being supported, or in the number of service recipients. To the extent that the material change can be easily accommodated by the robots, then such changes should not impact the managed service price or the service provider's ability to maintain quality standards and achieve service levels. However, to the extent that the composition of the service provider workforce is still predominantly human in nature, then material changes in volume must be addressed in the agreement. I would, therefore, recommend placing limiting language or provisions similar to the following to accommodate material changes in the services:

Material Events

As used in this Agreement, a **"Material Event"** means a circumstance in which an event or discrete set of events has occurred or is planned with respect to the business of Client that results or will result in a change in the scope, nature or volume of the Services that Client will require from Supplier, and which is expected to cause the average monthly amount of chargeable resource usage in the Services to increase or decrease by more than 20 percent (20%) for the foreseeable future. Examples of the types of events that might cause such increases or decreases include: (a) changes in locations where the Client operates; (b) changes in products of, or in markets served by, Client; (c) mergers, acquisitions or divestitures by Client; (d) changes in the method of service delivery, or changes in operational priorities; (e) changes in Client's market priorities; (f) unplanned changes in business conditions affecting Client's business that materially and negatively impact its need for the level of Services provided hereunder; or (g) changes in the number of business units being serviced by Supplier that were not anticipated as of the Effective Date.

Through the Change Order Procedures, Client may notify Supplier of any event or discrete set of events that it believes constitutes a Material Event. In the case of a Material Event, Supplier's Fees shall be adjusted in accordance with the following:

(a)   Supplier and Client will mutually determine on a reasonable basis those resources no longer required by Supplier to provide the Services ("**Targeted Resource Reductions**") and the costs that can be eliminated or reduced as and when the Targeted Resource Reductions are eliminated (the "**Targeted Cost Reductions**").

(b)   Supplier and Client will mutually determine on a reasonable basis those new or modified resources now required by Supplier to provide the Services ("**Targeted Resource Additions**") and the costs that would be incurred as and when the Targeted Resource Additions are placed in service (the "**Targeted Cost Increases**").

(c)   Immediately upon determination of the Targeted Resource Reductions, Supplier will proceed to eliminate the Targeted Resource Reductions as quickly as feasible. Immediately upon determination of the Targeted Resource Additions, Supplier will proceed to deploy the Targeted Resource Additions as necessary.

(d)   As the Targeted Resource Reductions are eliminated, the fees payable will be reduced by the full amount of the Targeted Cost Reductions applicable to the Targeted Resource Reductions as such Targeted Resource Reductions are eliminated, and the fees will be equitably adjusted. As the Targeted Resource Additions are placed into service, the fees payable will be increased by the full amount of the Targeted Cost Increases applicable to the Targeted Resource Additions as such Targeted Resource Increases are added.

If within sixty (60) days following notice under this Agreement, the Parties have not agreed upon an appropriate adjustment to the Fees, then Client shall have the right to terminate the relevant SOW, or this Agreement subject to a reduction of 25 percent (25%) in the applicable Termination Charge, such reduction not to apply in respect of the recovery by Supplier of unamortised or un-recovered investments or balance sheet items.

In addition to demanding an ironclad, fixed, managed service price that they expect to see declining over the delivery term as a result of productivity gains, clients are also seeking year-over-year improvements in the methods, processes, tools, and resources used to deliver the services. Clients are also seeking investments in the underlying technology used by service provider and, in some cases, want the opportunity to become early adopters for new service offerings or technology used by the service provider. The focus on continuous improvement and the governing contractual terms should address the following questions:

1. Will the method (extent and type of automation) by which the guaranteed productivity is achieved over the delivery term reside solely with the service provider?

2. Will there be any limitations placed upon how the service provider achieves the targets—x% robots or AI versus y% humans?

3. Why should the client wait for annual technology reviews to initiate changes when benefits can be immediately recognized from the deployment of emerging technologies?

4. Should the service provider be obligated to continually monitor and identify technology improvements, to implement new technologies that will improve performance, and to propose

methods by which higher standards, improved response times, and cost savings can be achieved?

When negotiating a provision that addresses these concerns and questions, it is important to establish a series of criteria that can be objectively measured to set expectations for improvements that occur during the delivery term. I am not a proponent of subjectivity, but I also acknowledge that when executing an outsourcing agreement, it is critical to pick your spots and focus on those terms and conditions that have the greatest impact on delivery risk. To that end, some subjectivity in these types of provisions does not have a substantial downside and meets the client's key interests in this area. It may be legitimate for a client to expect that the service provider will improve the services and take advantage of changes in technology, The focus, however, should be on the delivery of the services and the achievement of service levels. The agreement should not focus so heavily on subjective measures that may include the best practices of other IT vendors providing similarly situated services, the newest technology that is yet to be proven in the market, or the currency of the software used to achieve the same. It is always good to have the latest and greatest, but there is nothing wrong with what has been tried and true over time. To the extent that the service levels are being met and exceeded, this provision should not receive too much scrutiny.

An example of an improvements provision is as follows:

Services Improvements

Service Provider will cause the Services and all methods, processes, tools, software, equipment and other resources being used to provide the Services to evolve and to be modified, enhanced, supplemented and replaced as necessary for the Services and the Service Delivery Resources to meet or exceed the Service Levels. Any changes to the Services that are implemented in accordance with this provision will be deemed to be included within the scope of the Services at no additional charge to client.

Service Provider will meet with client at least twice annually throughout the Master Services Agreement Term to inform the client of: (a) any investments, modifications, enhancements, and improvements that it intends to implement with regard to the Services pursuant to this Section;

(b) new information processing technology or business processes Service Provider is developing; and (c) technology or process trends and directions of which Service Provider is otherwise aware that could reasonably be expected to have an impact on client's IT operations or business.

Another slightly more onerous provision that addresses the client's desire to have the option to get the latest and greatest is as follows:

Cost and Efficiency Reviews

On a semi-annual basis, Service Provider shall perform a cost and efficiency review of the Services and make recommendations to Client for reducing the cost of the Services. Service Provider's recommendations shall include methods to more efficiently utilize the resources that are chargeable to Client under this Agreement, including the following:

1. Fine-tuning or optimizing processes and systems used to perform the Services;

2. Use and analysis of the results of predictive modeling, trend analysis and monitoring tools;

3. Analysis and isolation of software, application and infrastructure design, configuration and implementation flaws;

4. Recommendations for aligning technology processes, tools, skills and organizational changes with Client's business requirements; and

5. Employing new technologies in use by Service Provider to replace existing technologies used by Service Provider to provide the Services, even if the use of such new technologies will result in a reduction in monthly revenues to Service Provider under the Agreement.

In the event Service Provider fails to include in its cost and efficiency recommendations the employment of new technologies (made Generally

WHAT ABOUT VARIANCES IN VOLUME?

Available by Service Provider to other customers for at least six (6) months) to replace existing technologies used by Service Provider to provide the Services, and (i) Client demonstrates through the internal dispute resolution process that employment of such new technologies would result in a reduction of the Service Fees for the Services, and (ii) if Client elects to implement such new technology in accordance with this Agreement, Client shall receive a thirty-five percent (35%) credit off of any Fee associated with the implementation of any such new technology by Service Provider.

While the 35 percent is not legitimate and completely arbitrary, this is another instance when complying with the requirement does not place an overly onerous burden on the service provider, meets the client's interest of wanting to be on the cutting edge of new technologies, and allows the service provider to pick its spots and focus upon more impactful components of the agreement.

CHAPTER 14

TO INSOURCE OR NOT TO INSOURCE

One other issue regarding the scope of the initial service to be outsourced is the ability of the client to insource or resource the services. Given the abundance of outsourcing service providers, it is rare to find one provider that can meet all of the client's needs. Even in a typical application outsourcing engagement, it is becoming much more common for a client to make multiple awards—different application bundle groupings—to different service providers. Under this construct, the client typically awards one bundle to a premium provider and another bundle to a lower-cost provider. If that lower-cost provider can meet the service levels, clients want to reserve the unfettered right to "lift and shift" applications from one provider to another. In addition, a client may want to reserve the right to insource or potentially resource the outsourced services. To that end, clients and their counsel are seeking a lack of restrictions on their ability to do the same. If an application or group of applications is removed from a bundle, then the parties must agree on the methodology by which the base monthly charges are reduced to accommodate the removal.

It may be legitimate for a client to have the ability to insource or resource an application or some portion of the services. There must be, however, in addition to the methodology previously referenced, some threshold identified that, once crossed, requires the client to continue to either pay at that threshold or renegotiate the base charges for the remaining scope of the outsourced service. If such a threshold did not exist, a client could continue to remove scope from a service provider with no consequences—in essence, a no-cost termination for convenience. In addition, at some point, the reduction in scope undermines the economics and financial viability of the opportunity for the service provider.

The deployment of robotic process automation raises a number of questions with regard to the client's ability to insource or lift and shift certain components of the services to another service provider. Service providers generally want to prohibit a client from removing scope at its discretion as they want to mitigate the cost of demobilization and redeployment for any impacted personnel, maintain the integrity of the initial deal shape, term, and price, and preserve sufficient in-scope services across which it can allocate its fixed delivery costs. Allowing the client to lift and shift scope without limitation is akin to a no-cost termination for convenience. Provisions which limit the client's ability to remove scope are focused on maintaining the integrity and composition of the FTE-based workforce over the contract term. To the extent the workforce is comprised substantially of robots (with limited human engagement) and the pricing model is transaction based, is it legitimate for the client to lift and shift scope (that is fully automated and being performed by the robots) at its discretion with limited notice and limited financial impact?

A two-pronged approach may be appropriate to answer this question as follows: (1) With humans, the FTE counts cannot drop below a contractually-stipulated floor (for example, 80 percent of the initially contracted monthly managed service price) without requiring payment for the remaining term at that 80 percent threshold or triggering a renegotiation; and (2) With robots, they can be lifted and shifted at will. The ability of the client to lift and shift the robots on an unlimited basis would be predicated on the client holding the license for the automation software and paying the service provider for the costs of designing, configuring, and implementing the automation at the on-set of the agreement. If both requirements were not met, a consolidated floor construct (the total fees paid can't drop below 80 percent of the initially contracted monthly managed service price) could be utilized to govern the client's rights in this area.

A sample provision from an applications maintenance agreement that reflects a nonexclusivity provision, the base charges pricing reduction methodology, and the floor structure is as follows:

Non-Exclusivity: Right to Insource and Re-Source the Services

Service Provider acknowledges and agrees that neither this Master Agreement nor any Service Agreement will give Service Provider any exclusive rights with respect to the provision of any products or services to the Client. Nothing under the Agreement will be construed as a requirements contract or be interpreted to prevent a Client from obtaining from third parties ("Re-Sourcing"), or providing to itself ("Insourcing"), any of the Services described in the Agreement. Client will have the right to Re-source or Insource any of the Services without cost or penalty and without the payment of any termination charges, subject to the charging methodology in the applicable Service Agreement.

Charging Methodology

The Base Charges will be reduced upon the elimination of an Application from an Application Bundle, whether as a result of Insourcing, Resourcing or any other reason. The amount of the reduction under this provision will be an amount equal to the allocated Base Charges for such Application, beginning upon the date of elimination of that specific Application, determined in accordance with the following:

The Time Tracking System will identify the Service Provider hours associated with each Application within the Application Bundle. The time tracked for the first 12 months following the Service Agreement effective date for Application Development and Maintenance non-discretionary services will be used to baseline the effort associated with each specific Application. This methodology will serve as the basis for allocating the Base Charges at the Application level within each Application Bundle.

In the event that an Application is eliminated, the Base Charges for the applicable Application Bundle will be reduced proportionately in accordance with the ratio of (a) the average monthly Productive Hours for ADM Non-Discretionary Services associated with the eliminated Application over the first 12 months after the applicable Service Commencement Date (or the total number of months since the Service Commencement Date for such Application, if less than 12) to (b) the average monthly Productive Hours for all ADM Non-Discretionary Services for such Application Bundle under such Statement of Work for the same months. In no event will the allocation described in this subsection result in an increase in the Base Charges.

Notwithstanding the foregoing, if for more than three consecutive months the Base Charges under this Service Agreement are less than 80 percent of the Base Charges for the applicable Service Agreement Year, excluding:

(a) the applicable Base Charge associated with Applications that are retired (versus insourced or resourced) and not replaced under this Service Agreement and

(b) any Base Charges with respect to Services that have been terminated in accordance with the Agreement, then:

Upon notice by service provider, the Parties will negotiate in good faith for not less than 60 days, an adjustment to the Base Charges to reallocate Service Provider's fixed costs to the lower volume of Services reflected in the reduced Base Charges; and

If the Parties are unable to reach an agreement on an adjustment to the Base Charges within 60 days, then this Services Agreement shall terminate as of the last day of such 60 period and client shall pay the applicable Termination for Convenience Charges.

The approach in this provision, namely, reducing the managed service fee by the number of hours associated with the eliminated set of applications, is a legitimate calculation. But this approach could undermine the cost and efficiency benefits of a managed service fee model (a staff roster of utility infielders that service multiple applications in the bundle) because service providers may begin to price by the application (a roster of specialists dedicated to a single application) in a more software-as-a-service, subscription-like model that will likely yield a less attractive price than a managed service fee.

CHAPTER 15

ACCEPT, REJECT, OR IT SHALL BE DEEMED

For acceptance provisions, a variety of procedural approaches and acceptance standards may be considered as viable and market-relevant options. That being said, I believe that five key components must be part of every acceptance provision. First and foremost, for every software and non-software deliverable, notwithstanding the underlying technology upon which it is based, as well as for any milestone, irrespective of the human or robot responsible for its achievement, there must be a set of objective, measurable, and verifiable acceptance criteria—capabilities, functions, specifications, descriptions, or standards against which the deliverable or the milestone achievement is reviewed and tested. Achieving this objective is just as important as a narrowly tailored statement of work, and a failure to do so is likely to result in a dispute.

The second component that is tightly interconnected with the development of acceptance criteria is the standard for acceptance. An example would be: "conforms to and performs in substantial (or material) accordance with the applicable specifications and acceptance criteria." To be clear, 100 percent conformance is neither realistic nor necessary. Substantial or material conformance is the market standard and should be used accordingly. In a recent negotiation, a client's legal counsel demanded 100 percent conformance as the acceptance standard as he believed the terms "substantial" and "material" were too subjective in nature and that 100 percent conformance provided the objective standard required for such an important component of the agreement. While I am always a proponent of objectivity, 100 percent conformance is not achievable, especially as it relates to software deliverables. No software developer claims its product to be 100 percent perfect as immaterial errors and bugs are commonplace. The next time you agree to the license terms for a commercial off the shelf software product, check the fine print. You will see that the software developer warrants that the product will work substantially or materially in conformance with the product documentation.

While I strive for perfection, agreeing to acceptance provisions that require 100 percent conformance with the acceptance criteria, especially for software deliverables, sets an unrealistic standard that will focus the service provider's efforts on a fool's errand. Another client concern from an acceptance testing perspective is to confirm that each component in a multiple deliverable statement of work can integrate with the other components that may have been previously accepted.

Allowing for this scenario is a reasonable request; the parties need to determine the implications of the interim acceptance of the initial components and how that acceptance impacts the beginning of the warranty period and payment throughout the build cycle.

Third, timeliness is an important factor in every engagement; because many deliverables build upon one another and must be completed sequentially, a reasonable acceptance window must be identified, with deemed acceptance as an absolute procedural requirement if the client refuses to respond with its acceptance or rejection of the deliverable in a timely manner. It always amazes me how clients avoid the notion of deemed acceptance like the plague. While I understand that they want to have sufficient opportunity to review and properly test, and accept or reject, each deliverable, they have an obligation to do so in a timely manner. Their failure to do so only delays forward momentum on the project and may result in service provider staff sitting idle.

Fourth, it is critical to identify what actions trigger acceptance and when the warranty period begins. And finally, the acceptance provisions must delineate what happens when a deliverable is rejected, how many attempts the vendor has to achieve acceptance, and what remedies the client has if the vendor is unable to do so.

Clients take extreme measures to avoid or significantly delay deemed acceptance. In one example, the client agreed to compensate the service provider on a time and materials basis for each service provider staff member who was forced to remain idle and could not proceed with the program while the service provider was awaiting acceptance notification. This occurred after a more than reasonable 30-day acceptance window. Another example reflects the multiple administrative steps and notices that must be met before acceptance will be deemed to have occurred. Let's stop this madness: Clients should be given sufficient time to review, test, and either accept or reject the deliverable or confirm achievement of the milestone, and to identify the deficiencies that are the basis for a rejection. It is in the best interests of both parties that the acceptance process occurs in a timely manner; therefore, let's step up to the plate, minimize administration, and focus on collaboration.

Let's first take a look at sample acceptance criteria language. In this example, a Deliverable Specifications Document was developed for each deliverable and milestone, and contains the acceptance criteria against which each deliverable and milestone are measured to determine acceptance.

Acceptance Criteria

General

The Parties will develop and agree upon Acceptance criteria and any applicable testing procedures for each Deliverable and Milestone and document them in the applicable Transition Plan, Project Statement of Work, Change Order or other agreement of the Parties. Acceptance Criteria will be objective and designed to verify compliance with applicable business requirements and performance specifications.

Software Deliverables

The Parties will develop and document Acceptance Criteria for each Software Deliverable and a detailed plan relating to the Acceptance testing period and procedures for each such Software Deliverable at least 30 days prior to the applicable Software Deliverable delivery date. At a minimum, such Acceptance Criteria will require a Software Deliverable to (1) be free from significant programming errors and (2) operate and comply in all material respects to the performance capabilities, functions, specifications and other descriptions and standards set forth in the applicable Deliverable Specifications Document.

Non-Software Deliverables

Acceptance Criteria for each Non-Software Deliverable will consist of applicable requirements as set forth in the applicable Deliverable Specifications Document.

Milestones

Acceptance Criteria for each Milestone will consist of applicable requirements as set forth in the applicable Deliverable Specifications Document.

Now, let's take a look at sample acceptance procedures that apply to software, non-software, and milestone deliverables. In this example, the acceptance testing process may include placing the software deliverable into production for a limited period to confirm conformity with the acceptance criteria. Placing a software deliverable into production prior to acceptance testing is atypical, because there would normally be a preproduction acceptance testing process; after that, the deliverable would be placed into production and the warranty period would begin. The general rule is that when a deliverable is placed into production, it has been accepted.

Acceptance Procedures—Software Deliverables

Upon delivery of any Software Deliverable, client will perform, and Service Provider will reasonably assist client in performing, Acceptance testing of each Software Deliverable in a timely manner to determine if such Software Deliverable satisfies the applicable Acceptance Criteria. Client will complete its review and Acceptance Testing within the timeframe specified in the applicable Deliverable Requirements Document (where no timeframe is specified, such time period will be 30 days after delivery). If a Software Deliverable is the final or sole component of Software specified by the Deliverable Requirements Document, the Acceptance Testing will include, at a minimum, the processing of sufficient test data to confirm the successful implementation and integration of each functional component of the Software.

As mentioned previously, this portion of the acceptance procedures specifies the default acceptance testing period of 30 days, if it has not already been stated in the deliverable requirements document. For non-software deliverables and milestones, the default period for the client to conduct its acceptance testing is likely to be 10 days. The deliverable specifications document may specify much shorter acceptance periods, especially for the transition or other efforts that are more time sensitive. These provisions also address the integration testing that may be required under a multiple-component build effort.

While it is not advised and not consistent with IT best practices, clients surprisingly want to reserve the right to place a software deliverable into a production environment before it is subject to testing and before it is accepted. Under this construct, a software deliverable would be placed into a production environment and tested, within the agreed upon acceptance window, against the acceptance criteria. If the deliverable fails to comply with the acceptance criteria, the client would notify the service provider as to the nature of any deficiency. Upon receiving that notification, the service provider would repair and retender the deliverable for acceptance.

Under this "testing in production" acceptance process, the client will typically agree to pay the service provider for the deliverable when it is placed into production but will reserve any acceptance decision until testing is completed. Depending upon the level of conformity with the criteria or performance specifications required for acceptance, this "testing in production" process could result in the client placing a software deliverable into production and receiving the benefit of utilizing the deliverable while still claiming that the deliverable does not conform to the acceptance criteria. Even though the service provider has been paid for the software deliverable and remains obligated to deliver it in accordance with the acceptance criteria, testing in a production environment could allow the client to receive the benefit of using the software deliverable in production while immaterial performance deficiencies are being remediated and could significantly delay the beginning of the warranty period.

A sample provision which captures this "testing in production" approach is as follows:

In addition, if specifically agreed by the Parties in the applicable Deliverable Specifications Document, the Acceptance Testing may include the successful operation of the Software in a production environment for the period specified in the applicable Deliverable Specifications Document (where no period is specified, such period will be for 15 consecutive days). If any Software Deliverable does not meet its Acceptance Criteria during the Software Acceptance Period, client will so notify Service Provider in writing, setting forth in reasonable detail (to the extent possible) any non-conformities with the Acceptance Criteria.

Including the successful operation of the software deliverable in a production environment as a part of the acceptance testing process is not typical, because a software deliverable would never be placed into a live production environment until after it passed the requisite level of acceptance testing. Placing into production a software deliverable that has not been accepted seems negligent, at best. If a service provider agrees to this type of provision, it is not unreasonable to expect and should demand a release from liability for any detrimental impact that it might cause. The general rule is that when acceptance testing is successfully completed, the deliverable is placed into production and the warranty period begins. An example is as follows:

During the Pre-Production Acceptance Testing Period, Service Provider shall conduct testing of each deliverable in a controlled "development environment" prior to implementation in a "Production Environment." As specified in the applicable Statement of Work, each Deliverable shall also undergo (1) beta, (2) functional, (3) system, (4) performance, (5) load, (6) stress, (7) integration, and (8) regression testing in a controlled "development environment" prior to implementation in a "Production Environment."

All acceptance testing shall be scheduled and executed in accordance with the work plan set forth in the applicable Statement of Work, or as otherwise agreed upon in writing by the parties. The Specifications (including the specifications set forth in the applicable Statement of Work) and any other acceptance criteria mutually agreed to by the parties shall collectively be referred to as the "Acceptance Criteria."

If Customer provides written notice to Service Provider that the Deliverable complies in all material respects with the Acceptance Criteria in Pre-Production Acceptance Testing, the Deliverable shall be deemed to have achieved pre-production acceptance ("**Pre-Production Acceptance**") or otherwise met the Acceptance Criteria. Customer may elect, in its sole discretion, to (i) eliminate Pre-Production Acceptance Testing, or (ii) test selected Acceptance Criteria as to any Deliverable. Unless otherwise specified in the applicable Work Order Package, final milestone payments will occur upon the completion of Pre-Production Acceptance or if the deliverable has otherwise complied in all material respects with all Acceptance Criteria.

(a)   Customer and Service Provider agree that implementation to the Production Environment shall not occur until the Deliverables comply with the Acceptance Criteria, or Customer elects to proceed to the Production Environment, despite the existence of an identified failure to comply with one or more Acceptance Criteria.

(b)   If Customer and Service Provider agree to proceed to the Production Environment despite the existence of any such identified issues, Service Provider will resolve such issues under the Production Warranty.

The following provisions address what occurs if the service provider tenders a deliverable that fails to meet the acceptance criteria.

Service Provider will correct or rework such Software Deliverable to satisfy its Acceptance Criteria, at no additional charge to client, within the period specified in the Deliverable Specifications Document (or where no such period is specified, within five business days of client's notice). Upon redelivery of such Software Deliverable to client, the Acceptance Testing will be repeated; provided however, that after the earlier of (a) three unsuccessful attempts by Service Provider to correct such Software Deliverable, and (b) three months after the initial Software Acceptance Period of such Software Deliverable, the procedure set forth in the Failure of Acceptance provisions will apply.

ACCEPT, REJECT, OR IT SHALL BE DEEMED

This provision is similar for non-software deliverables or milestones, but the limitation is likely to be the earlier of: two unsuccessful attempts by the service provider to correct the deliverable and bring it into alignment with the acceptance criteria; or 30 days after the initial non-software deliverable or milestone acceptance period. If the service provider still could not achieve acceptance, then the following failure of acceptance provisions apply:

Failure of Acceptance

With respect to any Software Deliverable, Non-Software Deliverable or Milestone provided pursuant to a Deliverable Specifications Document for which payment is contingent upon client's Acceptance of such Deliverable or Milestone, if such Software Deliverable fails Acceptance Testing, such Non-Software Deliverable does not conform to its Non-Software Specification Requirements or Service Provider fails to achieve a Milestone, then client will be entitled, at its option, to either:

With Respect to Deliverables

Accept the non-conforming Deliverable subject to a reduction in the applicable Charges payable for such Deliverable under the Service Agreement, as determined (a) by agreement of the Parties; or (b) pursuant to the dispute resolution procedures set forth in the Master Agreement if the Parties cannot agree to the amount of reduction within 30 days after client requests a reduction; or

Reject the Deliverable, terminate the applicable Deliverable Specification Document, if applicable, immediately upon notice to Service Provider, return the non-conforming Deliverable to Service Provider and be released from any obligation to pay Service Provider the Charges for such returned Deliverable; provided that if client retains the Deliverable, the amount payable to Service Provider will be determined (a) by agreement of the Parties; or (b) pursuant to the dispute resolution procedures set forth in the Master Agreement if the Parties cannot agree to the amount of reduction within 30 days after client requests a reduction; or

Reject the Deliverable and permit Service Provider to make one or more additional attempts to correct such Deliverable.

With Respect to Milestones

Unless the Milestone is a Transition Milestone, terminate the applicable Deliverable Requirements Document, if applicable, immediately upon notice to Service Provider and be released from any obligation to pay Service Provider the Charges for Service Provider's efforts to achieve such Milestone or (2) permit Service Provider to make one or more additional attempts to achieve such Milestone.

Hopefully, service providers will not have to deal with rejected deliverables, and clients will expeditiously determine that all deliverables meet the acceptance criteria and will provide timely notification thereof. However, as we all know, there may be instances when clients do not formally respond with a notification of acceptance or rejection in a timely manner. As I mentioned previously, clients and their counsel avoid deemed acceptance like the plague. I find that approach to be non-market relevant and not in the best interests of the parties. Such approach can significantly undermine an implementation or transition schedule, and stop a project dead in its tracks. Consider the hoops the service provider must jump through in the following example to achieve deemed acceptance if the client does not formally respond with an acceptance or rejection of the deliverable.

If client determines that the Software Deliverable satisfies the applicable Acceptance Criteria, or if prior to the end of the Software Acceptance Period client has not found any non-conformities with the Acceptance Criteria, client will notify Service Provider in writing of client's Acceptance of such Software Deliverable. If, at the end of the applicable Software Acceptance Period, client fails to provide Service Provider with written notice of Acceptance or rejection in accordance with this Section, Service Provider may provide written notice to the client that the applicable Software Acceptance Period has expired. If client does not provide written notice to Service Provider of Acceptance or rejection within five days following receipt of such notice from Service Provider, then Service Provider may provide a second written notice to the client that both the applicable Software Acceptance Period and the subsequent five-day period have expired. If client does not provide written notice to Service Provider of Acceptance or rejection within five days following receipt of such second notice from Service Provider, then as of the end of such second notice period, the Software Deliverable will be deemed Accepted by client.

Nothing contained in this Agreement will be deemed to prevent client from directing Service Provider to use a Software Deliverable in a production environment prior to Acceptance. Notwithstanding the foregoing, but subject to the applicable Deliverable Specification Document, if a Software Deliverable is placed into production with client's approval, such Software Deliverable will be deemed Accepted by client.

As I mentioned previously and if you have a client who seeks to avoid a deemed acceptance provision, you can suggest a provision similar to the following one under which the client must compensate the service provider for the client's delayed acceptance response:

For each day following the applicable Acceptance Review Period that client fails to provide Acceptance (or a Rejection Notice), client will pay the increased costs of Supplier for such delay based on the following: a daily amount for each of Supplier Personnel who was not able to continue working on any subsequent Deliverable or otherwise engage in meaningful work related to the Project due to such delay (the "**Daily Amount**").

The Daily Amount for each Supplier Personnel who was delayed will be calculated as follows: the applicable time and material hourly rate for the level of such Supplier Personnel (as indicated in the applicable SOW or Change Order) multiplied by 8 hours. (For example, for a delayed Supplier Personnel who is an "Analyst" with a $100 hourly rate, the Daily Amount for such personnel would be $800.)

I know what you are thinking—the client could reject the deliverable to avoid paying for a delay in conducting acceptance testing in a timely manner. To prevent that behavior, you can insert something similar to the following:

Client agrees and acknowledges that it will not issue a Rejection Notice in respect of a Deliverable where the client personnel who was responsible for the review of such Deliverable has not made any demonstrable review efforts (supported, where applicable, by written documentation regarding the review efforts taken) to review such Deliverable during the Acceptance Review Period.

While acceptance procedures and standards can vary, it is absolutely critical that the parties agree on the heart of this issue—objective, measurable, and verifiable acceptance criteria against which all deliverables and milestones are measured. Failing to do so leads to an expeditious and guaranteed path to a dispute. Although I typically never use the word guarantee, this is one time when I am comfortable with its application. In addition, make sure that the acceptance provisions are clear about these additional items:

1. Identify the standard by which acceptance is determined. For the reasons we discussed, 100 percent conformance with the acceptance criteria is neither realistic nor market relevant.

2. Define a reasonable time window during which the client can test the deliverables and milestones to determine if they conform to the acceptance criteria.

3. If the client does not respond after a reasonable time window has elapsed, acceptance should be deemed to have occurred.

4. Determine what, if any, actions taken by the client (such as placement into production) with regard to the deliverables trigger acceptance.

5. Identify the process that must be strictly adhered to by the parties when a deliverable is accepted, rejected, and repaired and retendered, and remedies available to the client if the service provider cannot achieve acceptance after multiple attempts have occurred.

CHAPTER 16

PLAYING NICELY IN THE SANDBOX

Given the delivery sweet spots, pricing structures, and levels of risk aversion of the major outsourcing service providers, it is a guarantee that you will be working in a multivendor environment side by side with your competitors. Because of this multivendor dynamic, clients have a strong interest in making sure that each of their vendors, even if they are fierce competitors in the marketplace, are cooperating and coordinating with one another, are sharing best practices, are communicating in a timely manner, and are sharing information as necessary so that each party's component of the services can be delivered in a timely, quality, and cost-effective manner. Ultimately, all actions taken by their vendors should be done in a way that lets clients receive the full benefit of services from their ecosystem. The whole should be much greater than the sum of the parts. In addition, clients have an even stronger interest in establishing a multivendor environment that, if a deficiency should arise, eradicates finger pointing by the affected vendors about the root cause of the dispute. Moreover, when the root cause is in doubt, clients want to make sure that they can direct vendors to fix the issue first, and allocate blame and address financial accountability later.

Many large clients have embraced the notion of forming a vendor collective, an approach focused on giving vendors an incentive to temper their competitive arousal and work together to help clients solve business problems. Royal Dutch Shell has taken this approach for some time, and its CIO, Alan Matula, agrees with my focus on collaboration and partnership. In a December 2011 *CIO Magazine* article, he stated: "Traditional methods on managing IT suppliers— mainly playing rival vendors off each other and negotiating ever-tighter contract terms—stymie creativity and ultimately limit the business benefits both sides get from the relationship." I have only one word in response: Amen.

To achieve that goal, Shell significantly streamlined its vendor base and created an ecosystem of 11 IT suppliers over three categories—foundation technology, infrastructure, and applications—and mandated that vendors cannot steal business from a fellow ecosystem vendor. In addition, all ecosystem vendors meet quarterly with Shell to discuss significant projects and collaborate on how they can advance Shell's strategic agenda. That Shell awards its ecosystem suppliers roughly half of its annual IT budget of $3.6 billion may help keep everyone on their best behavior. Irrespective of how Shell is able to motivate its vendors to play nicely together, I believe this vendor collective construct will continue to expand and will be an integral component of providing outsourcing services to large clients. Even if the client does not have a formal initiative like Shell's, the concept of playing nicely in the sandbox with other vendors should be a key component of every contract for outsourcing services.

To advance the notion of the vendor collective, Shell created Ecosystem Guiding Principles that help facilitate collaboration and partnership between aggressive competitors in the marketplace. According to the *CIO Magazine* article, those rules of engagement include the following:

1. Most sales professionals are banned from the office of the CIO.

2. Both Shell and the vendor staff shall respect the culture and heritage of each other's companies.

3. Senior executives must set a positive example for everyone else, in part by actively advocating for the ecosystem relationships.

4. Staff must work to solve problems at the lowest level possible, using escalation as a last resort.

5. Vendors must understand that although Shell wants to concentrate IT spending on ecosystem members, there are no guarantees of contract awards.

6.   Information gained through the ecosystem should not be used to win additional business at the expense of another member.

7.   Vendors should respect the intellectual property of other members and consider it confidential by default.

8.   All participants must do 360-degree reviews of one another and Shell.

The other key benefit of a vendor collective is that the key rules of engagement apply to the vendors as well as to Shell's procurement and IT organizations.

Boris Van der Weele, the supplier manager of Shell's consulting providers in 2011, clearly addressed this challenge in the 2011 *CIO Magazine* article. He stated: "There are people who will say that you shouldn't be too cozy with suppliers. Suppliers will take advantage of you. The Shell ecosystem aspiration is to be a system based on equality and trust and having a positive, respectful interaction. That isn't always easy because originally we were old school and hard-nosed in procurement. I'm not saying we've cracked the code, but our ecosystem is striving for it." Clearly, this approach is completely aligned with the key overarching theme for this book, namely, a focus on collaboration, trust, and mutual respect. With this as the backdrop, the negotiation of the terms and conditions in an outsourcing agreement should, hopefully, flow much more smoothly.

It certainly creates an interesting dynamic when a service provider is required to work in partnership with its most fierce competitors. The key is to find the appropriate balance between being maintaining good standing as a citizen of the multivendor ecosystem and sharing proprietary methods, tools, and other secret sauce components that yield a distinct competitive advantage in the marketplace. Clearly, the vendor collective rules of engagement are focused upon human interaction and behaviors across the ecosystem. As robots and AI become more broadly deployed into the delivery environment, it may be necessary to augment these rules to address how the robots and various neural networks will interact with each other if they are programmed to work side-by-side to solve business problems, process transactions, or remediate incidents. Just like their human counterparts, the robots and neural networks may find themselves in close quarters with their virtual peers. When faced with those circumstances, it will be critical that they also play nicely in the sandbox.

The bottom line is that the multivendor delivery environment is here to stay. Clients need to determine how to find the appropriate balance between achieving cooperation and quality delivery and allowing its service providers to maintain the integrity of their intellectual property. The challenge is making sure that the result does not yield an environment where service providers are not deploying innovation and newly developed best practices out of fear that they will be shared with and poached by their competitors, a situation that would marginalize the service providers' position in the market.

These cooperation provisions also reinforce the absolute requirement that statements of work be clear and concise about the roles and responsibilities of the parties. If there are discrete handoffs between different vendors, those lines of demarcation must be clearly drawn, especially when the clock is running, service levels are being measured, and service level defaults that may have a detrimental financial impact are likely.

An example of a cooperation provision is as follows:

Cooperation With Third Parties

Service Provider acknowledges that it is performing the Services in a multi-vendor environment and agrees that it may be necessary for Service Provider to coordinate its responsibilities with the efforts of third party providers or suppliers providing products or services to the client and that such coordination efforts may include proactively communicating with the Third Party Providers regarding service issues, acting as the single point of intake and resolution for Third Party Providers' questions and issues, scheduling meetings for discussion and exchange of information as appropriate, and providing guidance to Third Party Providers with respect to Service Provider's and the client's IT environment as it relates to the Services. Service Provider will cooperate with any Third Party Provider to the extent required for Service Provider to provide the Services in accordance with the Agreement and to the extent required for such Third Party Provider to provide its products or services to client.

Service Provider's obligation to coordinate and cooperate with Third Party Providers will include the following, to the extent requested by client or a Third Party Provider and as necessary for a Third Party Provider (as reasonably determined by client) to provide products and services to the Service Recipients:

providing information and data concerning the Services (including the manner in which the Services are provided), the Systems, and other resources used in providing the Services, including information regarding any System configurations and settings, operating environments, Systems constraints and other operating parameters;

providing access to and use of the Policies and Procedures Manuals; providing temporary access to any Service Locations; providing access to any Reports; and

providing access to and use of the Systems to which Service Provider controls access, Service Provider IP (subject to the IP provisions contained in the Master Services Agreement) and Service Delivery Resources;

provided, however, that provision of such information, access and use will be subject to such Third Party Provider (a) executing a non-disclosure agreement with client that is at least as restrictive as the confidentiality provisions set forth in this Master Services Agreement and (b) complying with Service Provider's security policies, to the same extent such policies are applicable to client under the Agreement.

This provision requires the third party to execute a nondisclosure agreement and to comply with any applicable security policies. However, these cooperation provisions, which are now more commonplace, are broad. Such provisions also typically include the requirement to work jointly with any third party to determine the root cause of a service deficiency and to provide reasonable cooperation and support for its prompt resolution. If there is a dispute related to cooperation or the party responsible for the deficiency, language similar to the following is used:

Disputes Related to Cooperation

Service Provider will use commercially reasonable efforts to resolve any dispute between Service Provider and a Third Party Provider without client's intervention no later than five days after receipt of notice of such Third Party Provider Dispute.

If Service Provider and the Third Party Provider are not able to resolve such Third Party Provider Dispute within such five-day period:

Service Provider will: (a) immediately advise client in writing of the Third Party Provider Dispute; (b) provide information to client concerning the Third Party Provider Dispute; and (c) provide Service Provider's recommendation for remedying the Third Party Provider Dispute. Client may request additional information concerning the Third Party Provider Dispute and require the Disputing Parties to attend meetings to determine the appropriate resolution of the Third Party Provider Dispute; and

Client may direct one of the Disputing Parties to begin to perform any services necessary to cure the Service Problem based on client's reasonable belief regarding which Disputing Party has responsibility to provide the disputed services. If client directs Service Provider to perform such services, client will so inform Service Provider and Service Provider will immediately commence performance of such services. Any such services performed by Service Provider will be performed at no additional cost or expense to client pending the final adjudication of the issue through the dispute resolution provisions of the Master Services Agreement.

The multivendor environment requires service providers to cooperate and to play nicely together in the collective services sandbox. Cooperation is a necessity: The key is finding the balance between being a good citizen and placing the client's interest in service delivery first and not undermining any service provider competitive advantage in the marketplace.

CHAPTER 17

YOU MUST FOLLOW THE LAW

I have participated in countless hours of discussions about the compliance-with-laws provisions in an outsourcing agreement. Frankly, 90 percent of those discussions have been a complete waste of time. They all end up in the same place, namely, that the service provider is responsible for complying with laws that apply to its business, and the client is responsible for all laws that apply to its business. If the client has outsourced a service that requires the service provider to comply with any laws that apply to the outsourced service, then the client gives the service provider a compliance directive that tells the service provider how to implement a particular law or regulation on the client's behalf. This principle will not change with the deployment of automation into the delivery model. Rather than directing its personnel to provide the underlying service in accordance with the compliance directive, the service provider will program such direction into the algorithm in the automation software. The bottom line is that the client remains fully responsible for interpreting laws or regulations that apply to its business operations.

A related regulatory issue that must be considered during the negotiation process is the legal obligations that arise when personnel are transferred from the client to the service provider in conjunction with the execution of the outsourcing agreement and are later displaced by robots for the delivery of certain components of the outsourced service. A number of laws have been enacted, particularly in the European Union with the Acquired Rights Directive ("ARD") and in the United Kingdom with the Transfer of Undertakings Protection of Employment ("TUPE"), the purpose of which is to safeguard and protect the rights of employees in the event of a transfer to another employer. To the extent the outsourced services include the transfer of employees in these jurisdictions and the agreement dictates their displacement in favor of automation, the obligations triggered by these laws need to be considered when negotiating transition plans and commercial terms.

This approach is straightforward and legitimate, right? Well, think again. Usually, a client wants the service provider to take responsibility for complying with and interpreting all laws, including those that apply to the client's business. I have never understood this request, because the client is in the best position to interpret any laws that apply to its business operations and is likely to employ or retain plenty of accountants, compliance experts, lawyers, and other subject matter experts to do so on its behalf. The idea that a client would want its outsourcing service provider to interpret and comply with laws that apply to the client's business across all of the geographies where the client may have a presence is not legitimate and is imprudent.

IT service providers are experts in outsourcing, and that is where they can deliver predictable results. But in interpreting tax laws, administrative provisions, and other regulations, I want to get advice from recognized experts in these areas. This goes back to the concept: "You can't outsource responsibility." The only viable option to offer a client is to have the service provider retain a law firm to provide a team of lawyers and other experts. These experts would focus on monitoring and interpreting all laws in all geographies where the client is engaged, and then directing the service provider to provide its services according to those interpretations. The client would, of course, be responsible for the cost of the legal team, and the service provider would probably want the law firm to indemnify it for any claims, demands, charges, actions, liabilities, damages, fines, penalties, costs, or other assessments that the client may incur as a result of the law firm's interpretation of the applicable law. The approach is cost-prohibitive and not in the client's best interest to pursue.

A sample provision that addresses this construct is as follows:

Compliance With and Changes in Applicable Laws

1.1 Client

Subject to **Section 1.2(b)**, client will comply with all Laws applicable to client and its business (i.e., Laws under which client would be liable in the case of non-compliance) that affect its receipt of the Services (collectively, "**Client Laws**").

1.2 Service Provider

(a)   Service Provider will comply with all Laws (1) applicable to Service Provider and its business and (2) applicable to Service Provider's provision of the Services (collectively, "**Service Provider Laws**").

(b)   Service Provider will comply with all Laws identified in a Client Compliance Directive.

(c)   Client may direct Service Provider on the method of compliance with any Client Compliance Directive. Service Provider will comply with all such directions. Service Provider will not be responsible to Client for a failure to comply with a Client Compliance Directive to the extent that Service Provider relies on, and complies with, Client's direction contained in such Client Compliance Directive.

(d)   If Service Provider reasonably determines that its compliance obligations require an interpretation of any Client Compliance Directive, Service Provider will present to Client the issue for interpretation and Client will provide such interpretation to Service Provider by notice signed by an authorized legal representative of Client with respect to such interpretation. Service Provider will not be responsible to Client for a failure to comply with such Client Compliance Directive to the extent that Service Provider relies on, and complies with, Client's interpretation pursuant to this Section in respect of such Client Compliance Directive.

(e)   If Service Provider is not in compliance with any Law with which it is required to comply, then Service Provider will immediately undertake such measures that are necessary to establish compliance with Service Provider Law. If Service Provider is not in compliance with a Client Compliance Directive after notice by Client, then (1) Service Provider will immediately undertake such measures that are necessary to establish compliance with such Client Compliance Directive, or

(f)   if Service Provider fails to immediately undertake such measures or such measures do not establish compliance with such Client Compliance Directive, then Client or its designee may undertake such measures as Client may require and that are necessary to establish compliance with the Client Compliance Directive and such measures will be at (a) Service Provider's cost if such measures to establish compliance are consistent with the direction or interpretation previously provided by Client to Service Provider.

Service Provider will be responsible for non-compliance with any Law to the extent such non-compliance arises from Service Provider's modification or enhancement of the Services or any Application that is not made pursuant to a request by Client and Service Provider failed to inquire of Client as to whether such modification or enhancement would have an impact on any Client Law.

This construct provides a clear line of demarcation of responsibility for compliance with applicable laws. It makes the service provider an order taker—which is exactly what it should be—in how the client wants a particular law interpreted on its behalf. Now that the responsibility issue has been settled, the next issue to be addressed is what happens when a law changes? The general rule is that each party is responsible for the cost of staying in compliance with laws applicable to its business. However, the service provider is generally responsible for notifying the client if it becomes aware of any change in a service provider law that may affect its performance of the services. In addition, it is not uncommon or unreasonable for the service provider to agree to notify the client if it becomes aware of any changes in a law affecting the client. Ultimately, the objective is to collaborate to determine the effect of any changes in laws that may impact the delivery of the services. The same approach applies to any change, namely, the client provides the service provider with a compliance directive that tells the service provider how to interpret the law on the client's behalf in its performance of the services.

A sample provision that captures the changes-in-laws concept is as follows:

Changes in Laws

(a)   Service Provider will promptly notify Client of any changes in Service Provider Law of which it becomes aware that may relate to Service Provider's performance of the Services. Service Provider will promptly notify Client of any changes in Client Law of which the Service Provider Account Executive becomes aware. The Parties will work together to identify the impact of changes in Law on the Service Recipients' use or receipt and Service Provider's performance of the Services.

(b)   Unless a change in Service Provider Law causes the performance of the Services to become illegal, Service Provider will perform the Services regardless of changes in Law.

(c)   Each Party will bear the cost of compliance with any changes in Laws (not related to the Services) applicable to such Party (e.g., Laws relating to the employment of its employees, employee tax withholding applicable to its employees or environmental and health and safety Laws relating to its employees or facilities).

(d)   Client will bear the costs to comply with any change in Client Laws provided, however, that with respect to any change in Client Law, Client will be responsible for only a pro rata share of such costs if Service Provider is required to comply with such change in Law for any of its other customers. Service Provider will bear the costs to comply with any change in Service Provider Laws.

While this provision provides that each party to the agreement will be responsible for the cost of compliance with any changes in laws, the parties may agree upon the inclusion of a termination right, with sufficient notice of at least 90 days, that would be triggered if the cost associated with compliance of a change in law exceeds a contractually-stipulated threshold, say 10 percent, and the parties are unable to agree upon a commercially reasonable change order to address the impact of the change in law. The service provider would have a termination right if the cost associated with compliance of a change in a service provider law increases the service provider's cost of delivering the services by more than 10 percent or if the change in law renders the service provider's performance of the services unlawful or impractical. The client would have a termination right if the cost associated with compliance of a change in client law or the implementation of a client compliance directive requires the client to pay the service provider an increase of greater than 10 percent of the annual charges for the services or results in a material reduction in the quality or scope of the services.

The net result is clear and concise. The compliance-with-laws portion of the agreement is a perfect example of where a market-relevant and industry-standard provision exists that is legitimate and commensurate with an outsourcing engagement for most services. There is no need to waste any time in this area. The bottom line is that each party is responsible for compliance with laws. Service providers provide outsourcing services; they are not accountants, lawyers, or compliance experts, and expecting them to serve in that capacity is negligent, at best. Use a compliance directive, collaborate when changes in laws materialize, allow for a materially threshold if the cost of compliance with a change in law will result in a material financial impact for either party, and focus on much more important portions of the agreement.

CHAPTER 18

BRING ME THE A-TEAM AND NO CRIMINALS, PLEASE

Every client wants its outsourcing service provider to bring its best and brightest to bear—from a delivery perspective. Each client wants the equivalent of the Ateam. While it might be optimal to deploy the all-star team to each account, they are called the all-star team for a reason, namely, because they are the best of the best and limited in number. Therefore, focus on having the service provider field a roster of staff members who can successfully deliver the services delineated in the service agreement. The contractual provisions which address the capabilities, qualifications, and eligibility of service provider personnel, the number of personnel that will be designated as "key" over the delivery term, and any restrictions on the ability of those personnel to perform services for client competitors will continue to be a focus during the negotiation process. However, the extent of automation to be deployed over the delivery term may mitigate some of the concern in this area as the robots, unlike their human counterparts, are equally qualified and capable and will pass any background check with flying colors.

Clients may want to include a quality or capability standard that must be met by each service provider staff member, but any such language is subjective. A client may want to retain the right to remove any service provider staff for what it believes may be a deficiency in the standard or any other reason. However, I believe that the client's ability to do so should be limited (at least in a managed-service environment) to when a particular service provider staff member repeatedly violates a client's policy or other requirements of the agreement, or engages in illegal conduct while deployed to the engagement.

If the client wants to remove a service provider staff member for any other reason, the service provider should review the request, determine if it is legitimate, and either replace the individual or take the necessary disciplinary action to prevent any recurrence of the behavior that was the basis for the request. The general rule is that most service providers defer to client requests of this kind, especially in a time and materials setting.

A sample provision that addresses the capabilities of service provider staff as well as the standard for removal is as follows:

Service Provider Personnel

Service Provider will assign an adequate number of Service Provider Personnel to perform the Services. Service Provider Personnel will possess the experience, skills and qualifications necessary to perform the Services in accordance with the Agreement and any additional experience, skills and qualifications agreed upon by the Parties. Service Provider acknowledges and agrees that it will be the responsibility of Service Provider to provide adequate levels of training and education so that the Service Provider Personnel remain current as to practices and technology at the level used by other top-tier IT providers in providing services similar to the Services to other customers, and developments and changes to the Services, Systems, Service Delivery Resources or any other resources, methods or processes used by Service Provider to provide the Services. If requested by client or otherwise required pursuant to a Service Agreement, Service Provider will cause Service Provider Personnel to attend training sessions provided by client.

Removal and Replacement

If client requests that any Service Provider Personnel be removed from the account (1) where such Service Provider Personnel is filling a Key Service Provider Position or (2) where client's request is the result of such individual's (a) tortious or illegal conduct or moral turpitude or (b) repeated violations of client rules and regulations regarding safety and health, personal and professional conduct, and business conduct and ethics policies or any other requirement of the Agreement, then Service Provider will immediately remove such individual from the client account.

If client requests that any Service Provider Personnel be removed from the client account for reasons other than as provided above, then upon receipt of such request, Service Provider will have a reasonable period of time (but in any event no more than five business days) to (1) investigate such matter and take appropriate action, which may include (a) removing the applicable person from the client account and providing client with prompt notice of such removal, and (b) replacing the applicable person with a similarly qualified individual; or (2) taking other appropriate disciplinary action to prevent a recurrence.

Service Provider will, as soon as reasonably possible, replace any individual Service Provider Personnel that is removed, terminated, resigns or otherwise ceases to perform the Services with an individual with equal or better qualifications to perform the Services and will otherwise maintain backup and replacement procedures for the Service Provider Personnel to maintain continuity of the Services.

In addition to wanting the A-team deployed, clients want to receive confirmation that the staff who are deployed to their site, have access to their systems, and are working with clients' staff have undergone an appropriate background check that verifies their identity, validates any educational degrees, confirms employment history, and provides a record of any prior criminal history. Conducting a background check on deployed staff meets a legitimate client interest. However, the scope, recurrence, and cost associated with such checks should be tempered by the scope of the services provided, the nature of the data to which the service provider team have access, and the industry in which the client resides.

In addition, the contract should stipulate when a service provider staff member cannot be deployed to the client. Standards may vary, but a general rule is that clients can exclude: any service provider staff member whose background check reflects data inconsistent with the information provided by that individual; any service provider staff member who has been convicted of, pleaded guilty or no contest to a crime involving a breach of trust, dishonesty, injury, or attempted injury to any property or person; anyone who refuses to consent to a background check; or any industry-specific exclusion including a debarment or restricted person list. An example of the scope of the background check is as follows:

> Provider further certifies that during the investigation of Provider's Representative's background, no information was discovered that would establish that Provider's Representative is anything other than qualified, honest, reliable, and non-violent and that the background check included an examination of criminal felony and misdemeanor and civil records of the Federal Courts and Municipal and Superior Courts of all Provider's Representative's counties of residence for the last seven years. In addition, if applicable, Provider certifies the background check included the following:

> Review of Department of Motor Vehicle records (applicable if Provider's Representative's assignment requires driving);

> Credit check and US Bankruptcy Court search (applicable if Provider's Representative's assignment is substantially related to financial or monetary functions);

> Verification of employment history for the past seven years (applicable if not completed at the time Provider hired Provider's Representative); and

> Verification of educational records for the highest degree received (applicable if educational background is relevant to Provider's Representative's assignment and such verification was not completed at the time Provider hired Provider's Representative).

> Provider further agrees that if it subsequently becomes aware of information that would establish that Provider's Representative is anything other than qualified and non-violent, it will report that information to the Company.

In addition to the more generic categories previously referenced, it might be legitimate to confirm that service provider staff members deployed to a life sciences client are not listed on an FDA Debarment list, but such a requirement would not apply to a retail client. Likewise, the scope of a background check for a staff person who would be deployed to a financial services client may include a credit check, although such a requirement may not be necessary in other circumstances. Similarly, including a requirement for drug testing should also be carefully considered, given the nature of the services being provided, the intrusion on the privacy of the personnel, and the continually evolving laws in that area. The key question should be: "What form of background check is required to ensure that the service personnel being deployed into the client environment have a history that is commensurate with and that would not jeopardize the level of trust and access they are being granted in conjunction with the delivery of the services?" I acknowledge that a background check is necessary, but these costs are typically borne by the service provider and can be costly, depending on the size of the staff roster. Therefore, I believe that the client should rely on any similar criminal or other background checks that were conducted by the service provider at the time of hire and should temper the scope of the check and the disqualification standard.

In addition to concerns about staff quality and background, it is legitimate and not uncommon for clients to try to include provisions stating that all deployed staff will be dedicated full time to providing the services; that all staff will comply with the confidentiality provisions of the agreement; that they comply with all client policies and other procedures when in a client facility; and that they receive a complete staff roster that includes the names of all staff members providing services under the agreement who will have access to client data and systems. Also, clients may even seek to include provisions that require their consent before the on-versus-offshore mix specified in the service agreement may be materially changed. Service levels may also be introduced that measure and target the on versus offshore mix during the delivery term.

Another key issue to be addressed about the service provider staff roster is which service provider personnel are deemed "key personnel" under the agreement? As per the label, key personnel play a critical role in managing the overall client relationship and striving to make sure that the services are delivered in a timely, quality, and cost-effective manner. Such personnel typically must be approved by the client before they are assigned to a key role, must be fully dedicated to the engagement, cannot be removed or replaced without the client's consent, and cannot provide substantially similar services to a named client competitor list during their tenure and for a period of 12 to 18 months after. As a result of their importance to the client relationship and delivery success, it is not uncommon to have a service level linked to key personnel turnover.

The number of key personnel under an outsourcing engagement, of course, varies, depending on the type and scope of the opportunity. At minimum, there is likely to be an overall service provider relationship manager who is responsible for the overall client relationship as well as service delivery. In addition, it is typical for a delivery manager to be identified for each service agreement executed by the parties. The scope of duties of the delivery manager is to oversee the successful delivery of the services within the manager's respective outsourcing tower. Moreover, additional service provider personnel could be labeled as key, including transition, contracts, or finance managers.

There is no standard for the number of key personnel. Given the importance of these roles and the restrictions placed on them, the roles and individuals should be carefully selected in a manner consistent with the nature, complexity, and scope of the services provided, and the respective career paths of these individuals. Although the number of key personnel is generally limited, a recent trend is to expand the definition of key personnel to include, "any vendor personnel whose continued performance of the services would reasonably be considered crucial to the success and timeliness with respect to the completion of such services." Unlike the more objective approach of naming a subset of service provider personnel as key personnel, this approach is much more subjective in nature as it is unclear which party is making the "crucial to the success" determination. A provision of this type could result in a significant number of the service provider's staff being designated as key personnel and could detrimentally impact the service provider's ability to manage its personnel, especially in a managed service environment. In addition, a key personnel provision of this type could serve as the basis for a breach of contract claim if the service provider removed a staff member that reasonably could have been determined to have met the "crucial to success" standard and that removal could be linked to a subsequent performance deficiency. To the extent that a service provider would agree to a provision of this type, the service provider should be able to remove any staff member at will without the client's consent so long as they notify the client of the change and provide a replacement resource with similar skills. By retaining the ability to remove staff, the service provider will have the flexibility to manage its personnel and focus on timely and successful service delivery.

The final personnel issue that should be addressed pertains to any restrictions on the solicitation of both service provider and client personnel. The general rule is that neither party should directly solicit or hire the other party's employees without the prior written consent of the other party. Such non-solicitation clauses should be modified to exclude employees responding to general advertisements for employment and be reasonable in both time and scope. An example of a nonsolicitation provision is as follows:

Non-Solicitation of Employees

Neither Party shall directly or indirectly on its own behalf solicit or hire, in any capacity whatsoever, any of the other Party's employees involved in a Statement of Work during the term of the applicable Statement of Work and for a period of one (1) year from the termination thereof, without the express written consent of the other Party. This prohibition shall not apply to hiring as a result from non-targeted solicitation, such as newspaper or Internet ads, or to employees who have been involuntarily separated from the Party seeking to enforce this provision of the Agreement, or to employees of a Party who have not been involved in the provision of Services under an applicable Statement of Work.

CHAPTER 19

WHO OWNS THE INTELLECTUAL PROPERTY?

The extent and scope of licenses granted both during and after the delivery term as well as the ownership of Intellectual Property (IP) developed during the delivery term are always outsourcing agreement components that receive a tremendous amount of scrutiny. At a macro level, both parties want to protect their pre-existing IP but must find the appropriate balance, given the delivery scope. Unlike a more traditional consulting or systems integration agreement, unique nuances are associated with an outsourcing engagement because the service provider truly steps into the shoes of the client during delivery. The parties must, therefore, prepare for how the service provider makes its IP available for the client to receive the benefit of the services, and for how the service provider shares its IP with other vendors in the client ecosystem. In addition, the parties must prepare for how they handle the service provider IP that becomes such an intricate part of the services that preparations for its survival post-termination or upon expiration of the service agreement must be addressed. Given that level of interconnectivity between the services and the IP used in their delivery, the focus on this area is legitimate, and key issues must be addressed in these provisions of the agreement.

The deployment of automation raises a number of unique questions as it relates to IP ownership as follows:

1. Who should own the algorithms and process automations and what happens after an expiration or termination event?

2. Were the automations specifically configured for a particular process within the client's environment? If not, should the client

care about ownership so long as they receive a perpetual license to use the automations for their internal business purposes?

3. If the service provider owns the automations, will they be able to utilize best practices to develop functional and industry specific automations that benefit multiple clients?

4. Will the client be disadvantaged if they relinquish ownership of the automations to the service provider?

5. Does the service provider have any interest in re-using or patenting the automation?

6. Will the client pay a fee for the upfront costs of developing, configuring, and implementing the automation?

7. Were the automations previously developed by the service provider?

8. What automation software is being utilized? Who holds and what is the scope of the license?

9. Does the service provider want its competitors to be able to utilize the automations after an expiration or termination event?

10. If the client does not own the automations, will they want to place any restrictions on the service provider's ability to use the automations with their competitors?

11. If the client owns the automations, will the service provider have a license to use the automations with other clients?

12. If the service provider owns the automations, will it grant a perpetual license to the client to use the automations? What will be the scope of that license?

13. How will the automations be defined in the contract?

Let's answer these questions one at a time. With regard to ownership of the algorithms and process automations, the answer depends upon the context under which they were created. If the automations were specifically configured for a particular client and a specific process within the client environment, then it is legitimate for the client to own them. Of course, any such ownership would be predicated upon the client paying an up-front fee for the costs of developing, configuring, and implementing the automation.

If the automations were not specifically configured for a particular client, then it may be legitimate for the service provider to own the IP but the client should receive a perpetual license to use the IP for its internal business purposes. The perpetual term of the license is important as the automations will likely become an inherent part of the client's operating environment and a termination or contract expiration event should not inhibit the client's ability to continue to receive the benefit of the services for which it paid. Allowing the service provider to own the IP, even in those instances where the automations were created for a specific client process or environment, may yield a long-term benefit for the client so long as the license is perpetual and irrevocable and includes an on-going maintenance and upgrade obligation as best practices evolve from a process perspective.

Agreeing to relinquish ownership of the automations is best suited for generic business processes. For those processes which are proprietary in nature, clients will have a legitimate interest in owning the automations and keeping them away from competitors. Even if the client agrees to relinquish ownership of the automations, they may seek to place some restrictions upon the service provider's ability to utilize the IP with a named list of direct competitors. The extent of any such list and the service provider's appetite for agreeing to any such restrictions would be predicated upon the development timeline— before or during the contract term—for the automation; any fees the service provider was paid to develop, configure, and implement the automation; and the downstream financial opportunity associated with ownership. If the client owns the automations, it could consider agreeing to a license back to the service provider that may contain restrictions similar to those discussed above.

WHO OWNS THE INTELLECTUAL PROPERTY?

From a service provider perspective, ownership is important as they may wish to patent the automations or utilize them with other clients. If the service provider were to relinquish ownership, it may seek to restrict the use of any automations by its competitors that may be engaged elsewhere in the client's ecosystem. Agreement to relinquish ownership to the client would be dependent upon any upfront payment the service provider received for developing, configuring, and implementing the automation in the client's environment. At a minimum, the service provider would expect to be fully compensated for those costs either at the time of delivery or over the term of the agreement. If the client were to terminate the agreement, then those costs would be included in the termination fee schedule.

The other consideration from a service provider perspective would be any restrictions upon its competitor's ability to access, utilize, and modify the automations after a termination or expiration event. While the answer to this question would most certainly be no, it may not be legitimate to implement a series of automations that are an integral part of the client's operating environment and then expect to remove them completely if the parties should go their separate ways. In the event of a termination or expiration event, it is also important to delineate how any service provider automation tools would be carved out from any ownership rights or license terms.

Other considerations in this area include deciding which party is best suited to license the automation software and understanding any assignment rights associated with that license as well as agreeing upon how process automations are defined under the agreement. Given the unique characteristics of the automations, they should be classified separately from other IP developed and brought to bear during the delivery term.

Now that we have reviewed the automation-specific IP rights of the parties, let's review how those rights are intertwined with the more general IP provisions we would likely see in a legacy outsourcing agreement.

First, the client must provide the service provider with a license to use any of its IP that is required in providing the services. An example is a license to use an application that the client uses to manage service tickets. A sample provision that addresses this requirement is as follows:

License to Service Provider

To the extent Service Provider requires use of client IP in connection with providing the Services, client hereby grants to Service Provider, during the applicable Service Agreement Term, a global, fully paid up, royalty-free, non-exclusive, non-transferable license for Service Provider and Service Provider Agents to Use the client IP, but only to the extent permitted by the terms of any applicable third party agreements (which client will communicate to Service Provider).

Second, clients can legitimately expect to receive a license to any software deployed by the service provider that is used in connection with the receipt of the services. This expectation applies to all software, including that owned by the service provider as well as that licensed by the service provider from a third party. In addition, in accordance with the concept of playing nicely in the sandbox, clients want to make sure that any software used in connection with the delivery of the services by one vendor can be used by third-party vendors in their ecosystem to the extent necessary for them to meet their delivery obligations. An example of a provision that addresses both scenarios is as follows:

License to Client

License of Service Provider Non-Software IP—During Term

With respect to Service Provider IP that is not Service Provider Software ("**Service Provider Non-Software IP**"), if any Service Provider Non-Software IP is used in connection with the receipt of the Services, Service Provider hereby grants, and will procure from any applicable third party the right to grant, a global, fully paid up, royalty-free, non-exclusive, irrevocable license to the Service Recipients to Use such Service Provider Non-Software IP during the applicable Service Agreement Term. Such license (1) extends to third parties providing services to client to the extent necessary for such services to be provided by such third parties, provided that such third parties are bound by confidentiality obligations similar to those of client under the Agreement.

License of Service Provider Software—During Term

With respect to Service Provider Software, if any Service Provider Software is used in connection with the receipt of the Services, Service Provider hereby grants, and will procure from any applicable third party the right to grant, a global, fully paid up, royalty-free, non-exclusive, irrevocable license for Client to Use the Service Provider Software during the applicable Service Agreement Term. Such license (a) extends to third parties providing services to client to the extent necessary for such services to be provided by such third parties, provided that such third parties are bound by confidentiality obligations similar to those of client under the Agreement. Such license will not include Microsoft Office products or other similar enterprise Software (e.g., Microsoft Word, where such Software is required to view reports developed by Service Provider), provided that Service Provider will identify such Software in Exhibit X to the applicable Service Agreement.

Prior to using any Service Provider Software that is not identified in the applicable Service Agreement to provide the Services, Service Provider will: (a) submit such Service Provider Software to client for client's review and approval; and (b) with respect to Service Provider Software that is licensed or leased from a third party, (i) use commercially reasonable efforts to obtain from the applicable third party the right to assign to client at no cost the applicable software license agreement and (ii) if Service Provider is unable to obtain such right, prior to using such Software, notify client of the approximate cost of obtaining such right or obtaining a separate license to such Service Provider Software. Upon client's request, Service Provider will provide client with a list of all Service Provider Software being used to provide the Services as of the date of such request.

Service providers want to protect their proprietary IP—their secret sauce—used during the delivery term from other competitors in the client ecosystem. To that end, they need to be mindful about how they deploy any IP that fits in the secret sauce category during delivery. Therefore, a service provider can designate any IP that will not be available to the client under the applicable service agreement. However, if any secret sauce IP is made available to the client in connection with its receipt of the services, then a license to both the client and any third-party vendors is likely to be required by the terms of the agreement. A provision that addresses this issue is as follows:

Limited License of Service Provider Software and Non-Software IP—During Term

Service Provider shall not make available to client the Service Provider IP set forth in Exhibit X to the applicable Service Agreement; provided, however, that if such IP is made available to client for its use in connection with receipt of the Services, Service Provider hereby grants, and will procure from any applicable third party the right to grant, a global, fully paid up, royalty-free, non-exclusive, irrevocable license to the Service Recipients to Use such Service Provider IP during the period of such use. Such license (1) extends to third parties providing services to Service Recipients to the extent necessary for such services to be provided by such third parties, provided that such third parties are bound by confidentiality obligations similar to those of client under the Agreement.

Although a key theme of this book focuses on collaboration and partnership, there are some areas where prudence dictates drafting a provision that will be enacted in the event of failure, either as a result of a termination event or the expiration of the service agreement. Under this umbrella, clients want to make sure they have a perpetual license to use any service provider IP incorporated into their systems or processes, and not commercially available following the expiration or termination of the agreement. In these instances, the client legitimately expects to receive a license to continue to use that IP after the service provider's delivery obligations are completed. It is important to note that the scope of any such license is limited to the receipt of services and excludes any stand-alone use of the IP. A provision that captures this approach is as follows:

Post-Termination and Expiration Rights

With respect to Service Provider IP that is (1) incorporated in client's systems or processes and (2) not commercially available to client following the expiration or termination of the applicable Service Agreement, Service Provider hereby grants, and will procure from any applicable third party the right to grant, a global, fully paid up, royalty-free, non-exclusive, perpetual, irrevocable license for client to Use such

Service Provider IP, provided that, with respect to the Service Provider IP described in this Section, such Service Provider IP may not be used on a stand-alone basis. Such license (a) extends to third parties providing services to Service Recipients to the extent necessary for such services to be provided by such third parties. Neither client nor any client Agent will decompile, disassemble or reverse engineer any Service Provider IP described in this Section without the consent of Service Provider.

We have addressed the licensing construct associated with service provider software used by the service provider during delivery and the implications of deploying service provider software that is required for the client to continue to receive the full benefit of the services in a post-termination environment. It is now important to address the ownership rights associated with any intellectual property first developed during the delivery term. Options relevant to developed IP include sole ownership by either party with a potential license back to the other, or joint ownership between the parties. Clients generally seek to own all developed IP. Service providers, however, prefer to own all of the developed IP and to provide a non-exclusive license to the client to use, maintain, copy, modify, enhance and prepare derivative works of the Developed IP for their internal business purposes only. Such an approach is not unreasonable as clients are not in the business of providing outsourcing services and have no desire to resell or license developed IP related to an outsourcing engagement in the marketplace. In addition, by agreeing to an ownership construct in which they would receive a broad license for all developed IP, clients receive the benefit of the developed IP from all prior service provider engagements—which would be classified as service provider pre-existing IP—with similar scope as well as the benefit of not having to pay the service provider to develop all IP from scratch.

To the extent that the service provider will not own all of the developed IP, their preference would be joint ownership of all developed IP. To the extent that the client will own all of the developed IP, then the service provider would seek a license back for all developed IP—excluding any confidential information of the client that may be embedded—or, at minimum, ownership of any derivatives or modifications originating in the service provider's pre-existing IP that are utilized in delivery. Developed IP is defined as follows: "Any IP developed by service provider pursuant to the agreement that is (1) a modification or enhancement of client IP or (2) an original non-derivative work provided to client under the agreement."

A provision that reflects client ownership of all developed IP is as follows:

Developed IP

Client will own and have all right, title and interest in and to the Developed IP. Service Provider hereby irrevocably assigns, transfers and conveys to Client all of its right, title and interest in and to the Developed IP, including all Intellectual Property Rights thereto. Service Provider will, and will cause all Service Provider Agents and Service Provider Personnel (whether former or current) to: (A) cooperate with and assist client, both during and after the applicable Service Agreement Term, in perfecting, maintaining, and enforcing client's rights in all right, title, and interest in any Developed IP, including all Intellectual Property Rights thereto, and (B) execute and deliver to client any documents or take any other actions as may reasonably be necessary, or as client may reasonably request, to perfect, maintain, protect, or enforce client's rights in such Developed IP.

Another area to be addressed is the scope of any license provided to the client if the service provider embeds any of its pre-existing IP into a deliverable or any developed IP. Identifying and establishing license terms for any service provider pre-existing IP embedded within developed IP is not an easy undertaking. As we discussed, the client may own all the developed IP, and it is not practical to highlight portions of that developed IP in which it has different ownership rights. Given this challenge, clients may seek to have service providers refrain from, or, at a minimum, identify and seek the clients' approval before including any service provider IP in any deliverables or developed IP to which the client retains ownership. If such service provider IP is embedded in a client deliverable, the next question is what is the scope of any license that the client receives with the embedded IP? Clients may seek to have an unrestricted license. In contrast, service providers generally seek to limit any such license to internal business purposes only or for use solely in connection with the deliverable in which it is contained. While the scope of the license for embedded service provider IP may grant the client the right to modify, enhance, and create derivative works from the embedded service provider IP, such a right will be limited to those instances in which such modification or enhancement is necessary to use or maintain the client deliverable. In no instance will the license allow the client to utilize the service provider embedded IP on a stand-alone basis. A sample provision that addresses this construct, but which does not include an internal business purposes limitation, is as follows:

License to Embedded Service Provider IP

Service Provider will not include or incorporate any Service Provider IP in any Deliverable or Developed IP unless: (A) Service Provider identifies such Service Provider IP to client in advance and in writing and (B) client agrees in advance to such inclusion or incorporation. Notwithstanding the foregoing, Service Provider hereby grants, and will procure from any applicable third party the right to grant, client a global, fully paid up, royalty-free, non-exclusive, sub-licensable, perpetual, irrevocable license for client to Use any Service Provider IP embedded in or required for the use of any Deliverable or Developed IP, solely in connection with such Deliverable or Developed IP.

If the client maintains ownership of all developed IP under the agreement, the inclusion of a residuals clause is beneficial to the service provider. Under such a clause, the service provider can use any general concepts, methodologies, or tools developed or disclosed by either party during the delivery term as long as such use does not infringe on the IP rights of the other party. A residuals provision is similar to the following:

Residual Knowledge

Nothing contained in this Master Agreement will restrict a Party from the use of any general ideas, concepts, know-how, methodologies, processes, technologies, algorithms or techniques retained in the unaided mental impressions of such Party's personnel relating to the Services that either Party, individually or jointly, develops or discloses under the Agreement, provided that in doing so such Party does not breach its obligations under the data protection provisions or infringe the Intellectual Property Rights of the other Party or third parties who have licensed or provided materials to the other Party.

The ownership of IP first developed by the service provider and any license rights granted between the parties must be carefully reviewed in light of the scope of the services outsourced. While the ownership rights related to first developed and embedded service provider IP may be straightforward, the now-commonplace multiple vendor ecosystem dictates that the parties address how IP is shared among vendors, and the implications and restrictions on its use in a termination, insourcing, or service agreement expiration event.

CHAPTER 20

YOU SHALL NOT MOVE SERVICE LOCATIONS WITHOUT MY CONSENT

The general rule is that each service agreement delineate the list of service locations as well as which component of the service is performed from each location. In many instances, the geographic delivery footprint of the service provider is a critical factor in the award decision because it affects service delivery as well as price.

In addition, given the sensitivity related to clients production data transmitted to and residing in the offshore service locations, clients typically specify a list of requirements in the areas of general and physical safety and security, network hosting, data-handling protocols, data transmissions and cryptography, facilities, equipment, and personnel and operations that must be strictly adhered to in each offshore location.

Although many of these requirements may seem stringent, the cost of a data breach can be significant, in terms of the direct and indirect costs of the breach and its remediation, and its effect on the client's reputation. Thus, including such security protocols in the agreement is consistent with industry best practices, should not be an afterthought, and, as long as they are reasonable in scope, should be agreed to by the service provider.

Given the absolute requirement to protect confidential information, particularly personal data, service providers seek to capitalize on this concern in the sales cycle. Consider a recent IBM cloud advertisement that states: "The IBM cloud is engineered to help deliver on the demands of data-intensive businesses. It's built on dozens of data centers across five continents, featuring a private fiber network that helps protect data as it moves between them. It offers dedicated, bare metal servers to avoid interference from outside users. And it includes the support of 6,000 security consultants in 10 operations centers."

With all of the scrutiny on service locations, data transmission, and security standards, clients want consistency in the service location footprint during the delivery term. Thus, it is typical and reasonable for the agreement to contain a provision that states that the service provider may not switch to a new service location without the prior written consent of the client. The client, when presented with such a move proposal, will certainly seek to understand the rationale for the proposed relocation, the risks and benefits associated with the move, and any operational, technical, security, or regulatory effect that may occur as a result. In addition, if the move reduces costs for the service provider, the client may expect that any such cost reduction be passed along as reduced charges.

Given the potential time associated with getting written consent for a move, I strongly recommend seeking pre-approval in each service agreement for a list of potential locations where service delivery may occur. Under this construct, the service provider must still notify the client of a potential move but retains the flexibility to provide its services from any of the pre-approved locations as long as there is no degradation in service quality. In addition, shifts in service location may also yield additional costs, taxes, and other expenses related to the move. The general rule is that the party initiating the move should bear the costs that may result.

In addition to obtaining pre-approval for potential site locations where the services are delivered, it is important to address the impact of changing a site location as a result of a change in law that affects the service provider or the client. As I have discussed, I support the notion that the service provider should be able to move among its pre-approved delivery locations, with notice to the client, as long as the service levels are not jeopardized. As for a change in laws, I say that the party who initiated the relocation request (you would expect this to be the party against whom the law is construed) carries the burden of any costs of any location change. For example, assume that a new Indian law is highly punitive toward outsourcing service providers. As a result of that law's enactment, the outsourcing provider that was delivering its services from an Indian delivery center decides to move its service location to the Philippines. In this instance, the service provider absorbs the cost of the change in location. Alternatively, consider a new law, enacted by the Canadian government that was targeted at and highly punitive toward utility companies that outsource any services to India. In that instance, the service provider moved the delivery of its services to a location outside of India, but the client, a Canadian utility company, absorbed the cost of the move because the client had requested the change in location. A sample provision that addressed issues related to site locations is as follows:

Site Locations

(a)   Each SOW will indicate the sites or facilities from which the Services performed under such SOW will be performed or delivered (a "**Site**"). Client must agree in writing in advance to any non-pre-approved Site from which Services are to be provided. Supplier will not change the location of any pre-approved Site, nor the type of Service to be performed at such Site, without providing 30 day advance notification of the move. Supplier will be responsible for all additional costs, taxes or expenses related to or resulting from any Supplier-initiated relocation of a Site due to a change in Supplier Applicable Law. Client will be responsible for all additional costs, taxes or expenses related to or resulting from a Client-initiated relocation of a Site due to a change in Client Applicable Law or due to a request by Client under paragraph 3 in this section.

(b)   In addition to the pre-approved Sites in Exhibit X and subject to Client's approval, Supplier may propose other sites to be set out in a SOW as facilities from which Supplier may provide Services. Client agrees to give due consideration to any such new sites that Supplier may propose. Exhibit X may also contain a list of countries pre-approved by Client (though specific Sites within such pre-approved countries would still require Client's prior written consent).

(c)   Client may require Supplier to locate (or relocate) certain Supplier Personnel, or otherwise deliver Services from, a Site in a particular jurisdiction in order to enhance Client's prospects for cost recovery in such jurisdiction (or for some similar reason). Prior to locating (or relocating) any Supplier Personnel within a particular jurisdiction pursuant to a Client request under this section, Supplier shall notify Client of potential cost impacts.

Another key issue with regard to the service provider locations is the frequency that they are subject to a controls audit report. Many clients want a controls audit report conducted annually at each facility where their services are provided. At a macro level, a controls audit report tests the security, availability, processing integrity, confidentiality, and privacy controls at each service location.

The challenge of this demand is that audits are costly, and many Tier 1 providers do not audit each facility annually; however, they do audit their largest facilities annually. If the client does not waiver from its annual audit requirement, the parties may agree to limit service provider locations to those subject to the annual audit program. Alternatively, if the client seeks the delivery of services from locations that are not a part of the annual program or seeks more frequent audits, then the client should absorb the cost of the more robust audit program.

CHAPTER 21

I NEED RELIEF—WHERE IS MY SAVINGS CLAUSE?

As I have discussed, it is critical to clearly articulate the roles and responsibilities of the parties in an outsourcing engagement. Doing this is especially important in a multivendor environment, where one vendor's success may be tied to the ability of another—either the client or a third party—to deliver its services in a timely and quality manner. One of the key reasons to do so is that if the client or a third party fails to comply with its responsibilities or does not meet its performance obligations, and that failure affects the service provider's ability to deliver its services in accordance with the service levels, then the service provider can seek relief and be excused from performance under a savings clause. I am not sure how the clause got the name, but it is probably rooted in its serving as a "saving grace" for the party seeking relief.

While a wide variety of actions may be required to be performed by the party seeking relief, the concept behind every savings clause is the same. The general rule is that a party is excused from its performance obligations under the agreement, including its obligations to meet service levels, if its ability to perform is prevented by the failure of the client or a third party to perform any of its obligations under the agreement or in the event of a force majeure event. In addition, and especially in a managed-service environment, clients are seeking the ability to reprioritize service provider staff as they may deem appropriate so they can focus on a particular high-priority initiative or to address a peak in volume. If clients desire that level of flexibility, that action should also be deemed a relief event for which performance should be excused.

For a savings clause to be successfully leveraged by the service provider, it is critical that it strictly adhere to the provisions that must be followed to obtain relief under the agreement. Those provisions generally require that (1) the service provider expeditiously notify the client of its inability to perform; (2) the service provider provide the client with a reasonable opportunity to correct the client's performance and, thereby, avoid the claimed non-performance; and (3) identify and pursue commercially reasonable means to avoid or mitigate the impact of its failure to perform. In addition, if there is some reasonable question about causation, it is not uncommon for the savings clause provision to require that the service provider perform a root cause analysis demonstrating that the client or third party's failure to perform is the cause of the service provider's non-performance.

Strictly adhering to the relief provisions is also an absolute requirement when contemplating the deployment of robotic process automation into a client delivery environment. The agreement must stipulate which party is responsible for the build specifications, maintenance, and management of the robots. In addition, deploying automation without the corresponding client obligation around compliance and change management will not yield the expected savings and process efficiencies. Failure to comply with and a refusal to accept changes in the underlying business process will only lengthen the list of exceptions that require human intervention and processing. As no party should absorb risks outside of its control, the agreement must clearly state the assumptions and dependencies upon which the achievement of any service levels, productivity guarantees, quality standards, and other savings or efficiencies are conditioned. The bottom line is that all the automation and artificial intelligence in the world is worthless if the humans that initiate incidents and tickets and provide the necessary inputs into the system fail miserably from a change management and compliance perspective.

I cannot stress enough the importance of strictly adhering to the provisions required in the savings clause to obtain relief. I facilitate many disputes that are the result of the client or a third party failing to meet its performance obligations or comply with its responsibilities under the agreement. I first confirm that the statement of work clarifies the roles and responsibilities of the parties and that the service levels are objective, measurable, and verifiable. Then, the first three questions I ask are as follows:

I NEED RELIEF—WHERE IS MY SAVINGS CLAUSE?

1. When did the service provider first identify that the client or third party failed to meet its performance obligations?

2. Once the service provider realized that the client's deficiency would cause its non-performance, did the service provider immediately notify the client? In writing?

3. Did the service provider take measures to mitigate the impact of the non-performance on its performance obligations?

Depending on the answers, it is easy to predict, with a high probability of success, the outcome of the dispute. An example of a savings clause is as follows:

> Service Provider's failure to perform its responsibilities under this SOW or the master agreement shall be excused if and to the extent such non-performance is caused by the performance or failure to perform of client or a client third party contractor to perform client's obligations under this SOW or the master agreement, but only if (i) service provider, upon becoming aware of such performance or failure to perform, expeditiously notifies client of its inability to perform under such circumstances, (ii) Service Provider provides client with a reasonable opportunity to correct such performance or failure to perform and thereby avoid such service provider non-performance, (iii) Service provider identifies and pursues commercially reasonable means to avoid or mitigate the impact of such performance or failure to perform, (iv) to the extent there are reasonable questions as to causation, service provider conducts a root cause analysis and thereby demonstrates that such performance or failure to perform is the cause of service provider's nonperformance.

Another example of a savings clause that addresses the reprioritization concept and contains an ongoing mitigation obligation is as follows:

> Service Provider's nonperformance of its obligations under the Agreement, including obligations to meet Service Levels, will be excused if, and to the extent, Service Provider's performance of an obligation pursuant to the Agreement is prevented by: (a) the failure of client to

perform any of its obligations pursuant to the Agreement, including those under the client Policies and Procedures Manual, or the acts or omissions of a Service Recipient or Third Party Provider; (b) Client reprioritization of Service Provider Personnel, provided Service Provider has notified client of the negative impact such reprioritization will have on Service Provider's performance of the Services and Service Levels; and (c) a Force Majeure Event (in each case, a "Relief Event"); provided, however, that Service Provider: (1) demonstrates via a root cause analysis that any such failure by client was the cause of such Relief Event, (2) uses commercially reasonable efforts to mitigate the impact of such Relief Event, (c) continues to use commercially reasonable efforts (including emergency fixes and workarounds performed by Existing Resources) to perform such obligation and (d) provides client with notice describing in reasonable detail the nature of such failure as soon as is practicable after Service Provider knows or should have known of such failure.

Finally, I have provided an example of a savings clause that is much more subjective about the relief that a service provider may receive when it is unable to perform as a result of the client failing to meet its own obligations under the agreement. In this instance, the client believed that a savings clause was not a necessity, given the aggressive timelines in the interim remedies provisions—primarily the dispute resolution and governance processes—in the agreement. While this approach was atypical because the concept of a savings clause is market-relevant, it may be an option in certain circumstances. Aptly, it was referred to as the "Compassionate CIO" provision when introduced by the client's counsel. It is as follows:

This outsourcing agreement utilizes a number of "interim remedies" (including Service Level remedies, dispute resolution processes, payment withholds, and credit assessment mechanisms) to assist the parties in effectively addressing performance issues that may arise during the Term. Customer deems the various remedies as essential tools to its management of this outsourcing agreement. Nevertheless, Vendor's effective ongoing performance is the critical behavior such remedies are designed to achieve.

Consequently, recognizing that circumstances may arise in which the imposition of the interim remedies as structured may not fairly reflect corrective and other efforts made by Vendor, subject to this Section, Customer, may, in its sole discretion waive, in an individual occurrence, Customer's right to use, or collect a credit resulting from, such interim remedies. Factors that will be considered by Customer in assessing whether to waive an interim remedy include: (i) Vendor's proactive involvement in identifying a problem before operational impacts are manifested; (ii) the timing, quality, and accuracy of communications from Vendor relating to the problem; (iii) the speed with which corrective actions are taken and the problem is fixed; (iv) the quality of Vendor's root cause analysis and the likelihood that appropriate steps have been taken to prevent a reoccurrence of the problem; (v) the quality of Vendor's overall performance at the time the remedy right accrues and during the Term; and (vi) the impact of other causal factors, including Customer's actions or inaction relating to the problem.

Any waiver under this Section must be in writing, expressly state that it is a waiver under this Section, and be signed by authorized Customer personnel.

Although aligning your fate with a Compassionate CIO may be an option with a long-term and trusted client, I prefer to have an objective savings clause that provides relief in these instances. As I discussed previously, one of the primary reasons IT projects are unsuccessful is the failure of the parties to clearly articulate their roles and responsibilities. The multivendor client ecosystem with an interconnected delivery scope has complicated this process. The likelihood that one vendor's ability to successfully deliver its services is conditioned on another vendor is high. The savings clause is, therefore, a necessity and truly a "saving grace." It provides a mechanism that a vendor can use to seek relief when it is unable to perform because of circumstances beyond its control.

CHAPTER 22

I WILL TAKE YOUR APPLICATIONS AND ARCHITECTURE AT FACE VALUE

It is always important to be mindful of the quality of the in-scope applications that will be transitioned to the service provider in an applications management outsourcing engagement. Also, it is equally important to pay attention to any client-mandated architectural standards which must be strictly adhered to during the delivery term. As for the applications, a client usually has a set of standards and policies to which all applications must conform to. These policies and standards are generally incorporated into the agreement, and compliance is not optional. However, many applications do not conform to that policy or standard, and that noncompliance may detrimentally impact the ability of the service provider to successfully transition the service. If this issue of noncompliance is overlooked, such an oversight can be costly. The client may expect the service provider to absorb any cost of making the applications conform to the standard or policy. In addition, many agreements state that an application cannot exit from the transition process until it conforms to the application standards in the agreement. To address this issue, I recommend including a provision similar to the following:

Application Compliance

During the Transition Period, Service Provider will identify to client any Application that is not in compliance with client Policies to the extent Service Provider becomes aware of any such non-compliance. After the applicable Service Commencement Date, Service Provider will continue, during the course of performing the Services, to identify any noncompliance with the client Policies. To the extent that an Application is not in compliance with client Policies, Service Provider will (a) provide notice to client of such noncompliance, (a) at least maintain the Application at its current state of compliance with the client Policies, and (c) if client requests that the Application be brought into compliance with the client Policies, Service Provider will do so as Discretionary Work.

In addition to the state of the applications, it is important to focus on the client's architectural standards for the delivery of services. This seems like an easy issue to address, but a client often introduces modifications to the architecture and assumes that the service provider will then amend its provisions of the service to comply with those changes, even if the cost is significant. Although architectural standards may change, the service provider should not have to absorb the costs of the change. This is yet another example of the proposition that a party should never absorb a risk it does not control. Therefore, I would include a provision similar to the following:

Architecture, Standards and Strategic Direction

Service Provider will comply with the client Architecture and any modifications to the client Architecture made available to Service Provider. To the extent that such modifications materially increase or decrease Service Provider's costs to provide the Services, the Parties will negotiate an equitable adjustment to the Charges with respect to such increased or decreased cost in accordance with the Change Control Procedure.

CHAPTER 23

TO WHOM DO WE COMPLAIN WHEN WE ARE UNHAPPY?

An effective governance process is a critical component of any successful outsourcing engagement for a number of reasons. When executed properly, the governance structure under an outsourcing agreement should facilitate the timely, quality, and cost-effective delivery of the services, and the resolution of conflicts or disputes in a timely manner. The ultimate objective of a strong governance program should be to maintain open lines of communication at all hierarchical and functional levels, to collaborate and partner for success, to innovate and focus on continuous improvement of the delivery of the services, and, hopefully, to prevent any dispute or conflict from leaving the governance process and entering a more formal dispute resolution process.

First, a strong governance process should require the appointment of a number of key roles by both the client and the service provider; such roles incorporate varying levels of responsibility to ensure that services are delivered in a timely, quality, and cost-effective manner. These roles may include a relationship manager, a contract manager, a transition manager, a service delivery manager, and a finance manager. These individuals in these roles should align closely with one another and communicate on a recurring basis throughout the delivery term. I am a proponent of a "no surprises" approach to successful contract management. A key tenet is an open channel whereby both the client and service provider proactively address potential problems before they materialize into formal disputes. Therefore, collaborating and partnering for success is the first requirement for a strong governance program.

Second, and of equal importance, is the requirement to establish a series of joint governance committees to oversee the performance of the services and to help facilitate the interaction of the parties during the delivery term. The governance committees typically include a steering committee responsible for the oversight of the agreement and the overall relationship between the parties. At a macro level, the committees focus on key activities, including the following:

- Monitor and resolve disagreements about the provision of the services and the performance standards.
- Review and approve any changes to the agreement.
- Review the service provider's performance under the agreement.
- Resolve escalated issues and disputes.
- Review current trends and best practices in the market and any changes in the client's business and IT strategy to determine any impact on service delivery.
- Manage the overall client relationship and focus on alignment of goals and objectives.

In addition to the steering committee that operates at a global project level, it is advisable to form additional committees at the service agreement level. These may include a management committee, a contract administration committee, and a service delivery management committee. Members of each committee and their specific roles and responsibilities can be agreed upon by the parties. However, the key objective is that the committees are formally established, that they meet on a recurring basis, that they proactively manage issues that arise during delivery, and that any conflicts or disputes that they are unable to resolve are promptly escalated to the next level in the hierarchy of the governance structure.

The last component of a successful governance process is absolute clarity about the hierarchy of the committee structure and the timeline under which disputes are escalated to the next level in the hierarchy for resolution. Optimally, that process should facilitate the timely facilitation, escalation, and resolution of delivery issues before they materialize into formal disputes. In the spirit of resolving disputes in a timely manner, it is critical to identify the individuals who make decisions on behalf of the parties. While committees are valuable, bring diverse insight into problem resolution, and can make recommendations, there must be one individual responsible for making decisions.

CHAPTER 24

LET'S FOLLOW THE PLAYBOOK

Although it is not a mechanical process per se, from a delivery perspective, outsourcing services are rigid and disciplined in process and approach. Given this dynamic, for each service agreement, the service provider develops a policy and procedures manual that describes how the service provider performs and delivers the services under the agreement, any equipment and software used in delivery, and any documentation, including operations manuals, end user guides, and other specifications that provide further details of its delivery activities. In essence, it becomes the bible that is strictly adhered to during the delivery term. However, unlike the Bible, the policies and procedures manual evolves during service delivery to reflect any changes in the services as well as in the IT environment, operations, and business process.

As I have previously discussed, the timely development of a policy and procedures manual is typically a critical deliverable to which deliverable credits apply. Depending on the scope and recurrence of the credit structure, the inability of the service provider to properly complete the policy and procedures manual can have significant implications on the overall outsourcing engagement. In addition to the financial penalties that may accrue, the final completion and acceptance of the policies and procedures manual is typically a required deliverable in the stabilization phase of the transition. Thus, the failure to complete and achieve acceptance of this deliverable can leave the service provider stuck in no man's land—unable to graduate from the transition and begin the steady-state phase of the engagement.

Although there is no standard format for a policies and procedures manual, the typical sections include the following:

1.   **Organizational Review:** governance, organization, and scope.

2.   **Transition Activities and Responsibilities:** deliverables and milestones.

3.   **Steady State Procedures:** performance, contractual, and financial management.

4.   **Performance Management Processes:** service level measurement and reporting, security management, architecture and standards management, incident management, and change management.

5.   **Financial Management:** financial analysis and planning, service level credits, invoice management, pricing adjustments, and regulatory and tax compliance.

6.   **Contract Management Process:** contract administration, change control, dispute resolution, audits, and governance.

7.   **Relationship Management Process:** governance, forecasting and demand management, customer satisfaction and workplace services, and third-party providers.

8.   **Other Operational Processes:** application on-boarding, knowledge management, quality management, risk management, data protection, compliance with policies and laws, and project and process management.

Clearly, the policies and procedures manual crosses multiple dimensions. It not only describes the method by which the services will be delivered but also serves as a valuable resource when faced with a termination, re-sourcing, or service agreement expiration event.

CHAPTER 25

CHANGE CAN BE GOOD

As I discussed previously, any agreement for outsourcing services must contain a formal change order process that must be strictly adhered to for **any** change instituted during the delivery term. Please note that I underlined and put in boldface the term "any" in the previous sentence. The failure to do so absolutely yields a speedy path to the dispute resolution provisions in the agreement and frankly, reflects poor project management practices and, in my opinion, is negligent.

Never lose sight of the fact that the primary reason IT projects fail is the failure to properly define project scope at the time of contract execution. Highly connected to this issue is the failure of the parties to strictly comply with the contractually stipulated change order process. I am not going to spend a lot of time addressing the need for a change order process that is strictly adhered to by the parties. It must be a formal process whereby any change from the original agreed upon scope is identified. Of course, this approach is contingent on both parties having read the statement of work, and clearly understanding the scope of delivery and their roles and responsibilities.

Only then can the parties articulate any deviations from that original scope. Therefore, before the delivery of services begins, each member of the client and service delivery team should be required to read the contract and be absolutely clear about the delivery responsibilities of the parties. Strict discipline is a necessity here because there is no tolerance for error. To use a football analogy, this is basic blocking and tackling. If you cannot do this, then you should ride the bench for the entire game.

When the change request is made and the parties agree that it is legitimate, the service provider should have the opportunity to clearly document the services, deliverables, milestones, and performance standards associated with the change, any applicable acceptance criteria, and any associated price increase. In essence, the service provider offers a proposal in the change order request form that articulates the scope and the price of services to be delivered under the change request.

When the change order request is received by the client, the parties can review the scope of services consistent with the change and the price, and can negotiate scope and price as needed. When the terms are agreed on, the parties formally execute the change order, and the work may begin. No matter what promises are made or whatever the reason, do not, under any circumstance, begin the delivery of the services until the formal change order has been fully executed by the parties. Failure to do so is a guaranteed path to a dispute. Trying to execute a retroactive change order after the services have been delivered never goes as smoothly as expected, and is not in the best interests of either party. For that reason, strict discipline is a priority.

I have seen countless disputes arise because the parties failed to adhere to the change order process. The question now arises: Why bother executing a narrowly tailored statement of work with clarity on roles and responsibilities if you are not going to document any changes made during the delivery term? The answers I have received to this question have varied over the years, but some are as follows:

- It was just a minor change, and I did not want to deal with the paperwork.
- It was just a minor change, and I did it to preserve my relationship with the client. I didn't want the client to think I was nickel and diming him.
- We intended to execute the change order but just didn't have time to get it done.
- The client told us that he would compensate us accordingly at the end of the phase and that there was no need to execute the change.
- We figured that we would "true-up" with the client at the end of the program because there would likely be lots of changes.

The general rule I propose is that shortly after the agreement is executed, identify a minor change required in the agreement. It might be refining the timeline in the transition plan or as simple as changing a notification address in the agreement, both having no associated cost impact. Irrespective of the nature of the change, I encourage you to execute a change order in strict compliance with the process in the contract. By doing so, you instill the proper level of discipline in both the client and service provider teams, and reinforce the notion that change is OK but must be clearly documented and agreed to in writing by the parties.

When in doubt, remember the Standish Group statistics that reflect the primary reason IT projects fail: scope creep. How, might you ask, do scope creep and change occur in a vacuum? The answer is: when the parties fail to memorialize changes to the statement of work, both changes in the scope of services as well as the price. To avoid scope creep, change should be broadly defined, as in the following example:

Definition of Change; Scope of Application of Change Control Procedures

The terms and conditions set out in the Change Control Procedures will apply to the following (each, a "**Change**"):

(a)   any Modification or other alteration to any Deliverable that results in a change to the Specifications therefor or to any other requirement therefor set out in this Agreement other than a Modification or other alteration made by Supplier in order to provide the Services in accordance with the Service Levels or to address emergency security issues;

(b)   any change to the nature or scope of any Services currently being provided, or any change to any Specifications or other requirements in respect of a Service that is currently being provided;

(c)   the removal of any Service or part thereof;

(d)   any change to any existing Service Level;

(e)   any change to a Milestone or Milestone Deadline; or

(f)   any other change to this Agreement that is expressly stated to be made, or would be reasonable under the circumstances to be, in accordance with the **Change Control Procedures**.

Each request for a Change will be made and implemented only in accordance with the terms and conditions set out in the Change Control Procedures.

I am not sure what else to tell you here. I can say that what may seem like basic blocking and tackling is typically an afterthought or ignored altogether until it is time to true-up for the change and the service provider wants to be paid. It is right about then that the client comes down with an acute case of amnesia about the reason why the change was initiated, and a dispute arises shortly after. We know the path from there well: Relationships are damaged, service providers work under duress, and financial settlements are reached and none are optimal for either party.

CHAPTER 26

CAN I GET SOME HELP?

A service provider typically subcontracts a portion of the services that it is responsible for delivering. The general rule is that the client wants to retain the right to approve any subcontractor or third party that the service provider intends to use during the delivery term. I believe it is legitimate for the client to expect that the service provider will deliver the overwhelming majority of the client's delivery scope, especially in a competitive procurement where the skills and delivery acumen of the service provider were a key component of the selection decision. However, requiring consent for each subcontractor seems unnecessary. Getting prior consent should not be required as long as the agreement stipulates the following terms: that a subcontract does not release the service provider from its responsibility for delivery of the services; that any work performed by the subcontractor is deemed to be work performed by the service provider; that any subcontractor comply with the terms of the master agreement; that all applicable terms, including the disclosure and handling of confidential and personal information, flows down to the applicable subcontract; that the service provider is responsible for all payments to the subcontractor; and that the portion of the services subcontracted is in a limited range. Obtaining consent for subcontractors is not an issue that requires lots of time in the negotiation process. I advise the service provider to identify all subcontractors it intends to use during the delivery term and, as with service locations, get blanket approval for them.

Even with blanket approval, the client should retain the right to revoke its approval of any third party if that third party does not comply with the terms and conditions of the agreement, if its performance is materially deficient, or if any misrepresentations have been made regarding the third party.

Finally, there should be a reasonable standard for using a third party to deliver the services. If a third party is engaged for its technical expertise or geographic footprint, then I see no reason why the client should not freely offer its consent. However, if the service provider is subcontracting key components of its delivery scope that it claimed to be its delivery sweet spots during the sales cycle, then it is legitimate for the client to seek to understand the rationale for engaging and seeking the assistance of the third party, and to withhold its consent as necessary.

CHAPTER 27

IF YOU CHANGE, YOU WILL PAY

A recent trend I have encountered is clients seeking to avoid the change control process—primarily, the cost of the change—with regard to changes in client policies and procedures identified or referenced in the master agreement. I have little tolerance for a client seeking to have its outsourcing service provider be financially responsible for amending the delivery of its services solely as a result of a unilateral change the client has made in the client's policies and procedures. This is not a legitimate position. The price proposed by the service provider was developed in accordance with the scope of services provided as well as any other requirements, including the client-mandated policies and procedures that must be followed during the delivery term. Given the highly competitive nature of outsourcing engagements, any unforeseen costs that the service provider would be required to absorb could have a detrimental impact on the financial viability of the engagement.

Expecting the service provider to absorb the additional costs associated with a change in client policies or procedures is not a legitimate request. The service provider should be responsible for absorbing only those risks within its control, and these types of changes in client policies and procedures clearly do not meet that requirement. In addition, if the service provider is readily available to absorb what could be significant costs of such changes, a question arises about the credibility and financial legitimacy of the initial proposal. If the cost of such a change can be readily absorbed by the service provider, questions about the client's ability to trust the service provider and the legitimacy of the service provider's original proposal are likely to follow. Ultimately, if your client does not trust you, you might as well call it a day and play golf.

Agreeing to amend the services in a contractually stipulated timeline is one thing; agreeing to absorb the cost of compliance is another. In addressing this issue, a few options can be considered. The first is objective and straightforward, namely, that any change in the areas previously articulated yield a change order that identifies any change in delivery process and associated costs. While this is the most objective approach, it may yield unnecessary levels of change control administration because of the potential of frequent changes. However, we should not forget one of our key contracting principles: If you make a change, you execute a written change order to reflect it. This key principle should not be set aside to reduce the time spent on contract administration.

The second option is to include a provision that yields an equitable adjustment to the charges if that change in policy or procedure materially increases or decreases the service provider's cost of providing the services. While the inclusion of the term "material" may reduce unnecessary administration, it may equally facilitate a dispute because the interpretation of material is subjective. In this instance, a change order would still be executed, but it could be a no-cost change order if the change was not deemed material. In addition, this example provides the client with the option to provide relief to the service provider as it relates to compliance with a particular policy or procedure. It is as follows:

> Prior to the Master Agreement Effective Date, Client will make available to Service Provider in writing all Client Policies with which Service Provider is obligated to comply. Service Provider will comply with all such Client Policies, as well as subsequent additions and changes to such Client Policies that are made available in writing to Service Provider during the Master Services Agreement Term, provided that, to the extent that such additions and changes materially increase or decrease Service Provider costs to provide the Services, the Charges will be equitably adjusted (in accordance with the applicable Charges Methodology) with respect to such increased or decreased costs in accordance with the Change Control Procedure. If client provides relief to Service Provider from performing the Services in compliance with a requirement of the client Policies, such relief will only be valid if client provides a written variance approved by the person designated by client.

IF YOU CHANGE, YOU WILL PAY

I have seen parties agree to a dollar threshold that results in an adjustment to the charges only when that threshold is exceeded. This kind of agreement avoids pricing negotiations related to slight deviations in client policies and procedures, and avoids any potential disputes about the impact of any change in policies and procedures for the services and the materiality of any related price impact. Any costs incurred by the service provider below this threshold result in the execution of a change order, but there is no cost adjustment until the threshold is exceeded.

With advance notice of this type of provision, the service provider may be able to incorporate the impact of this requirement into its staffing roster and managed service price submission. It is as follows:

As of the Effective Date and continuing throughout the Term, the Service Provider shall provide Services to Client and the Authorized Users as such Services may evolve or are otherwise supplemented, enhanced, modified, or replaced in accordance with this Master Services Agreement. Except as specifically set forth in the applicable Statement of Work or the Master Services Agreement, Service Provider shall provide all Service Provider Equipment, Software and all other resources necessary to provide the Services in accordance with the Service Levels and other Requirements of this Statement of Work and the Master Agreement. To the extent specific Equipment, Software, Intellectual Property, tools, Customer Policies and Procedures, or guidelines are identified, referenced, or referred to in this Statement of Work, the Master Services Agreement or any Exhibits, such Equipment, Software, Intellectual Property, tools, Customer Policies and Procedures, and guidelines shall include any amendments, modifications, updates, and replacements to such Equipment, Software, Intellectual Property, tools, Client Policies and Procedures and guidelines identified by Customer from time-to-time during the Term of this Statement of Work, provided that Service Provider shall not be required to incur more than Fifty Thousand Dollars ($50,000) in documented expenses in any Contract Year (and no more than Twenty Thousand Dollars ($20,000) as to any single change) as a direct result of any amendments, modifications, updates and replacements to Client Policies and Procedures.

CHAPTER 28

I DON'T TRUST YOU—
WHAT ABOUT MY AUDIT RIGHTS?

I am frustrated with having to spend days, weeks, and, sometimes, months negotiating client audit rights that are rarely exercised during an outsourcing engagement. The general rule is that service providers must maintain an audit trail of all financial transactions and non-financial operational records, including transactions, authorizations, system changes, implementations, reports, analyses, as well as data created, collected, or processed and stored by the service provider in the performance of its obligations under the agreement. Similarly, clients must have a broad contractual right to audit their service providers in the following areas:

- To verify the accuracy of any charges and invoices.
- To verify the integrity of their data and to examine any facilities and systems that process, store, secure, support and transmit that data.
- To review the service providers' performance of the services in the areas of process and procedures, systems, equipment, and software, calculations regarding performance standards, general controls and security practices, and disaster recovery and backup procedures.

When both parties can get past the general parameters of the audit, then the focus can shift to determining the frequency, scope, and cost of audits done during the delivery term. As it relates to the overall audit rights of the client, a "reasonableness" standard should apply that should be grounded in the following core principles:

I DON'T TRUST YOU—WHAT ABOUT MY AUDIT RIGHTS?

1. The service provider assists the client auditors as reasonably necessary for them to complete their audit program.

2. The frequency of any such audits must be reasonable in scope—once a year is a reasonable standard. If the client seeks to audit more frequently, then it reimburses the service provider for the costs and expenses of supporting the audit. The support of an audit should never result in degradation of the services.

3. The service provider auditor cannot be a competitor of the service provider. The parties must agree on a reasonable list of service provider competitors.

4. No auditor has access to service provider cost information, internal quality assurance, or other management reports, or the proprietary information of any other service provider client.

5. If the auditors seek to load audit software onto service provider equipment, they are allowed to do so on client-dedicated equipment only.

6. The service provider conducts its own internal audits and shares a summary of the results to the extent relevant to its provision of the services.

7. Annually, the service provider conducts a controls audit for each approved service location from which the services are provided in accordance with the relevant standard.

8. If the client seeks to conduct an additional controls audit at a service provider location or seeks delivery from a location that does not undergo an annual controls audit, the client is responsible for the costs of such audit, including the cost of service provider personnel assisting in such audit.

9.   If an audit reveals deficiencies in the service provider's internal controls or procedures relating to the services, the service provider will develop a remediation plan to address the deficiencies within a reasonable time, will submit the remediation plan to the client for its review and comment, and will execute against the plan accordingly.

10.   If the service provider fails to develop a remediation plan or remediate a deficiency within the timeline in the remediation plan, the client may terminate the agreement for cause without cost or penalty, and without the payment of any termination charges.

In addition to these key principles, the parties should agree on a reasonable timeline as it relates to records retention and what level of support and any associated cost are required that result from a litigation request, governmental investigation, or other request or demand for information.

The deployment of automation into the delivery environment raises a number of audit related issues that must be addressed during the negotiation process. As we have discussed, automation increases compliance and decreases risk as the robot is free from human bias, incapable of being bribed or committing malfeasance, and performs its obligations in a highly accurate manner. However, because the robot always acts consistently, an error can quickly become systemic and widespread. Thus, it is important to ensure that the automation is routinely updated to reflect any change in business process and that the proper security protocols exist so that a rogue employee or other bad actor is unable to gain access to the robot and alter its program to conduct unauthorized processing.

Generally, the audit provisions in a legacy outsourcing agreement focus on the audit rights of the client as the outsourced service will generally be delivered from a service provider-controlled facility in an offshore location. Under that construct, it is the service provider's obligation to maintain the appropriate level of controls and procedures required to properly perform the services. The deployment of automation in the client's environment raises a number of additional issues and changes to the audit program that must be addressed by the parties during the negotiation process including controlling the robot's access to systems and data, testing to confirm the robots are functioning as programmed, implementing any changes to the underlying business processes in a timely manner, and monitoring the robot's performance to confirm compliance with applicable laws and regulations. Given this shift in the environment where the robots will reside, audit obligations will likely be much more evenly balanced as the level of automation increases.

CHAPTER 29

THE TAXMAN COMETH

My general rule is not to provide tax advice, and I will stick with that approach in this Chapter. Unlike many of the other provisions in the agreement, there is no industry standard for a tax provision other than to mitigate the taxes paid by either party under the agreement. I will state only that each party should be responsible for its own income taxes and taxes on its personal property, capital, and employment. The parties should be able to agree to include a provision that they will work together to minimize any taxes imposed on either party.

The tax implications in an outsourcing engagement can be complex. They can depend on the locations where the services are provided and any post-execution changes in those locations, any client invoicing requirements that might seek to allocate the cost associated with using the services or issuing invoices across multiple geographies, executing any local country agreements, and leveraging any applicable tax treaties.

This may be the only provision in the agreement where it is appropriate for the parties to think carefully about the consequences of failure and to collaborate in a manner that yields a tax strategy whereby neither party pays a dollar more in taxes than absolutely necessary.

CHAPTER 30

LET'S BENCHMARK YOUR PRICE

A benchmarking provision is also an area that receives a tremendous amount of scrutiny in the negotiation process. In its simplest form, a benchmarking provision allows the client to benchmark the price it pays to a service provider for its services against similar services delivered by similar providers in the marketplace. The idea behind this provision is to confirm that the client is receiving competitive market pricing during the delivery term. Despite the attention it receives, the benchmarking provision is seldom exercised by clients because it is expensive, time consuming for both parties, and the client does not need to rely on it to seek changes to the agreement's related terms, conditions, or price.

Like the audit provisions, benchmarking is a contractual right that the client may seek to exercise during the term of the agreement. Although benchmarking is a contractual right, there are parameters to be addressed as follows: (1) which party has responsibility for the cost of the benchmarking exercise; (2) how frequently the client can conduct a benchmarking exercise; (3) the procedures used by the benchmarking entity; (4) any benchmarking moratorium for a period after contract execution; (5) how the benchmarking results are gathered; (6) the legitimacy of the benchmarking exercise, namely, the ability to find a similarly situated engagement delivered by a similar service provider; (7) how the results are interpreted; (8) how a benchmarking condition is identified, namely, are the charges being paid by the client within a certain percentage of the representative sample; and (9) what events occur and what remedies the parties may have after a benchmarking condition is identified.

As stated above, price is generally the focus of a typical benchmarking provision. In some instances, the provision is expanded to include service levels against which the service provider will be measured over the delivery term. With the rapid pace at which technology is evolving and the deployment of automation into the delivery environment, the benchmarking provision of the future will likely be expanded even further to include the method (FTE versus automation percentage) and pace (have generally available technologies been utilized to maximize efficiency gains?) at which the service provider is deploying new technologies in relation to other engagements in the sample. In addition to expanding the scope of the benchmarking process, clients may also seek to expand the frequency and conditions under which a benchmarking exercise can be initiated.

The benchmarking concept does not always sit well with service providers that have just been subject to a highly competitive and lengthy procurement process conducted by the client, their external counsel, and their third-party advisor. Given the highly competitive market for outsourcing services, multiple down-selections and decision gates are common, parallel negotiations are routinely conducted, and threats of disqualification are frequently asserted, all with the hope of securing services under the most favorable terms and at the most competitive price. Imagine how a service provider must feel after it has put its best foot forward in the negotiation process and agreed on an aggressive pricing structure, only to find that the client intends to benchmark its competitive pricing shortly after contract execution. Ultimately, if the price is deemed non-competitive by the benchmarking entity, the client may seek an automatic adjustment to its price, even though price was a key component of the bargain.

Despite challenges previously identified, benchmarking remains a legitimate contractual right that the client can exercise during the delivery term. If the client exercises that right, the following core principles should be used for the logistics of benchmarking and for the results in the benchmarking report:

1.   The client should not be able to benchmark more than once a year during the term of the agreement, and the first opportunity to benchmark should not occur until one year after the transition is completed. Since a competitive process just occurred, the client

should have some level of comfort that it has selected a vendor under terms and prices that are market-relevant and competitive.

2.   Both parties should agree on a pre-approved list of acceptable third parties that can conduct the benchmarking exercise.

3.   The cost of the benchmarker should be shared equally among the parties. That way, all parties can participate in developing the instructions for the benchmarker, identifying the number and type of entities and similar service offerings against which the service provider's price is being evaluated. Finally, the agreement must specify what result (typically, the service provider's price is not within a certain quartile of the representative sample) triggers a benchmarking condition.

4.   The focus of the benchmarking exercise should be to benchmark the price and rates paid by the client against the rates paid for similar services from similar providers elsewhere in the market.

5.   The benchmarking process should be objective, measurable, and verifiable, and should be normalized to account for differences in the volume of services, the scope of services, service levels, financing or payment streams, and other terms and conditions.

6.   The benchmarking exercise should not seek to measure more subjective areas, such as delivery quality or the service levels and targets. These areas typically can be fine-tuned under the terms of the agreement by changing the service levels and the measurement methodology, or by agreeing to an annual increase in the expected and minimum targets based on productivity gains and continuous improvement. Technology currency also should not be the focus of the benchmarking exercise because it is not a controlling factor in the timely and quality delivery of the services.

7.   When the benchmarking entity completes the initial report, the parties should have the opportunity to review, comment upon, and

request changes to the proposed findings. After this period, which should last no more than 30 days, the final report should be issued.

8. If the charges for the services are not within the quartile stipulated in the agreement, then a benchmarking condition exists. If the charges are within the stipulated quartile, no further action is required.

9. If a benchmarking condition exists, the service provider should be given the option within a reasonable time—no more than 90 days—to develop a plan to bring the charges within the top quartile.

10. If the service provider does not provide such a plan and the parties cannot agree on any adjustment to the charges through the governance or dispute resolution process, the client can terminate the agreement for its convenience.

If the benchmarking report reflects that the services do not fall within the contractually stipulated quartile, clients will seek to include an auto-adjustment provision in the agreement. Such a provision allows for the automatic downward adjustment of the charges or rates to bring them within the approved quartile. Such an auto-adjustment provision may also be limited to no more than a certain percentage, say 5 percent.

I am not a proponent of an auto-adjustment provision because I do not believe that it is legitimate for a third party to introduce a report that automatically resets service provider price. Even the greatest commodity providers would not agree to such a provision, and outsourcing services are different than selling pencils or coffee mugs. As I have discussed, price is just one component of the bargain with the client. Price cannot be viewed in isolation and dictate an adjustment without considering the terms, market conditions, and competitive environment at the time the original agreement was executed. In addition, the benchmarking process is very difficult to conduct in an objective, measurable, and verifiable manner as a result of the significant number of variables that impact price. And given the highly competitive nature of outsourcing procurements and the ability of the client to select multiple vendors to provide similar services under one outsourcing tower, it has many options to pursue if a benchmarking condition has been identified.

Finding a similar engagement can be extremely challenging, and attempts at normalization go only so far. Even the most highly regarded third-party advisors have acknowledged this point. Thus, if a benchmarking condition is identified, the parties should discuss options to address what, if any, measures can be taken to bring the charges within the approved quartile or other threshold. Let's be clear—neither the service provider nor the client wants to terminate the agreement; doing so does not yield rainbows and lollipops for either party. Therefore, I believe that both parties have an equal incentive to develop an appropriate plan that allows them to move forward. However, if they are unable to agree, the client should be able to terminate the agreement within a reasonable time after those discussions conclude. Termination should be at its convenience but with the payment of any termination charges in the agreement. When faced with this set of circumstances, I am also a proponent of providing the client a discount from the termination fee prevailing at the time it pursues this option.

A sample benchmarking provision that reflects most of these key principles is as follows:

Benchmarking

With respect to each Service Agreement, Client will have the right, commencing, with respect to a Service, after the applicable Transition for such Service and no more frequently than once per year thereafter during the applicable Service Agreement Term, to benchmark the Charges for all or a portion of the Services under such Service Agreement. The purpose of any benchmarking exercise is to confirm that Client is receiving competitive market pricing and quality with respect to the management, delivery and receipt of the Services.

A benchmarking under this Section will be conducted by an independent industry-recognized benchmarking service provider designated by Client and approved by Service Provider (the "**Benchmarker**"). Service Provider agrees that the following companies are acceptable as Benchmarkers as of the Master Agreement Effective Date: X, Y, and Z. The Parties and the Benchmarker may negotiate reasonable changes to such form and, provided that such agreement includes confidentiality obligations that are at least as restrictive as the confidentiality provisions set forth in this Master Agreement, Service Provider will execute such agreement. Client will provide to Service Provider a copy of any instructions that Client provides to the Benchmarker. Service Provider may suggest instructions to Client, which Client may provide to the Benchmarker.

The fees and costs of the Benchmarker will be shared equally by Client and Service Provider. The Parties will reasonably cooperate with the Benchmarker, including, as appropriate, by making available knowledgeable personnel and pertinent documents and records. Service Provider will notify Client if such cooperation requires a material amount of effort and Service Provider cannot provide such cooperation using Existing Resources. Such notice will specify the reasons that such cooperation cannot be provided with Existing Resources and the specific impacts use of Existing Resources would have upon Service Provider's performance of the Services and Service Levels. Client may (1) limit such cooperation to a non-material level of effort (and no additional Charges will apply) or (2) direct Service Provider to provide such cooperation (a) using Existing Resources, subject to an agreed upon degradation of the Services or Service Levels or (b) to the extent such cooperation cannot be performed without degradation, with additional resources, as approved by Client, at the rates set forth in the applicable Service Agreement.

The Benchmarker will perform the benchmarking in accordance with the Benchmarker's documented procedures, which will be provided to the Parties prior to the start of the benchmarking process. The Benchmarker will compare the Charges and Service Levels under the Service Agreement applicable to the Services being benchmarked to the costs being incurred, and service levels being provided, in a representative sample of similar IT operations for other entities by top-tier IT providers. The Benchmarker will select the representative sample from entities identified by the Benchmarker and approved by the Parties and (2) identified by a Party and approved by the Benchmarker. The following conditions apply to the representative sample: (a) it will include at least five and no more than eight entities, (b) it will not include entities that have not outsourced IT operations, and (c) it may include entities that are outsourcing customers of Service Provider. Service Provider will not be required to provide the Benchmarker (i) any information relating to Service Provider's internal costs or (ii) any proprietary information regarding Service Provider's other customers.

The Benchmarker will commence the benchmarking exercise within 30 days of receipt of Client's request and issue its initial report to the Parties within 120 days of receipt of Client's request. In conducting the benchmarking, the Benchmarker will normalize the data used to perform the benchmarking to accommodate, as appropriate, differences in volume of services, scope of services, service levels, financing or payment streams, and other pertinent factors. Each Party will be provided a reasonable opportunity (but no more than 30 days) to review, comment on and request changes to the Benchmarker's proposed findings. Within 10 days of receiving any comments from the Parties, the Benchmarker will issue a final report of its findings and conclusions.

If, in the final report of the Benchmarker, the Charges for the Services under the applicable Service Agreement for the benchmarked Services are not in the top quartile of the representative sample (viewed from the perspective most favorable to Client), then Service Provider will develop a plan for Client's review and approval to bring the Charges within the top quartile within 90 days after the Benchmarker's issuance of the final report. Service Provider will implement such plan once approved by Client. If, in the final report of the Benchmarker, the Charges under the applicable Service Agreement for the benchmarked Services are within the top quartile of the representative sample (viewed from the perspective most favorable to Client), then no further action will be required. If Service Provider does not provide such plan or implement such plan to reduce the Charges as required by this Section and the Parties cannot agree on an adjustment to the Charges through the informal dispute resolution procedure, Client may, upon 30 days' notice to Service Provider, terminate the applicable Service Agreement (and any related Service Agreement) or the applicable Statement of Work (and any related Statement of Work), as of the termination date specified in the notice of termination, with payment of any termination charges set forth in the applicable Service Agreement.

So there you have it. Benchmarking is a contractual right that the client should have under the terms of an outsourcing engagement. That right can be dangerous though, given the complexities I have just discussed. It is, therefore, important to address the frequency of undertaking a benchmarking exercise and to stipulate how the benchmarker's results are used. Rather than viewing it as the client's using the process to get an automatic price adjustment, benchmarking should be viewed as one datapoint whereby the client can evaluate the overall value it is receiving from its outsourcing provider. Remember the old saying: "The bitterness of poor quality is remembered long after the sweetness of low prices is forgotten."

CHAPTER 31

DON'T YOU DARE OVERBILL ME

You would think that the time charging and subsequent invoice process in an outsourcing engagement would be straightforward. If the services were going to be delivered on a time-and-materials basis, service provider personnel would charge their time to the applicable service agreement, and the client would be billed for the number of hours worked in the prior period at the applicable labor category rate for each individual. By contrast, if the services were delivered on a fixed-price or managed-service basis, the parties would agree to a monthly managed-service price (at a bundle level, for example, in an application outsourcing effort), and the invoice would reflect the monthly managed service fee without any details related to actual hours worked. Well, think again. In the delivery of outsourcing services, the line between managed service and time and materials has become blurred. The introduction of automation into the delivery environment and a corresponding migration from a managed service to a transaction or outcome based pricing model should alleviate much of the client concern in this area. While the pricing model is evolving, I will review a number of the key considerations in this area.

First, service providers typically have an obligation to implement a time-charging system to log all time spent by service provider personnel in performing the services. Along with that requirement, service provider personnel often are required to record their time based on the specific application they support so it can be consolidated at the bundle level to calculate how the base charges will be reduced if an application if insourced, resourced, or retired. When you combine that level of transparency with monthly and annual limitations on the number of service provider productive hours that may be used for invoicing, the client has complete insight into the service provider's ability to deliver the services and meet the service levels within its fixed managed-service price. Also, the client may use that data to right-size the team roster or renegotiate its managed-service price as it deems appropriate.

In addition, when you combine that data with a detailed personnel projection matrix (on and off-site service provider head count of those deployed monthly during the delivery term) required as a part of the RFP process, the ability of the service provider to overachieve financially, based on a managed-service contractual construct, is mitigated. While there is typically no disagreement about the definition of a time-and-material vs. fixed-price engagement from an invoicing perspective, clients have complete transparency about the staff roster and actual hours worked in support of delivery.

I have discussed how the consolidated hours required to support a specific application are used to address the effect of a retirement or resourcing event on the base charges. However, this level of transparency undermines the construct typically associated with a fixed-price/managed-service engagement. Although I am not necessarily questioning the legitimacy of this approach, the traditional boundaries of a managed-service engagement are being tested. Clients seem to be driving toward an "outsourcing as a service" delivery construct. In this construct, clients identify the monthly managed-service price of a specific application or bundle, and retain the ability to lift and shift applications or services either back in-house or to other vendors, as necessary, with no impact on the agreement.

In addition to these requirements, the invoicing and payment provisions include the frequency of the invoices (typically, monthly), the level of detail to be included in the invoice, any supporting data that may be required, and the payment term. For the payment term, clients seek to establish a new market standard of 60 or even 90 days from the receipt of a valid invoice. From my perspective, 30 days should be the standard, especially for clients flush with cash. If they want their service provider to act as a bank, the carrying cost should be factored into the rate structure. In addition to addressing the payment term and level of detail contained in the invoice, the agreement should specify that in addition to its payment responsibility for retained expenses that will be billed directly to the client by the applicable third party vendor, the client will be responsible for the payment of any pass-through expenses that are incurred by the service provider on behalf of the client.

In addition to the managed service or time and materials fees associated with the services being delivered, the agreement should specify the process by which the service provider will be reimbursed for travel, lodging, and other expenses it incurs in its performance of the services. While there is generally no question that the service provider should be reimbursed for legitimate expenses it incurs during the delivery term, the key issues to be addressed include how expenses will be invoiced to the client, either on a cost-reimbursable basis or as a fixed percentage of the service fees. While the actual amount of travel and related expenses will vary depending upon the delivery model, a reasonable fixed percentage of fees range for expenses would be from 10 to 15 percent. Beyond the certainty of the amount of the expenses for which the client will be responsible, the key advantages of invoicing for expenses on a fixed percentage of fees basis are that it eliminates the administration required with maintaining receipts and the need to carefully scrutinize expenses for which the service provider seeks reimbursement against the governing travel and expense policy requirements.

To the extent a cost-reimbursable approach is preferred, the parties will need to agree upon whose travel policy will govern the delivery of services, the threshold above which receipts will need to be provided, and the scope of expenses that will be eligible for reimbursement. The bottom line is that travel and expenses are a component of every outsourcing engagement and any governing travel and expense policy should be grounded in good judgment. My recommendation is that the parties agree upon a travel and expense reimbursement and invoice policy that minimizes administration, that places reasonable limitations on service providers when incurring travel and related expenses, and that is neutral to both parties from a financial perspective.

Two other components that impact the total charges associated with an outsourcing agreement include cost of living adjustments (COLA) and foreign currency exchange risk (Fx). Both COLA and Fx are unpredictable cost elements that can expose the parties to significant financial risk during the contract term and must be carefully considered during the negotiation process.

COLA, or inflation risk, is a relatively straightforward concept. Given that the typical outsourcing engagement spans multiple years, it is incumbent on the parties to determine if the prices paid under the agreement will be adjusted periodically for inflation and which party will bear that risk. Service providers generally seek recurring COLA adjustments while clients, their counsel, and third party advisors believe COLA adjustments are unnecessary and that inflation risk is a component of the service provider's responsibility in managing its global workforce and delivery costs. As a result of this divergent perspective, there are a variety of options that can be utilized to manage COLA risk. Those options range from managing COLA through a cost of living index—the agreement would specify the frequency and applicable geographic indices utilized to calculate any COLA adjustment, how the risk will be allocated among the parties, and any applicable increase limitations—to having the service provider include all inflation risk in its managed service fee or rate card over the full delivery term.

Fx risk arises when a service provider incurs costs in the currency of one country but is paid in the currency of a different country. An example would be an outsourcing services agreement under which a U.S. company has decided to outsource a business process to its preferred IT services provider. The services will be delivered from India and the agreement specifies that all invoices will be issued and paid in U.S. dollars. Despite the fact that the service provider will be paid in U.S. dollars, the service provider leases space, pays for its offshore resources, and makes other commitments in the local currency, Indian rupees, where the services will be delivered. While this may sound harmless, if the value of that local currency drops in relation to the invoicing currency, the service provider's costs would decrease significantly and the client would end up paying more in U.S. dollars for the services provided than the services actually cost in the foreign currency.

Assume that the service provider's cost to deliver in India is 50,000 Indian rupees per month and that the contract provides for the payment of fees of $1,000 per month, payable in U.S. dollars. Also assume that at the beginning of the contract term, the foreign exchange rate was approximately 55 Indian rupees per one U.S. dollar. Under the agreement, the service provider would receive $1,000 from the client, and exchange it for 55,000 Indian rupees, of which it would use 50,000 to pay its costs and retain 5,000 Indian rupees in profit. Fast forward a few months and the value of the U.S. dollar has now fallen and the exchange rate between the Indian rupee and U.S. dollar is now 40 Indian rupees per one U.S. dollar. The $1,000 payment received by the service provider will, once converted, only yield 40,000 Indian rupees and will be insufficient to cover the service provider's costs and provide any profit. To the extent that the U.S. dollar was to strengthen and the exchange rate is greater than 55 Indian rupees to one U.S. dollar, the service provider would generate a significant profit.

The purpose of an Fx provision is to determine the method by which the risk and cost associated with currency fluctuations will be managed and allocated among the parties during the delivery term. Like COLA, the options for managing Fx risk vary and range from allocating the risk to one party to sharing the risk throughout the contract term. Other options include having the client pay for the services in the local currency in which the costs were incurred, deploying a hedging strategy against fluctuations in exchange rates, or applying some average historical currency fluctuation between the local currency and the invoicing currency to future payments. Given the unpredictability of currency markets, Fx risk can be significant and the parties must contemplate what impact currency fluctuations may have over the term of the agreement. Based upon the complexities associated with currency fluctuations, I encourage you to engage your finance and treasury subject matter experts when negotiating Fx terms.

The other issue in this area that receives a lot of scrutiny is the handling of disputed charges. Naturally, clients expect to retain the absolute right to dispute and withhold from payment charges for disputed services they receive under the agreement. The challenge to the client's ability to withhold payment for disputed charges with no limit is that the service provider could be forced to continue to provide services with no payment (all of the charges could be disputed on a recurring basis) until the dispute is resolved. Since the service provider is likely to be able to terminate the agreement only when the client fails to pay undisputed charges in a timely manner, the service provider could be held hostage and forced to work under duress until the dispute is resolved.

To address this issue, the standard approach is to place a limitation on the amount of disputed charges that can be withheld by the client. This may be some number of an average month's fees (I have seen anywhere from two to four) or some percentage of the service agreement (I have seen anywhere from 15 percent to 25 percent) where the disputed charges arose. In either case, when the threshold is crossed, the client can continue to dispute the charges but must resume payment (it can pay under protest) to the service provider. Another option is to temporarily suspend the disputed portion of the services until the parties have been able to meet and discuss resolution.

If the withheld amount exceeds the disputed fees cap, the client has a contractually stipulated period to bring the amount withheld within the threshold; failure to do so enables the service provider to exercise a termination right. Irrespective of the withholding threshold, the parties should agree on an expedited dispute resolution process to facilitate these types of disputes in a timely manner. If the parties are able to do so, any disputed charges withheld from a previous period should be addressed and resolved before the withholding threshold is breached and before any additional disputed charges might arise.

I have included two provisions that address the disputed charges threshold, the first with a monthly withholding limit and the second with a percentage of the statement of work. They are as follows:

Disputed Charges—Monthly Fees Threshold

Client will pay undisputed Charges when such payments are due under this Article. Client may withhold the portion of a payment for particular Charges that Client disputes in good faith, pending resolution of such dispute, up to an aggregate amount equal to four months' Charges under the relevant Services Agreement based on such average monthly Charges due during the previous rolling six-month period multiplied by four, provided that Client notifies Service Provider in writing of the nature of the dispute. Client will pay any disputed amounts in excess of such four-month threshold (i.e., in excess of four months' Charges in the aggregate) without prejudice to Client's right to dispute the applicable Charges.

Disputed Charges—Statement of Work Percentage

Each party agrees to continue performing its obligations under this Master Services Agreement while any billing dispute is being resolved unless and until such obligations are terminated by the termination or expiration of this Master Services Agreement. Neither the failure to dispute any Service Fees or amounts prior to payment nor the failure to withhold any amount shall constitute, operate, or be construed as a waiver of any right Client may otherwise have to dispute any Fee or amount or recover any amount previously paid. As to any Statement of Work, Client shall not withhold an amount greater than twenty percent (20%) of the total Fees to be paid under such Statement of Work. Upon reaching the twenty percent (20%) withhold amount, Client's obligations to pay shall resume as if there were not an existing dispute.

CHAPTER 32

YOU WILL PROTECT MY DATA AT ALL COST

Entering the words "data breach" into a Google search pretty much says it all. With resulting headlines such as "The Target Data Breach Is Becoming a Nightmare," "Goodwill, Feds Investigate Possible Data Breach," and "Fears of a Sony Pictures Entertainment-Style Attack Spread," it is clear that high blood pressure results when discussing the handling of confidential and personal information. The failure to implement a data security program that has the appropriate level of security and data-handling protocols that mitigate the unauthorized release of confidential or personal information has had a detrimental impact on profitability, brand awareness, and customer loyalty. Such failure also strains the relationship between the service provider and the client. Thus, it is critical to place the appropriate level of scrutiny on the provisions that govern the exchange, handling, and protection of data between the parties.

The May 2018 enactment of the General Data Protection Regulation (GDPR), which applies to all member states in the European Union (EU) will require additional scrutiny for both clients that control personal data and service providers that process the personal data of individuals in the EU. The GDPR is the most significant change to worldwide data privacy laws and its reach extends well beyond the borders of the EU, as it applies regardless of where the personal data is processed or stored. The regulation is aimed at standardizing data privacy laws across the EU and protecting, strengthening, and empowering the data privacy rights of individuals in the EU with regard to the processing of their personal data.

At a macro-level, the GDPR will require all organizations to implement robust handling protocols; to train its personnel with regard to the handling of personal data; to have a legitimate basis (contractual requirement, compliance with a legal obligation, or necessary to protect the individual) for collecting and using personal information; to obtain consent before processing personal data; to audit its compliance with the law; to maintain records of the data being processed; to adhere to specific standards as it relates to data transfers; to define retention periods for personal data; and to promptly notify the EU regulators in the event of a breach. The GDPR also gives individuals a number of rights as its relates to their personal data including the right to access the data, to correct any inaccurate or missing data, to request a copy of their data, to restrict the use of their data, and to request the deletion of their personal data.

The GDPR places increased obligations on data controllers (the entity that determines what data is collected, from whom, the purpose for collecting the data, and how long the data will be retained) and data processors (the entity contracted by the data controller to process personal data on its behalf) and allows for the levying of significant fines (up to 4 percent of total worldwide annual revenue) and enhanced regulatory scrutiny if an entity fails to comply with its obligations under the law. Under the GDPR, the definition of both personal data (any information that identify or relates to an identifiable individual) and the processing of that data (any operation or set of operations which is performed on personal data) are very broadly defined. Ultimately, the GDPR reinforces the necessity that both parties take all necessary measures to mitigate the occurrence of a data breach.

While the impact of a data breach can be significant, it is important to balance the fear-inspiring media headlines with the actual cost of remediation. In June of 2016, the Ponemon Institute released its annual Cost of Data Breach Study in which it documented the average total cost of a data breach by 383 companies across 12 countries and 16 industry sectors that experienced the loss or theft—ranging from 3,000 to in excess of 101,500 compromised records—of protected personal data. In determining the average cost of a data breach, the Ponemon Institute interviewed some 1500 individuals at the impacted companies and recorded the direct and indirect expenses incurred by the company to remediate the breach as well as the extrapolated value of customer loss resulting from turnover or diminished customer acquisition rates. According to the research, the average total cost of a data breach for the 383 companies participating in the study increased from $3.79 million in 2015 to $4 million in 2016 and the average cost paid for each lost or stolen record containing sensitive and confidential information increased from $154 in 2015 to $158 in 2016. In addition, the study evaluated the likelihood of a company having one or more data breach occurrences in the next 24 months. On this issue, the study reported that there is a 26 percent probability of a material data breach involving 10,000 lost or stolen records during that time period. This prediction is quite concerning and, in light of GDPR and future legislation, it is critical that companies take all reasonable measures to maintain the integrity of any confidential and personal information in its possession.

The study noted that U.S. companies had the most costly data breaches with an average of 29,611 breached records, an average remediation cost of $221 per record and an average total organizational cost (which includes the direct costs of engaging forensic experts, telephone support, and credit monitoring services plus the indirect costs of in-house investigations and communications and expected customer loss) of $7.01 million to remediate the breach. The least costly breaches occurred in India and South Africa where the average total cost was $1.6 million and $1.87 million respectively. The report also highlights those factors that result in the greatest decrease in the cost of data breach. Those factors include an incident response team, extensive use of encryption, employee training, implementing a threat sharing and business continuity management plan, and the appointment of a chief information security officer. The report provides valuable insight into the overall cost of a data breach and I encourage you to review it in greater detail.

For purposes of our discussion here, it is critical to be mindful of the actual costs of a data breach and the key mitigating factors when contemplating the importance of data handling protocols and the liability construct to which the service provider would be subject in the event of a breach. Given the circumstances that may result from an unauthorized release of a client's confidential information, it is critical that the parties agree on the appropriate safeguards for exchanging and maintaining data. To determine which information is subject to any restrictions, it is important to understand the scope of the confidential information umbrella and any discrete components—primarily personal data—that may require unique treatment.

Let's discuss the definition of confidential information. The definition is generally broad and includes the following: any information in any form exchanged between or made available to the parties, and is marked "confidential," "restricted," or a similar designation. I think of a big box of confidential information that must be handled according to the standards agreed on by the parties. In a small section of that box, I segregate an area for personal information that is the most sensitive, and must be held to and protected by an even higher standard.

In addition, clients may seek to expand the confidential information umbrella to include additional categories of their information that may be exchanged between the parties, and that may or may not be designated as "confidential." This approach would include a provision which states that confidential information includes information marked with a restricted legend or identified as confidential at the time of receipt or which a reasonable person would understand to be confidential. I am not a proponent of this approach. If data are confidential or personal, I want the data legitimately marked as such so it immediately alerts the individual handling the data that the data are subject to safeguards or protocols. Because any damages from the failure of the service provider to properly protect this data are likely to be excluded from the liability cap and, therefore, are unlimited, the "confidential" designation is critical.

Given the sensitivity of the data and the harm that may occur on release, I want to avoid any subjective decision-making about the proper classification and handling of the data exchanged. Both parties must be jointly committed to protecting confidential information, and that process must begin with labeling it. Failing to do so or seeking to include information not properly marked under this umbrella undermines the integrity of the entire data protection program and violates the notion that data-handling protocols should be objective, measurable, and verifiable.

Information exchanged between the parties that should be marked as confidential should include the following: client and service provider intellectual property; any intellectual property developed under the agreement; any proprietary specifications, designs, documentation, correspondence, software, tools, or methodologies; any information concerning the non-public business and financial operations of a party; any customer data; any data that may be stored or maintained by the service provider in its provision of the services; and any personal information.

When information has been marked as confidential, both parties use such information solely to meet their obligations or exercise their rights under the agreement; refrain from disclosing any confidential information of the other party to a third party; and protect the confidential information with at least the same degree of care they employ to protect their own similar, confidential information, and expend—at the very least—commercially reasonable efforts to prevent the disclosure of the confidential information to a third party.

The receiving party is relieved of its protection obligations for confidential information only when it can demonstrate that the information was:

- In the public domain at the time of the disclosure.
- Published or became part of the public domain through no fault of the receiving party after disclosure.
- Already in the possession of the receiving party at the time of disclosure.
- Received from a third party who had a lawful right to disclose the information.
- Was independently developed by the receiving party without any reference to the confidential information of the disclosing party.

Let's assume we have properly labeled the covered information as confidential and identified what, if any, exclusions exist from a protection perspective. Now let us discuss the extent of the data security program as well as any audit rights that the client may seek so it can evaluate and confirm the security of its data. To prevent the unauthorized access to or disclosure of any client data or any destruction, loss, or alteration to the data, the service provider needs to establish a data security program to accomplish this. Any such security program uses the necessary tools, methodologies, policies and procedures, and controls required to protect the data. In addition to installing the requisite software and implementing the necessary access controls, it is important for all data exchange channels to be secure and consistent with industry standards, and for the appropriate security measures to be in place to encrypt any client data transmitted to and from the various service provider locations.

In addition to the aforementioned features, other key components of the security program include ensuring that the data processed, maintained, and stored for one client are segregated from another's data either through using dedicated systems or logical partitions; that any data are not stored in an unsecure area; that the appropriate levels of encryption are used for all client data; and that a monitoring program to ensure compliance is implemented. And, of course, the security program and all procedures are clearly documented in the policies and procedures manual.

Given the importance of properly securing data, I am OK with the subjective concept of an ongoing requirement that the service provider monitor developments and trends in technology and data security, and update the data security program as needed to have it comply with current market standards and best practices.

As it relates to the ongoing monitoring program, it is important for the agreement to stipulate what access the client has so it can maintain its comfort level that its data are secure, that the service provider is complying with the security program, and that its data have not been subject to intrusion or interception. In addition to having access to any alerts, logs, and data feeds from the service provider's network intrusion systems, it is typical for the client to have the right, at its cost and expense, to conduct an annual security audit of the systems used to deliver the services, which may include vulnerability assessment and penetration testing. Finally, the agreement should provide a set of procedures that occur if a security incident were to happen. The general rule is that the service provider must promptly notify the client of the incident, perform a root cause analysis and develop a corrective action plan, and remediate the security incident and take commercially reasonable actions to prevent its recurrence.

Now that our security program is in place, it is important to consider the impact of any personal information exchanged between the parties during delivery.

While many service providers seek to avoid handling any personal data during delivery, this is not always a viable option. Even performing generic application development services in an SAP financial system, for example, is likely to expose the service provider to personal information of the client's customers, suppliers, or employees. And given the very broad umbrella used to define personal data— up to and including a zip code—it is highly unlikely for a service provider to deliver any form of outsourcing services without being exposed to personal data.

Given the likelihood of exposure to personal data and the potential applicability of the GDPR, key questions must be answered, including:

1. What can be done to limit access to such data in a manner commensurate with the services provided?

2. What unique data-handling protocols should be established for how personal data are exchanged and handled between the parties?

3. What happens if there is an unauthorized release of personal information?

For the first question, I am a proponent of giving access to personal information only to those personnel whose responsibilities under the agreement require such access. In addition, I also recommend instituting an additional layer of protection, namely, least-privileged access for the limited subset of individuals who have access to the personal information. Least-privileged access should be a client's affirmative obligation to provide only the level of personal information required by the service provider to complete its obligations under the agreement. Examples are as follows:

*   The service provider needs only 5,000 records to meet its delivery obligations, but the client provides 50,000 records and the records are lost.

*   The service provider requires only five people to have access to certain data to meet its delivery obligations. The client provides

access to 50 individuals, and one of the individuals who did not require access misappropriates the data.

- The service provider requires only "read" access to the personal data, and the client provides administrator-level access with copy and download capability.

As for the second question, the parties should agree on the specific data-handling protocols that should be instituted and agree to them before any personal data exchange occurs. The protocols may be the client's data handling protocols, the protocols recommended by the service provider, or a hybrid set of protocols that are developed jointly by the parties. Ultimately, the parties should agree that the protocols will protect any personal data to be handled or exchanged during the delivery term, mitigate the likelihood of a breach, and comply with any applicable laws. Given that many data protection laws are not crystal clear, the parties will need to agree that the protocols they have developed contain appropriate measures to comply with the law. The protocols will include specific requirements in a number of areas including data transfer, access limitations, personnel training, network and physical security, storage, retention, and disposal. In addition, the protocols should articulate any restrictions on the ability of the service provider to transfer personal data among its service locations. When the protocols have been established, they must be strictly adhered to because there is no tolerance for error. If there is an unauthorized release, a root cause analysis will be completed to determine which party failed to comply with the protocols and the requirements of the data security program. It is typically from the results of this root cause analysis that fault is apportioned (on a comparative basis).

There are a few components for Question 3 above, namely, what happens in the event of an unauthorized release of personal information. As we have seen recently with AOL, Target, eBay, Global Payments, Adobe, and even Goodwill, this is the doomsday scenario. First, time is of the essence. If there is a security incident or security threat involving personal information, the service provider should have an affirmative obligation to immediately—but no more than a few hours after learning of the occurrence—notify the client about all known details related to the incident. In addition, the service provider should do an investigation to determine the scope of the systems and data that were compromised and should conduct a root cause analysis to determine the cause of the incident. The results of the investigation and root-cause analysis are then given to the client, and the parties work jointly to further investigate the incident, coordinate with law enforcement as necessary, and take all measures to prevent a recurrence.

With that process, the client should be responsible for determining the following: if any notice of a personal security occurrence should be given to any individuals, government authorities, consumer reporting agencies, or others; the contents of any such notice; if any remediation is to be offered to the affected individuals; and the nature and extent of the remediation.

Now that the service provider has timely notified the client of the nature of the personal information breach and any affected individuals have been identified, the next questions to be asked are as follows:

1. Which party caused the breach?

2. To the extent that both parties were responsible, can liability be apportioned?

3. Once responsibility has been determined, what, if any, liability limitations is the service provider subject to for direct and indirect damages that result from the unauthorized release of the data?

Assuming that we have identified which party caused the breach or apportioned liability to the extent that both parties contributed to the breach, the question of liability is likely to arise. Although this is another instance where we are preparing for the consequences of failure, prudence dictates that adequate focus be dedicated to this issue, given the detrimental impact that results if personal information is released.

When establishing the liability construct related to a data breach, I am a proponent of establishing a different liability limitation for a breach of personal information versus a breach of confidential information. The rationale behind this approach is that the consequences of breaches of personal information are different from breaches of confidential information. A breach of confidential information can result in irreparable and potentially unlimited loss to the client, which legitimately justifies a level of unlimited liability. A personal information breach will generally not result in irreparable harm or unlimited loss, may be statutory or regulatory in nature, and may trigger regulatory enforcement, penalties, and individual claims. Given that the liability associated with a personal information breach is different than a confidential information breach and the potential damages of a personal information breach are more foreseeable and quantifiable in nature, I believe it is legitimate to establish a different liability construct for a personal information breach versus the unlimited liability standard that would apply to a breach of confidential information.

From a personal data breach liability perspective, I believe the market-relevant standard will continue to evolve as GDPR-like legislation (and the potential fines that can be levied thereunder) is enacted on a global basis. Any standard in this area should be predicated on two key components, namely protecting personal information from unauthorized disclosure while maintaining a reasonable balance of risk and reward between the contracting parties. Achieving that objective can be accomplished with a construct under which the service provider agrees to be responsible for unlimited direct damages (excluding or with some limitation for fines levied under GDPR) resulting from the breach and indemnifies the client for losses to the extent arising from third party claims relating to the service provider's breach of the data handling protocols up to a contractually stipulated cap. These losses stemming from third party claims may include both direct and indirect damages. Although clients may seek unlimited liability for damages arising from the breach, including losses related to reputation and lost revenue or profits, I believe the construct I have identified is market-relevant and acknowledges the impact of and reasonably apportions accountability for an unauthorized release of personal information.

Another construct which yields a reasonable balance of risk and reward and which is straightforward in its operation is establishing an enhanced liability cap, or super-cap, that would apply in the event of a data breach. The limit for such a super-cap could be set based upon some multiple (100 to 300 percent) of the total fees paid under the applicable contract, the total fees paid during some prior rolling monthly period (24 to 36 months), or some multiple (two to three times) of the standard liability cap for general claims under the agreement. The super-cap construct would be an all-inclusive liability cap and would not distinguish between direct damages claims from the client or an indemnity obligation for third-party claims from the individuals that were impacted by the data breach. Irrespective of which approach you prefer, both would exclude any damages stemming from lost profits, loss of reputation, or loss of business which results from the data breach.

As for unlimited direct damages, the scope should be broad and certain types of damages that could be determined to be indirect damages by a court of competent jurisdiction should be deemed as direct for purposes of this provision. A sample of the types of damages included in this umbrella is as follows:

- Fines, penalties, interest, and other amounts required to be paid by company under any applicable law or by governmental authority, or incurred to satisfy an order or directive of a governmental authority (given the magnitude of potential fines that could be levied by the EU under GDPR, this category of damages would need to be limited, not deemed a direct damage, or covered under the indemnity component of a super-cap if the personal data of EU citizens is in scope);

- Amounts paid by Company to third parties, including Company's customers and their customers, Company vendors and employees, to the extent such amounts are direct damages finally awarded by a court (including, if awarded damages for identity theft insurance, reimbursement for credit freezes, fraud resolution services, and identity restoration services;

- Any similar services that corporate entities that maintain or store Personal Data make available to impacted individuals in the event of a breach of such information required by Applicable Law, including but not limited to expenses incurred to provide credit monitoring services to individuals affected by a Personal Data Breach;

- Expenses incurred to provide warning or notice to Company's employees, customers, law-enforcement agencies, regulatory bodies or other third parties;

- Expenses incurred to investigate, assess, or remediate a Personal Data Breach, or failure to comply with Privacy Laws or Regulations and/or relevant industry standards; or

- Expenses incurred to retain a call center to respond to inquiries regarding a Personal Data Breach.

Now that we have addressed the direct component of any damages that may result from the unauthorized release of personal data, the question then becomes what, if any, indemnity obligation the service provider has for losses paid by the client for third-party claims arising from the data breach? As for a standard in this area, I believe it is evolving as personal data breaches have become frequent occurrences, and the damages can be significant. Although a year ago, most clients, their counsel, and third-party advisors would have agreed to only unlimited direct damages and no indemnity for losses related to third-party claims, this is no longer the case. The recent trend I have encountered is for the client to initially seek completely unlimited liability for losses related to third-party claims but ultimately settle for an indemnity cap negotiated by the parties. From a service provider perspective, agreeing to unlimited liability for losses for third-party claims can be troublesome and does not yield a reasonable allocation of risk and reward.

In addition to a broad indemnity for third party claims related to the data breach, clients are seeking unlimited liability for lost profits, loss of reputation, or loss of business which results from the data breach. Agreeing to unlimited liability for lost profits, loss of reputation, or loss of business is not legitimate as these losses may not necessarily be directly linked to the data breach. A client's relationship with its customers crosses over multiple dimensions and linking a single data breach to the loss of customers, business, and profits is unclear. In addition, expecting the service provider to accept unlimited liability is not a legitimate approach as the act of outsourcing a service does not mean that all operational risk is outsourced as well.

Ultimately, the client remains responsible for the security of the personal data—both in the eyes of its customers and the law—and the client should work with the service provider to minimize any operational risk associated with its handling in connection with the outsourced service. To the extent that the service provider adheres to the same data handling protocols that the client followed historically and a data breach occurs, the residual risk associated with that data breach should still reside with the client. It is neither reasonable nor legitimate to expect the service provider to accept unlimited liability for risks that can't be mitigated or controlled through strict adherence to the protocols.

While clients may assert that the service provider caused the breach and should, therefore, be subject to all related losses, the connection to these types of damages seems overly broad. And while buying more insurance may seem like a possibility, I have yet to encounter a policy for unlimited coverage. In addition, service providers legitimately seek to balance risk and reward across their active engagements, and to maintain a liability construct commensurate with the scope of the agreement. It is therefore not unreasonable for a service provider to have a clear line of sight and a level of predictability for the scope and extent of its liability if a breach occurs.

One emerging technology that will assist service providers in maintaining data security is blockchain. Simply put, blockchain is a digital transaction record that is stored on thousands of computers across the Internet. Because blockchain's distributed ledger network involves no centralized control over data, it is far less subject to cyberattacks. A key data integrity feature is that once a record is posted to the ledger, it can't be changed. Blockchain uses a cryptography-based digital signature to verify identities. Users execute transactions with a private key that is generated at the time an account is established. The private key, a lengthy and random alphanumeric code, is known only to the person who controls the account. Blockchain does allow for the creation of public keys to share information with third parties.

Both service providers and clients will welcome the adoption of blockchain technology given the impact its key features—the lack of centralized control over data, the inability to change records once they are created, and the cryptography-based authentication process—will have on maintaining data security.

YOU WILL PROTECT MY DATA AT ALL COST

I have seen this shift to clients demanding unlimited liability in the event of a data breach across all industries, but primarily in the life sciences and health arena, given the nature, extent, and sensitivity of data that may be exchanged during the delivery term and the detrimental impact that may occur on release. In addition, I believe that it is legitimate for the client to have a no-cost termination right for the entire master agreement and any service agreements executed under it, if the service provider violates a material obligation of the data security program that cannot be cured within a contractually stipulated time period.

In order to meet the service provider's interest of predictability for the scope and extent of its liability and the client's interest of mitigating the detrimental impact that may occur in the event of a breach, I believe an indemnity cap is a market-relevant approach to solving this issue.

The key components of this type of indemnity provision are as follows:

1. The service provider will indemnify the client for losses to the extent arising from third party claims relating to service provider's breach of the data security protocols (which may include both direct and indirect damages) up to a contractually stipulated cap.

2. The cap will be determined on a statement of work basis in a manner consistent with the nature of the services being provided and the nature, extent, and sensitivity of personal data that will be exchanged between the parties during the delivery term.

3. The parties will be required to agree upon a cap prior to the execution of a statement of work with a default provision to the extent they are unable to do so prior to the commencement of service delivery.

4. To the extent that a cap is not agreed to and documented, the following will apply to such SOW: the greater of: (a) XX million dollars ($XX,000,000) or (b) the charges for Services paid or payable to service provider under such SOW during the twenty-

four (24) month period immediately preceding the most recent event giving rise to the claim [or if twenty-four (24) months have not elapsed at the time of the claim, the average monthly fees paid by Client to service provider as of the time of the claim, multiplied by twenty-four (24)].

5. Losses are defined as all claims, demands, charges, actions, liabilities, damages, lost premiums, fines, penalties, costs, assessments, and all related costs and expenses (including any and all reasonable attorneys' fees, expert fees, court costs, reasonable costs of investigation, litigation, settlement, judgment, appeal, interest, penalties, and attorneys' fees to enforce any right under this Agreement) presented to, brought against or incurred and obligated to pay by way of adjudication, settlement, or through some other form of mutually agreed dispute resolution.

6. A violation by service provider of a material obligation of the data security program will constitute a material breach by service provider of the agreement, and service provider will cure the cause of such breach within five days after service provider first discovers or is notified of such breach, provided that, if such failure is not capable of being cured within five days, service provider will provide a plan to cure such failure within three days, pursuant to which service provider will cure such failure no later than 10 days after service provider first discovers or is notified of such breach.

7. If the cause of such breach is not cured in the required timeframe, the client may, upon notice to the service provider, terminate for cause, in whole or in part, the master agreement or the applicable service agreement, as of the termination date specified in the notice, without cost or penalty and without the payment of any termination charges.

Given the amount of real estate the unauthorized release of client confidential information—particularly personal data—breaches occupy on the front page of the *Wall Street Journal*, it is critical that the parties collaborate in developing appropriate data-handling protocols. The protocols will govern the exchange and handling of all personal data, and must be followed strictly during the delivery term. Based on the significant detrimental impact that may occur in the event of a breach, the parties must work together to mitigate the effects of an unauthorized release versus spinning cycles focused on the consequences of failure and the allocation of blame.

CHAPTER 33

DO I GET A WARRANTY WITH THAT?

The typical outsourcing agreement will contain a series of representations, warranties, and covenants that the parties agree to comply with during the delivery term. It is important for both parties to carefully review the warranties being offered in order to confirm compliance during the delivery term. In addition, it is important that both parties understand the potential liability associated with any such obligations. It is not uncommon for a client to seek an indemnity from a service provider for any breach of its warranty obligations under the agreement. As the indemnity provisions of the agreement will generally be excluded from the liability cap, a breach of any warranty obligations would not be subject to the liability cap specified in the agreement.

The master agreement typically contains macro-level and general warranties in the following areas:

1.   That each party is duly incorporated or properly registered, validly existing, and in good standing in its respective jurisdiction.

2.   That each party has the power and authority to execute, deliver, and perform its obligations under the agreement.

3.   That each party is duly licensed, authorized, and qualified to do business, and is in good standing in each jurisdiction in which it has a presence.

4.   That each party is in compliance with all laws applicable to its obligations under the agreement and has obtained all permits and licenses required of it in connection with its obligations under the agreement.

5.   That there is no outstanding litigation, arbitrated matter, or dispute that, if decided unfavorably to the party, would be expected to have a material adverse impact on the party's ability to fulfill its obligations under the agreement.

Offering a warranty in these areas is not reasonable as for the most part, they can be measured in an objective, measurable, and verifiable manner. In addition, and possibly with the exception of the warranty related to compliance with laws, offering an indemnity in these areas would not be unreasonable.

Once the parties have agreed upon the high-level representations and warranties in the master agreement, the warranty related to the services themselves must be established. From a services warranty perspective, each statement of work or service agreement typically designates the warranty period that begins when any deliverables are formally accepted with the acceptance protocols. There is no standard for the term of the warranty period but the typical warranty term ranges from 30 to 90 days. However, the period should align with the nature of the deliverable provided. It should also accommodate extended warranty claims if the deliverable is linked to a quarterly or year-end process that would not occur until the default warranty period has expired.

Generally, the methods and techniques utilized to satisfy the warranty claim will be at the sole discretion of the service provider so long as deliverable meets the specifications contained in the statement of work. In addition, the warranty obligations will not extend to any defects or non-conformance resulting from: (a) changes or modifications to the deliverable by a third party without the service provider's prior written consent; (b) changes or modifications to third-party software following creation of the detailed specifications for the deliverable; or (c) the client operating the deliverable other than in accordance with the applicable documentation or as otherwise described, directed or allowed by service provider, for the purpose for which it was designed, or on hardware recommended, supplied or approved in writing by service provider.

The agreement should also dictate the remedy if the service provider, after taking commercially reasonable efforts to do so, is unable to satisfy the warranty claim and determines in its reasonable business judgment that any repair, adjustment, modification, or replacement is not feasible. In this instance, the client will generally have a number of options it can elect in its discretion including requiring the service provider to completely replace the deliverable for another which has the same capabilities and functionality or returning the deliverable for a full refund of fees. To the extent that the client seeks a refund of fees, it could still pursue other remedies under the agreement related to the non-functioning deliverable.

When establishing the standard for a warranty claim, it is important to distinguish the warranty standard for the overarching services themselves versus that of a specific deliverable. Where there are no specific deliverables, it may be necessary to establish a generic warranty for the delivery of the services. The challenge with these types of warranties is that they tend to be extremely subjective in nature. For example, consider the following services warranty provision:

> Vendor represents, warrants and covenants as follows:
>
> Vendor will execute the Services in a good and workmanlike manner by skilled individuals in accordance with good industry practice adopted by reputable global providers providing similar services. Unless otherwise agreed in an SOW, Vendor will reperform any Services not in compliance with this warranty brought to its attention in writing within sixty days after those Services are performed.

Replacing the "good and workmanlike" standard with "timely and professional" or some other designation still results in a rather subjective warranty standard against which a valid warranty claim would be filed.

Establishing the legitimacy of a warranty claim for a specific software or non-software deliverable is a rather straightforward process as follows:

DO I GET A WARRANTY WITH THAT?

1. The service provider submits a software or non-software deliverable to the client.

2. The client tests or reviews the deliverable to determine if it conforms to the acceptance criteria or performance specifications.

3. If the deliverable conforms to the acceptance criteria, the client accepts the deliverable.

4. The warranty period would begin immediately after acceptance.

5. If the deliverable fails to operate in accordance with or conform to the acceptance criteria or performance specifications during the warranty period, the client would file a warranty claim that the service provider would satisfy.

6. The service provider is only obligated to satisfy warranty claims filed within the contractually-stipulated warranty period.

It is important to carefully review any performance specifications to which the deliverable is expected to conform during the warranty period. One method by which conformity can be measured is to track defects and categorize them into severity ratings. Once the defects are categorized, the warranty term can stipulate that the service provider may not exit the warranty period until such time as all or a limited number of defects within certain categories have been remediated. This same construct can also be used as the standard for acceptance before a software deliverable is placed into production.

Before we can address the legitimacy of this approach, let's take a look at a sample set of severity ratings as follows:

• **Severity 1 (Critical):** The failure causes a system crash or irrecoverable data loss or causes impairment of critical system functions. The customer cannot continue using the software. No acceptable work-around exists.

- **Severity 2 (High):** The failure causes impairment of system function. The customer can still access the software but cannot perform a critical task and no work around solution exists for that task.

- **Severity 3 (Medium):** The failure causes impairment of a system function. The customer can use the software (an acceptable work around exists) but the defect is very annoying.

- **Severity 4 (Low):** The failure causes inconvenience or mild annoyance. A work-around exists, and can be used in production until the defect is resolved in the next major release.

As we have discussed, acceptance criteria must be objective, measurable, and verifiable. Severity ratings should also meet that standard. The challenge is for the parties to agree upon a warranty standard that balances the performance of the underlying deliverable with the service provider's ability to exit the warranty period within a reasonable time. It is not legitimate for a service provider to exit the warranty period with any outstanding severity 1 defects given the impact such defects have on critical system and business functions. It also seems reasonable to allow for a similar standard for severity 2 defects given their impact on performing critical business tasks.

Although clients may demand perfection, software is never perfect. Check the license agreement for any of the software packages installed on your computer. You will find a warranty provision which states that the software is not error or bug free and that it will function substantially or materially in accordance with the product documentation. To that end, the existence of any severity 3 or 4 defects should generally not function as warranty exit barriers. There is no right answer in terms of how the warranty provision should be structured; both parties simply need to be clear on the proper standard and level of effort required to satisfy any warranty obligations.

In addition to providing a warranty that the deliverables will substantially or materially conform to their applicable specifications, the client will also seek a warranty that the deliverables will not infringe upon the IP rights of a third party. While an IP infringement warranty is a legitimate client request, it is likely that an IP indemnity will also be contained in the agreement. From my perspective, it is acceptable to offer both the warranty and the indemnity so long as the sole remedy under the warranty provision is the same as that offered under the indemnity, namely that the service provider will use reasonable efforts to procure for the client the right to use and continue using the deliverable or replace it with a non-infringing equivalent or modify it to make its use non-infringing. Any non-infringing equivalent should not result in the degradation of the performance or quality of such deliverable. If the option to procure, repair or replace the deliverable is not available on commercially reasonable terms, then the client will stop using the infringing deliverable and receive a refund of its fees for the deliverable.

In addition to the warranties for infringement and conformance with the applicable performance specifications, clients may seek some form of anti-virus warranty as well. A warranty of this type is not unreasonable so long as the warranty is tied to the utilization of anti-virus software as well the vendor's knowledge at the time of delivery. An example of such an anti-virus warranty is as follows:

> As of the date of delivery to client, to Vendor's knowledge, each Deliverable will be virus free. If Vendor has failed to have or maintain current, industry recognized virus protection and a virus is found to have been introduced into any Deliverable, by virtue of Vendor's failure to maintain industry-recognized virus protection, Vendor will (at no additional charge) replace the portion of the Deliverable that contains a virus.

In addition to the macro-level warranties in the master agreement, clients will typically seek to include additional representations, warranties, or covenants that bind the service provider during the term of the agreement. I am not a strong proponent of including such a list, because the substance of the additional representations, warranties, or covenants is typically subjective and is likely to be addressed more specifically elsewhere in the agreement. Clients may also seek to rely upon the unnecessary and subjective obligations and standards in this lengthy list of additional representations, warranties or covenants for a performance deficiency claim. Given my affinity for the four corners rule and my aversion to disputes that lack substance, I strive for an agreement that is clear about the performance obligations of the parties and that contains objective, measurable, and verifiable acceptance criteria and performance standards. If that requirement is met, there is no need to include subjective covenants into the body of the agreement. Examples of this subjective standard that should not be used are as follows:

Service Provider will provide the Services with promptness, diligence and in a professional manner, in accordance with the practices and professional standards used in well-managed operations performing services similar to the Services, and Service Provider will use adequate numbers of qualified individuals with suitable training, education, experience and skill to perform the Services;

Service Provider will use commercially reasonable efforts to (1) use efficiently the resources or services necessary to provide the Services and (2) perform the Services in the most cost-effective manner consistent with the required level of quality and performance;

Service Provider will, in its performance of the Services, use commercially reasonable efforts to reduce the impact on the environment, reduce power consumption, and otherwise provide the Services in an environmentally-friendly manner;

Service Provider will provide the Services using proven, current technology, Equipment and Software that is consistent with technology, Equipment and Software used by top-tier IT providers performing services similar to the Services pursuant to similar terms and conditions to support the Service Recipients' efforts to maintain competitiveness in the markets in which they compete.

This is another area where the parties need to strive for an objective, measurable, and verifiable outcome.

CHAPTER 34

MAY I PLEASE SEE YOUR PROOF OF INSURANCE?

A disagreement over insurance provisions should never impede the successful completion of a negotiation for outsourcing services. If this happens, it is time to immediately retire and focus on qualifying for the Senior PGA Tour. My only advice is that the client's insurance requirements should be reasonable and align with the services provided. Every service provider has qualified insurance and risk management experts on its payroll who can review the insurance requirements requested by the client. These experts can, hopefully, meet those requirements or find an acceptable option based upon the service provider's insurance coverage. Thus, let the insurance subject matter experts agree on the provisions, and do not allow insurance provisions to detrimentally impact the negotiations or the relationship between the parties.

I will say the following about insurance:

- As they do with the tax and audit provisions, let the insurance experts deal with the insurance provisions.

- Clients must be reasonable about their insurance requirements, which need to align with the services provided.

- All Tier 1 service providers, given the size and global scope of their operations, maintain adequate commercial liability coverage consistent with the level of risk in their operation. Thus, clients should not expect service providers to get additional insurance policies on the clients' behalf.

- I have never been a party to an outsourcing or any other consulting agreement that has failed to close because of a disagreement over insurance provisions. Let's continue with this trend.

CHAPTER 35

WILL YOU INDEMNIFY ME?

The indemnification provisions in an outsourcing agreement are a perfect example of an agreement component squarely concentrated on the consequences of failure, namely, making the client whole for any losses it incurs in a third-party claim resulting from a breach, harm, behavior, or deficiency caused by the service provider in its performance of the services. Ultimately, the indemnity discussion, irrespective of client and industry, always focuses on the depth and breadth of the indemnity obligation that the service provider accepts in performing its services. As you can imagine, the client and its counsel seek as broad an indemnity obligation as possible, and the service provider seeks the polar opposite. Indemnity provisions are excluded from the liability cap. Therefore, an overly broad indemnity provision that includes each representation and warranty in the agreement under the indemnity umbrella nullifies the liability provisions in the agreement. It may also subject the service provider to a liability construct that does not yield a balanced level of risk and reward for the parties.

To quickly recap, *indemnity* is the act of making a party "whole" or holding it harmless for any damages or losses it has incurred or will incur as a result of the conduct of the party that caused the harm. The indemnity provisions are predicated on the notion that a party should not be held liable if it did not contribute to the underlying action which caused the harm. Along with the scope of the indemnities requested, the other issue negotiated under a general indemnity provision is the standard of conduct—any conduct (good, bad, or otherwise) to any negligent, grossly negligent, or intentionally wrongful acts or omissions—related to the delivery of services that, when breached, triggers the indemnity obligations in the agreement. In addition to the general indemnity provisions, the parties must agree on the scope of any patent and copyright indemnity. Historically, these two areas comprise the scope of the indemnity obligation in an outsourcing services agreement.

To establish the scope of the indemnity provision, I take an approach based on two broad questions and one core principle, as follows:

Questions:

1. Is the "action / omission / event" that the client requests indemnity for in the service provider's control?

2. Are the "general" or "broad" indemnities that the client requests covered by one or more of the specific indemnities requested?

Core Principle:

Indemnities, which are excluded from the liability cap, must be reasonable and limited in a service contract; otherwise, the liability cap is, in essence, meaningless.

The indemnity provision can be broken down into the two components I mentioned previously: IP indemnity and general indemnity. An IP indemnity is exactly what it sounds like, specifically, the service provider indemnifies the client if the service provider tenders any deliverables or introduces any IP to the client that infringes upon a copyright, trademark, or patent, or misappropriates a trade secret of a third party. I believe it is appropriate for the patent component of the indemnity to extend to a patent in any designated patent country—a party to the Patent Cooperation Treaty—and to patents issued or published during the term of the agreement. While clients may expect the patent component of the IP indemnity to be perpetual, this expectation is unrealistic. Patent applications are confidential, and the service provider has no way of knowing if a future patent application could render its work product into one that infringes. Moreover, the client likely owns the IP according to the terms of the agreement, and the client is not paying an on-going premium to address this risk. Therefore, such a perpetual indemnity violates the core principle previously identified and functions as an insurance policy, which is not the objective of this type of provision.

WILL YOU INDEMNIFY ME?

An example of a limited patent indemnity which captures these concepts is as follows:

> Service Provider shall indemnify, defend and hold harmless client, its directors, officers, employees and agents from and against any and all third party claims, liabilities, and costs, including reasonable attorneys' fees, in connection with any claim brought against client by a third party alleging that the Services, or Deliverables infringe or misappropriate any patent, copyright, trademark or trade secret rights of such third party; provided, with respect to patent infringement, service provider's indemnity shall only extend to patents issued or published during the Term in any country that is a party to the Patent Cooperation Treaty.

The IP indemnity has exclusions, and there is no service provider indemnity obligation if the third-party claim results from any of the following:

- The modification, combination, operation, or utilization by the client of the IP with that from another provider—where such action was not contemplated under the agreement—in the documentation accompanying the IP, or authorized by the service provider when it was tendered.
- The failure of the client to comply with the written specifications provided to the client by the service provider.
- The failure of the client to use a non-infringing version of the deliverable after notification by the service provider that such use is required to avoid a possible infringement claim.
- The client distributes or uses the deliverable as part of a business venture or program for the benefit of a third party.

We have looked at the market-relevant standard for the IP indemnity. Now I should briefly discuss what remedy the client has if any service provider IP is found to be infringing. Unlike a general indemnity claim, which I will discuss next, the IP indemnity claim requires actions above and beyond cutting a check to the client for any losses it may incur as a result of the infringement. In addition to possibly writing a check for damages to the party whose intellectual property rights were infringed on, the service provider must address what options it may pursue to allow the client to continue to use the deliverable and receive the full benefit of the services. The three key options are as follows:

1.   Secure the right for the client to continue using the infringing work product.

2.   If the first option cannot be done with commercially reasonably efforts, then the service provider can replace or modify the infringing work product to make it non-infringing, as long as that modification does not degrade service performance or quality.

3.   If the first two options cannot be done using commercially reasonable efforts, the service provider can remove the infringing work product, and the charges can be adjusted—a refund of fees paid for the infringing work product—to reflect the removal.

In the preceding list of options, the process is sequential. At its own expense, the service provider was required to secure the right—possibly through a license—for the client to continue to use the infringing work product subject to a commercially reasonable standard. Under this construct, the service provider can only proceed to option 2, replacing or modifying the infringing work product to make it non-infringing, if it is unable to secure the right for the client to continue using the infringing work product under option 1. The only challenge in this construct is that "commercially reasonable" strikes at the heart of my aversion to subjectivity, because the term is incapable of having a precise definition. To avoid any dispute about the definition of the term—i.e., fair, done in good faith, and corresponding to commonly accepted commercial practices—I prefer that the service provider be given the autonomy to navigate through these options as it deems appropriate, by taking into account the importance of the infringing work product and its impact on the client's ability to fully receive the benefit of the services. My perspective is that as long as the client can continue to receive the full benefit of the services, then the client should be indifferent as to how the service provider secures their ability to do so.

Now, let's turn to the general indemnity. As I previously discussed, I believe that the general indemnities should be agreed on in a manner consistent with the two questions and core principle. In addition, the triggering standard for any general indemnity obligation should be that the indemnifying party's actions violated the stipulated standard of care (ranging from ordinary negligence to recklessness to intentional or willful misconduct) and caused (not arising from or related to) the type of harm (personal injury, death, or property damage) for which the indemnified party seeks to be indemnified. I am not a proponent of an indemnity provision whose sole purpose is to establish an unlimited liability back door to a general contractual breach claim. A master agreement provides ample opportunity for such general contractual breach claims to be asserted and more than adequate remedies, including termination, exist for the non-breaching party if the breach is not cured. Also, for any indemnity provision, it is critical to carefully define the term "claims" to be third-party claims. Finally, the amount of the indemnity itself should be defined as amounts finally awarded against an indemnified party by a court or arbitral panel of competent jurisdiction, or the amount agreed to by the indemnifying party as part of a settlement with the third party. Let's take a look at a preamble to a supplier indemnity provision which captures these concepts:

> **Supplier Indemnity:** Supplier will indemnify, defend and hold Client, its officers, directors, employees, agents, and Affiliates, and their respective officers, directors, employees and agents (collectively, the "Client Indemnitees"), harmless from and against, any Claims by third parties and reimburse the Client Indemnitees for final amounts to the extent caused by:

Let's assume that the indemnity requested is within the service provider's control and is not overly broad. In that case, I strongly believe that a reasonableness standard should be used for the scope of the indemnity. As previously mentioned, clients or their counsel may seek to expand the scope of the service provider's indemnity obligation to include a breach of the terms in the overarching master agreement or a service agreement executed thereunder. Turning the entire contract into one big indemnity makes the limitation on liability meaningless and may yield an inequitable balance of risk and reward for the parties.

With the deployment of automation, it is important to consider the possibility that a robot goes rogue and engages in an action which causes harm to a third party that brings a claim against the client? While the likelihood of such an event may be slim, would the robot be covered within the scope of the indemnity obligation? Is the robot an agent of the service provider or the client? The answer would likely depend upon a number of factors including which party was in control of the robot, which party was responsible for programming the robot to act in the manner which resulted in the damages and ensuing claim, and within whose IT environment the robot resided. To address this issue, indemnity provisions will likely need to be amended to explicitly state whether the scope of the indemnity obligation extends to third party claims where the underlying damages were caused by a robot or some other form of AI.

One approach that clearly violates this principle of reasonable and limited indemnities is seeking to embed each representation and warranty in the agreement's indemnity umbrella. An example of that type of indemnity is as follows:

> *To the extent caused by:*
> The inaccuracy, untruthfulness or breach of any warranty or representation made by Supplier under this Agreement;

As I have discussed, this type of indemnity is overly broad. Typically, clients and their counsel request many broad representations and warranty obligations related to the performance of the services that yield a more robust contractual remedy upon a breach by the service provider. In this example, the client is seeking to include every representation, and warranty in the agreement—even those related to the performance of the services—under the indemnity umbrella, all of which are excluded from the liability cap. Although it may be appropriate to include non-performance-related representations and warranties under the indemnity umbrella, this provision extends well beyond that threshold and creates one big indemnity obligation. Although this option may be too broad, it would be appropriate to agree to a more limited indemnity tied to the following representations and warranties:

- That the service provider is duly incorporated (or appropriate corporate form), validly existing, and in good standing under the laws of the state identified in the preamble to the agreement.
- That the service provider has the power and authority to execute, deliver, and perform its obligations under the agreement.

- That the service provider is duly licensed, authorized, or qualified to do business in each location from which the services will be delivered.
- That the service provider has the full power and authority to grant any rights contained in the agreement without the consent of any other party.

This list is clearly tied to non-performance-related issues and is much more limited in scope. An example of two other overly broad indemnity obligations is the following:

To the extent caused by:
Supplier's errors, omissions or failure(s) to perform the Services

To the extent caused by:
Negligence, gross negligence, recklessness, fraud or willful misconduct by Supplier, its employees or agents

These provisions are also troubling because they include any errors or omissions of the service provider related to the delivery of the services in the indemnity provision and thereby exclude any future indemnity obligations from the liability cap. This approach is not legitimate as the client has a multitude of contractual claims it can assert if the service provider fails to properly perform the services. In addition, the negligence standard is too low for the aforementioned reasons, especially given the broad scope of this indemnity. As written, this becomes a catchall and overly broad indemnity that includes more specific indemnities. The provisions therefore violate Question 2 above and should be amended.

I would limit this indemnity to bodily injury and death, or personal and tangible property loss or damage and would consider agreeing to the ordinary negligence standard. The rationale is that if the service provider acts in a negligent manner that yields these results, then it should indemnify the client. Examples of this indemnity include the following:

To the extent caused by:
(a)   any death, bodily injury, sickness, disease or personal injury of any kind, of any Person (including any client

(b)   Indemnitees or Supplier Personnel), to the extent directly caused by the negligence or willful misconduct of Supplier or Supplier Personnel;

(c)   any damage, loss or destruction of any tangible, real or personal property, to the extent caused by the negligence or willful misconduct of Supplier or Supplier Personnel;

(d)   any crime, fraudulent or dishonest acts committed by any current Supplier Personnel (whether within or outside the scope of their employment or consulting retainer), acting alone or in collusion with others;

What about an indemnity caused by the service provider failing to obtain or maintain any authorizations or consents under the agreement, failing to comply with a supplier law, or breaching the confidentiality provisions of the agreement? I believe such an indemnity is appropriate only for the authorizations and consents that the service provider is responsible for getting under the terms of the agreement. An indemnity is also legitimate if the service provider fails to comply with a law, but only if it violates a law that applies to the service provider under the agreement. In addition, it is reasonable and market-relevant to agree to an indemnity when the service provider fails to comply with a Client Compliance Directive—see Chapter 17—including any fine or penalty for such failure. Finally, a breach of the confidentiality provisions of the agreement, excluding a breach regarding personal data as per our discussion in Chapter 32, is also a reasonable indemnity for the service provider to offer the client.

In addition, it may be appropriate to include an indemnity for the following:

1.   The work-related injuries of the supplier's employees or its subcontractors, unless such injuries are caused by the client.

2.   Claims asserted by the service provider's subcontractors, unless such claims are caused by the client.

3.   Employee benefit claims of the supplier's employees.

4.   Claims made in connection with any assigned or managed agreements resulting from the service provider's breach of any obligation under the agreement, assuming that the cause of action arose during the term when the service provider began managing the agreement or after the agreement has been assigned.

5.   Claims caused by the shared use of facilities, hardware, software, or other resources with other service provider's customers.

6.   Claims for any monetary amounts, including taxes, interest, and penalties, assessed against the client that are the obligation of the service provider under the agreement.

I have spent most of this Chapter discussing service provider indemnities that flow to the client. What about client indemnities? While perfect parallelism is not the standard in an outsourcing agreement, I would expect to see a parallel client indemnity for the following:

- Monetary amounts assessed against the service provider that are the obligation of the client.
- Personal injury, death, and property damage resulting from the client's negligent acts or omissions.
- Failure to comply with client laws applicable to its receipt of the services, including any fines or penalties imposed from such failure.
- Failure to obtain or maintain any client-required consents and authorizations.
- Failure to comply with any obligations under an assigned contract before it made its transition to the service provider.
- An IP indemnity for any client intellectual property.
- Fraud, willful misconduct, and gross negligence committed by the client or its agents during the delivery term.

The bottom line as it relates to the indemnity provisions is that the parties need to use a reasonableness standard when agreeing on the size of the indemnity umbrella. If you ask the two questions and stick with the core principle, both parties should get the protection they need to stay out of the rain.

CHAPTER 36

WHAT COULD POSSIBLY BE MORE FUN THAN AN INDEMNITY DISCUSSION?

Why, Liability Limitations, Of Course

Limitation on Liability is the provision in an outsourcing agreement that is the most focused on the allocation of blame and the consequences of failure, and gets the most scrutiny. This provision is much more complex than picking the number of months of fees that will be accumulated in the direct damages cap to compensate the non-breaching party for damages. The parties must also agree on the types of damages to include in or exclude from the liability cap. A breach of any provisions of the agreement which are excluded from the liability cap would result in unlimited liability for the breaching party and can have a significant, detrimental financial impact. Given that potential impact, the list of exclusions should be carefully determined by the parties. To that end, liability limitations must devised in a way to be market-relevant and aligned with the services provided.

As we discussed when considering the scope of an indemnity obligation, the parties must also consider fault and the apportionment of liability if the robots destroy data, fail to comply with data handling or other protocols that results in the unauthorized disclosure of confidential or personal information, or engage in some other action which results in a security violation at a facility, an audit deficiency, or some other breach of the agreement. Alternately, what if the robots simply provide an answer or process a transaction that yields a sub-optimal result? While RPA and AI are not new technologies, they have not been widely deployed in the outsourcing world and market-relevant standards to address liability have not been established. When negotiating this issue, my advice would be to apportion liability in a manner consistent with a situation involving a human actor. To that end, I would ask the following questions:

1. Who was in control of the robot at the time the incident occurred?

2. Within whose IT environment did the robot reside at the time of the incident?

3. Who was responsible for developing, configuring, and implementing the robot?

4. Was there some human intervention (perpetrated by either party or by a third-party actor) which caused the robot to go rogue?

Once you address the types of damages to include or exclude from the liability cap and have identified a process by which fault can be determined, the liability provisions are straightforward and must address the following key areas:

1. The liability limit that applies to the outsourced services—the total fees paid or payable by the client during a specified number of months preceding the event causing the claim.

2. At what level is the liability cap established—at the service agreement or SOW level under which the claim arose, at a consolidated level for related service agreements and SOWs, or at the master agreement level for all active engagements?

3. The liability limit for any project or other work that may be provided in conjunction with the outsourced services.

4. What types of damages or losses are the parties not liable for under the agreement?

5. To what provisions in the agreement does the liability cap not apply? Under what circumstances are the parties subject to unlimited liability?

6. Is there any sort of replenishment provision if the liability for damages awarded by a court exceeds a threshold of the cap as established in No. 1 above?

7. Will service level credits be counted toward the liability cap?

First, let's discuss the liability limit. The current market-relevant standard is that the liability cap in an outsourcing engagement is based on a rolling monthly multiple of the fees paid or payable by the client under the agreement or the statement of work under which the claim arose. You may ask why the monthly fee construct is used, and I have no answer other than that is the way it has always been done. This answer troubles me because I agree with the thinking represented by a recent quote: "Just because you've always done it that way doesn't mean it's not incredibly stupid." There are many options, including establishing a hard dollar limitation for each claim under the agreement. This limit would be separate from fees paid under the agreement or the statement of work under which the claim arose. It would specify a different liability cap, either per claim or in the aggregate, in a hard dollar amount which could vary based upon the type of claim—contract, negligence, or tort. The limit could be set based upon the average actual damages similarly situated parties have incurred in the event of a breach. The limits could vary depending upon industry, geography, and the scope of the services being delivered. Or the approach could be a project-based construct, limiting liability to the fees paid under the overall master agreement or statement of work. Or an option could be to refuse to set a cap and require all claims to go directly to a binding arbitration panel that would apportion liability appropriate to the claim and the actual damages incurred by the non-breaching party. The optimal result would be a liability limitation that is commensurate with or within the relative range of the actual damages incurred by the non-breaching party.

During a recent client negotiation, a well-regarded third-party advisor commented that the monthly fees construct makes no sense as it is not legitimately related to the actual damages that the non-breaching party may incur. From this perspective, it may be time for a change in this area. The purpose of this provision is to allow a party to be legitimately compensated for actual damages it incurs as a result of the breaching party's failure to perform its obligations under the agreement. If the current liability construct does not achieve that objective, then why does the industry continue with this madness and refuse to implement the necessary changes? Maybe we need to print up T-shirts that say: "Live less out of habit and more out of intent."

While the T-shirts are being printed and all of my suggestions are being considered, for now we can stick with the market-relevant construct of some rolling multiple of the fees paid or payable by the client under the agreement or statement of work under which the claim arose. The standard has been a moving target fluctuating anywhere from 12 to 15 months. Clearly, service providers want to maintain a 12-months-of-fees standard, whereas clients and their counsel want to move the standard and the market to a 15- or even 18-month target.

It is not possible to agree to a monthly fee multiple without also considering the level where the liability cap is established for the agreement. Will it be 12 months of fees paid under the entire agreement, 12 months of fees paid under the statement of work under which the claim arose, or 12 months of fees for a series of related statements of work, possibly for each statement of work executed in a particular outsourcing tower? While having this discussion, it is also important to discuss the liability limit for any project engagements in separate statements of work delivered in conjunction with the outsourced services. Will the liability limitation for these projects be limited to the fees paid under the specific project statement of work under which the claim arose, or will the project fees be included in the overall liability cap set at the master or service agreement level?

Although myriad options are used in practice, I advocate that the market-relevant standard be as follows: The liability cap should be set as the total charges payable to the service provider under all service agreements or statements of work, except project work—in effect, under the particular outsourcing tower (Application Development and Maintenance, Infrastructure, BPO, etc.)—for the 12 months before the month when the most recent event that caused the liability occurred. If the event causing the liability occurs during the first 12 months of the engagement, then the total fees payable to the service provider are calculated by taking 12 times the average monthly fees payable to the service provider in that particular tower when the incident that caused the liability occurred. As I mentioned previously, the pendulum continues to swing between the 12- and 15-month thresholds and the level at which total fees are calculated—entire master agreement, statement of work from which the claim arose, or related statements of work—will also have an impact on where the pendulum comes to rest. Given my perspective on the correlation between actual damages incurred and the dollar amount reflected in the 12- or 15-month construct, I say that monthly multiple should be established based upon the services provided and in light of the other connected terms in the agreement. Also, to set a limitation at an appropriate level to satisfy a damages claim, the parties may agree to include a slightly different construct that states that the limitation is the greater of the fees payable during the prior 12-month period or a hard dollar amount agreed to by the parties.

Liability related to project work (Question 3) should be a separate liability cap and be limited to the fees paid under the statement of work where the claim arose. For project work, the parties can consider options from a liability cap perspective, including the type of services provided, the extent and nature of a potential damages claim, and the impact of the claim on any other terms in the agreement it is connected to. In the interest of clarity, I am a strong proponent of including in the master agreement a menu construct that articulates the liability construct for each tower and engagement type delivered under the contract term. An example of a menu provision that embodies these concepts is as follows:

(a)   **Direct Damages Cap—Application Development Services:** With respect to all SOWs that are identified as AD Services SOWs, liability will be limited to an amount equal to the aggregate Fees paid by Client for all AD Services SOWs then in effect during the 12 months immediately preceding the event giving rise to the liability; provided that if the event giving rise to liability occurs during the first 12 months after the Effective Date, liability will be limited to an amount equal to the average of the aggregate monthly Fees paid to Supplier pursuant to the applicable AD Services SOWs multiplied by 12. AD Services are defined as project type Work where the final deliverable involves the development or implementation of custom software or modifications.

(b) **Direct Damages Cap—Managed Services:** With respect to all SOWs that are identified as Managed Services SOWs, liability will be limited to an amount equal to the aggregate Fees paid by Client for all Managed Services SOWs then in effect during the 12 months immediately preceding the event giving rise to the liability; provided that if the event giving rise to liability occurs during the first 12 months after the Effective Date, liability will be limited to an amount equal to the average of the aggregate monthly Fees paid to Supplier pursuant to the applicable Managed Services SOWs multiplied by 12. Managed Services are defined as any services that are long term, recurring services regarding an information technology function, including application management.

(c) **Direct Damages Cap—BPO Services:** With respect to all SOWs that are identified as BPO Services SOWs and which each have total fees estimated of $20,000,000 (over the life of each SOW) or less, liability will be limited to an amount equal to the aggregate Fees paid by Client for all such BPO Services SOWs then in effect during the 12 months immediately preceding the event giving rise to the liability; provided that if the event giving rise to liability occurs during the first 12 months after the Effective Date, liability will be limited to an amount equal to the average of the aggregate monthly Fees paid to Supplier pursuant to the applicable BPO Services SOWs multiplied by 12. With respect to a SOW that has total fees estimated of more than $20,000,000, then, an amount equal to the aggregate Fees paid by Client for such BPO Services SOW then in effect during the 12 months immediately preceding the event giving rise to the liability; provided that if the event giving rise to liability occurs during the first 12 months after the Effective Date, liability will be limited to an amount equal to the average of the aggregate monthly Fees paid to Supplier pursuant to such BPO Services SOW multiplied by 12. BPO Services are defined as any services that involve contracting for the operations and responsibilities of specific business functions or processes.

(d)   **Direct Damages Cap—Consulting Services:** With respect to all SOWs that are identified as Consulting Services SOWs, liability will be limited to an amount equal to the greater of: (i) $1,000,000; or (ii) the aggregate Fees paid by Client for all Consulting Services SOWs then in effect immediately preceding the event giving rise to the liability. Consulting Services are defined as Project type work where the final Deliverable does not include custom software or modifications.

(e)   **Direct Damages Cap—SOWs with No Classification:** If a SOW is not or cannot be classified as an AD Services SOW, or a Managed Services SOW, or a BPO SOW, or a Consulting Services SOW, then, liability will be limited to an amount equal to the greater of: (i) $1,000,000; or (ii) the aggregate Fees paid by Client for Consulting Services SOWs then in effect immediately preceding the event giving rise to the liability.

(f)   **SOWs with Mixed Services:** If a SOW includes two or more mixed classifications (e.g. AD Services, Managed Services, BPO Services and/or Consulting Services), the SOW will be classified on the basis of which of these Services is estimated to generate the highest Fees over the duration of the SOW, and all Fees under such SOW will be allocated to such classification. For example, if a SOW includes AD Services and Managed Services and the Fees for the AD Services are $2,000,000 and the Fees for Managed Services are $1,000,000, the SOW will be classified as an AD Services SOW and $3,000,000 would be added to the direct damages cap applicable to AD Services SOW.

Related to the aforementioned Question 4, it is important that the liability provisions clearly articulate any specific types of damages the parties will not be held liable for under the agreement. The general rule is that neither party is responsible for any indirect, special, incidental, punitive or consequential damages, or lost profits arising from or relating to a party's performance under the agreement. A few sample provisions that reflect these exclusions are as follows:

> **Liability Restrictions:** IN NO EVENT, WHETHER BASED ON AN ACTION OR CLAIM IN CONTRACT, EQUITY, NEGLIGENCE, TORT OR OTHERWISE (INCLUDING BREACH OF WARRANTY, NEGLIGENCE AND STRICT LIABILITY IN TORT), WILL A PARTY BE LIABLE FOR CONSEQUENTIAL, EXEMPLARY, PUNITIVE OR SPECIAL DAMAGES, WHETHER ARISING FROM OR RELATED TO THE AGREEMENT, WHETHER OR NOT FORESEEABLE AND EVEN IF SUCH PARTY HAS BEEN ADVISED OF THE POSSIBILITY OF SUCH DAMAGES IN ADVANCE.

> **Disclaimer of Indirect or Consequential Damages:** In no event will a Party be liable for (i) any loss of profits, loss of revenue, loss of anticipated savings, loss of or corruption to data provided Supplier has an obligation to back-up data and is in compliance with its obligations to back data up under this Agreement, loss of goodwill or (ii) any other indirect, incidental or consequential, exemplary, punitive or special damages, whether in any case arising from or related to this Agreement or otherwise, regardless of the type of claim, whether in contract, tort (including negligence), warranty, misrepresentation, strict liability, under an indemnity or other legal or equitable theory, whether or not foreseeable, and regardless of the cause of such Losses even if such Party has been advised of the possibility of such damages in advance.

With regard to Question 5, i.e., exclusions from the liability cap, some provisions in the agreement are excluded. Therefore, any claims asserted and ultimately adjudicated under these provisions are subject to unlimited liability, including any consequential, exemplary, and punitive damages to boot. As I have discussed previously, it is important to use restraint because a lengthy list of exclusions from the liability cap renders it meaningless and exposes the parties to a level of liability that does not align with the allocation of risk and reward under the agreement. In a typical exception provision, it is common to find the following exceptions:

1. Any losses caused by fraud, willful misconduct, or gross negligence of a party, including their employees, affiliates, subsidiaries, officers, subcontractors, consultants, or agents.

2. Third-party claims that are the subject of the indemnification provisions.

3. Losses caused by a party's breach of its obligations with respect to confidential information, except for a breach of its obligations with respect to personal information. (See Chapter 32 on establishing a different liability construct for damages claims resulting from the unauthorized release of confidential vs. personal information.)

4. Losses caused by a service provider's breach of its obligations with regard to personal information, as long as a service provider's liability is limited to the losses described in the applicable portion of the agreement. (See Chapter 32—unlimited direct damages and an indemnification for losses related to third-party claims—both direct and indirect damages—subject to a contractually stipulated cap.)

5. Losses incurred by either party resulting from its failure to comply with any applicable laws.

In addition to or instead of the aforementioned exceptions, it is possible to carve out other provisions that are not subject to either the liability cap or unlimited liability. Examples may include abandonment or breaches of confidential information whereby the liability of the breaching party could increase to some greater direct damages limitation—a super-cap, if you will—given the potential impact associated with a breach. An example of this type of provision is as follows:

Special Liability Provision for Claims Relating to Breach of Confidentiality Provisions: In relation to the liability of either Party for any misuse, disclosure or other misappropriation of the other Party's Confidential Information in breach of, each of Supplier's and Client's liability for all Losses will be limited to the following, as applicable:

for Consulting Services SOWs, liability will be limited to an amount equal to two times the Fees paid (or payable) for such Consulting Services SOW, or if there is more than one Consulting Services SOW then in effect, liability will be limited to two times the aggregate of all Fees paid (or payable) under all applicable Consulting SOWs then in effect immediately preceding the event giving rise to the liability; or

for all AD Services SOWs or Managed Services SOWs or BPO Services SOWs, the Fees paid or payable by Client under all AD Services SOWs or Managed Services SOWs or BPO Services SOWs, respectively, during the 24 months immediately preceding the event giving rise to the liability; provided that if the event giving rise to liability occurs during the first 24 months after the Effective Date, liability will be limited to an amount equal to the total Fees paid and that would be payable to Supplier pursuant to the applicable SOW for proper performance of the Services during such 24 month period; or

for all those SOWs with no classification, liability will be limited to two times the limit specified in such Section.

For purposes of this Section only, the term "Confidential Information" will not include Personal Information. For clarity, liability for breaches of Personal Information is subject to the limitations on liability contained in the Personal Information Liability Schedule.

Related to Question 6, it is typical to have a cap replenishment provision in the agreement. Such a provision states that if during the term of the agreement the aggregate liability of the service provider for damages exceeds a percentage of the liability cap, say, 80 percent, the service provider is obligated to increase the available cap to the amount originally contemplated by the agreement. If the service provider fails to do so, the client may exercise a no-cost termination right. An example of a replenishment provision is as follows:

If, at any time during the Master Agreement Term and for any reason, the total aggregate liability of Service Provider for damages (acknowledged in writing by Service Provider or awarded by a court upon the first judgment obtained to pay on the claim) under or in connection with the Agreement exceeds 80 percent of the liability cap and, upon receipt of client's request, Service Provider refuses to waive such cap or increase the available cap to an amount at least equal to the original liability cap set forth in this section, then client may, upon notice to Service Provider, terminate for cause, this Master Agreement or the applicable Service Agreement, as of the termination date specified in the notice, without cost or penalty and without the payment of any termination charges.

Regarding Question 7, the provision should clarify if service level credits count against the cap. The parties can determine the appropriate inclusion or exclusion of service credits against the cap in light of the overall service credit construct. Although I understand the service provider's preference to have such credits count against the cap, I do not necessarily believe that the two concepts are interconnected and, would, therefore exclude any such credits from counting against the liability cap.

Although myriad options may be considered for the liability construct, the foundation remains constant in setting the liability construct and any corresponding exclusions. As I like to say, it is that simple and that complex. The key is to review the liability provisions with the other provisions in the agreement with which they are so tightly interconnected.

CHAPTER 37

WHAT ARE WE GOING TO DO WHEN MOTHER NATURE COMES KNOCKING?

Negotiating terms and conditions that address the allocation of blame and the consequences of failure takes up time that is better spent on other matters. However, it is legitimate and time well spent to focus on what should happen if a catastrophic event occurs that impedes the ability of the parties to perform their obligations under the agreement. In a typical management consulting or systems integration engagement, a catastrophic event—that one always hopes to avoid—most likely would have a detrimental impact on the project schedule or the implementation timeline. Any such delay may have a significant impact on these types of engagements, but the stakes are much higher in an outsourcing engagement. Irrespective of the event and the affected geography, business must continue, and the impact on the critical infrastructure, applications, or processes that have been outsourced must be mitigated. It is critical that disaster recovery and business continuity plans are thorough and ready to be deployed against when necessary.

So let's start by discussing a force majeure event. A legal term, it refers to a catastrophic event, such as fire, flood, earthquake, acts of God, riots, civil disorders, terrorism, acts of government authorities, pandemics, or any other cause beyond the control of the parties to the agreement. If such an event occurs, neither party is liable for any default or delay in the performance of its obligations under the agreement. This outcome, of course, assumes that the nonperforming party is not at fault in causing the delay. Or, the delay could have been prevented by taking the appropriate precautions that may include performing disaster recovery services according to the plan agreed to by the parties. In a force majeure event, the nonperforming party is excused from further performance for as long as the force majeure prevails and the nonperforming party continues to use commercially reasonable efforts to begin performance again without delay.

To properly prepare for the impact of a force majeure event, the service provider is required to develop a business continuity and disaster recovery plan acceptable to the client. Each plan should identify and be designed to facilitate achieving the appropriate recovery time objectives—the targeted time frame when service must be restored after a disaster or disruption in service. When the plan is approved by the client, it should be implemented, updated, tested, and fully operational so it can be used when a disaster occurs.

The focus of a legacy business continuity and disaster recovery plan is the way in which the service provider intends to re-engage (work from another floor, work from another building in the same city, work from home, or deploy workers in another city) its workforce after a force majeure event in order to meet the appropriate recovery time objectives stipulated in the agreement. While a force majeure event may impact the ability of service provider personnel to resume delivery of their services, any robots that have been deployed into the delivery environment are already at work, and absent a complete loss of power, can continue working seamlessly before, during, and after the force majeure event. Recovery time objectives should therefore be updated during the delivery term to account for the level of automation that has been deployed across each outsourced service area.

The contents of the plan include an invocation process and communication plan. It also has descriptions of the different disaster and disruption levels that are likely to run the gamut from local site incidents to broader building incidents to incidents that impact the city or country from which the service was being delivered. For each incident type, the plan should define the disaster level; determine the recovery time objective; identify the critical service delivery components that must be restored in that time period (references to the specific requirements in the statement of work are typical); and the actual plan of action, which may range from resuming the services elsewhere in the same building to temporarily relocating the services to another service provider delivery center that would support them until normal operations began again. To fulfill that plan of action, the plan should state the address of the alternate location where the services are provided until the disaster ends. In addition, the business continuity plan should address any relief that the service provider will receive with regard to the achievement of service levels during the service disruption period.

The plan should also specify which services would resume in the recovery time objective (RTO). The RTO may range from 24 to 72 hours from the time of disruption depending upon the service location and the scope—site incident versus building incident—of the disaster. This issue receives much scrutiny because the client typically wants 100 percent of its services restored in the RTO. However, it may be feasible for the service provider to restore only some minimal level, say, 10 percent to 20 percent of the seats assigned to the client at an alternate location, as it is trying to restore a basic level of service to all clients serviced at the impacted location. In addition, service providers may seek to include a provision in the business continuity plan which allows them to utilize normal course client production seats for recovery in the event of a disaster not related to the client. While that request may be legitimate, it should not include service level relief during the recovery period. An example of a disaster recovery plan for a site incident is as follows:

Disaster Level 1: Site Incident

Description: A Level 1 Disaster represents a local technical failure that can be mitigated with redundant availability and connectivity ("**Disaster Level 1**"). An example would be a local area network failure, such as a malfunction of a distribution switch that affects availability of the LAN from which the services are delivered.

Recovery Time Objective: Resumption of critical Service delivery for all applications in a Disaster Level 1 situation will be provided within 24 hours from time of disruption. Critical Service delivery consists of the activities described in Sections x, y, and z of the statement of work. All other Services will be restored as capacity comes back online as mutually agreed with the client.

Disaster Recovery Plan: The response to the declaration of a Disaster Level 1 will be to execute the appropriate support process with the appropriate provider (facilities management, IT infrastructure support, etc.), managing the event as a Severity Level 1. Service delivery leadership will receive frequent updates as to the status of resolution of the event.

If resolution of the event will not be possible within the RTO period then appropriate measures will be taken to resume the affected services elsewhere within the same building, or promotion of the event to Disaster Level 2 will be performed should the Services and Service Provider Personnel need to be temporarily relocated to another Service Provider delivery center location to support Services until the Disaster is over.

Ten to fifteen percent of a single location's seats assigned to the client will be recovered to an alternative location. Basic technology set up: Workstation with standard Service Provider desktop configuration, VPN connectivity at the recovery location (does not include dedicated bandwidth), access to shared printer/fax machine, telephones as per location telephone policy. In addition to such ten to fifteen percent of recovered seats, offshore Service Provider Personnel will access VPN connections from home using portable PCs working in shifts to provide the Services. Onshore Service Provider Personnel will provide Services from the applicable Service Location and by accessing VPN connections from home using portable PCs.

Alternate Service Location: Resumption of critical Services during a Level 1 disaster event will be elsewhere within the same building.

For business continuity and disaster recovery plans, clients want to be reassured, at some level, that when a force majeure occurs in one geographic region, their services can resume within the appropriate RTO in another location or in another delivery center that was not affected. In addition, if a disaster happens, clients want to ensure that the service provider not increase its charges for the affected services or charge for any additional usage fees during the recovery period. These are legitimate requests, and the agreement should reflect this requirement.

In addition, all clients believe that they are of the utmost importance and should be given treatment as favorable as that given to any other client serviced from the affected facility. To address that concern, it is typical to include a provision that states that no other service provider customer receives priority in having its services restored. Such a provision addresses a legitimate request and lowers the client's blood pressure during this discussion. A sample that captures this approach is as follows:

> Whenever a Force Majeure Event or a Disaster causes Service Provider to allocate limited resources between or among Service Provider's customers, Service Provider will not give any other customers of Service Provider priority over client. Service Provider will not redeploy or reassign any individual in a Key Service Provider Position to another account in the event of a Force Majeure Event.

Things get interesting when a client seeks a provision that states that the service provider is responsible for the additional costs of any substitute services incurred by the client as a result of the service provider's failure to meet any RTO in the business continuity and disaster recovery plan. This seems to be a reasonable request. However, agreeing to such a provision could put the service provider in a situation where the client seeks the services of the only service provider in the affected area that can provide the necessary product or service required to restore the affected service, and that service provider is charging an exorbitant price premium. Given this potential for price gouging, I am not a proponent of this type of provision. It is clearly in the best interests of both parties that the services be restored in as timely a manner as possible, and I assure you that the service provider is doing everything possible to achieve this goal. This provision should have a "reasonableness" limitation or other restrictions to mitigate the impact on a client under duress and the impact of an alternate service provider looking to capitalize on those circumstances.

So let's assume that a force majeure event has occurred and that the service provider has been unable to restore the critical services in the RTO. Or, let's assume that the performance of a material portion of the services does not have a specified RTO and is delayed for an extended time. So what happens next? Under these circumstances, I would say that it is legitimate for the client to have a no-cost termination right for the service agreement and any related service agreements. I believe that the key focus should be on the materiality of the unrestored services because termination is not a cakewalk for either party and should be exercised only when absolutely necessary.

In this instance, I prefer to use a step-like approach. If a significant force majeure event occurs, the service provider will be doing everything possible to restore services to all of its clients in as timely a manner as possible. I am in favor of offering the client a termination-for-convenience option after seven to 10 days. This termination for convenience is not a no-cost option, but I would offer a 50 percent reduction of the termination fee, given the nature of the issue triggering the termination right—Mother Nature—and the fact that neither party is at fault. When a more lengthy time period has passed, say, 20 days, and the service provider is still unable to restore service delivery, then I would offer the client a no-cost termination right. Although I would still focus on reasonableness and materiality, I would be more tolerant of a client seeking to exercise its termination right in this instance, even if only a small portion of the services still had to be restored. An example of a provision that captures this step-like approach is as follows:

Alternate Source; Termination

If (a) the performance of all or a portion of the Services is prevented, hindered or delayed for more than the amount of time specified in the applicable Service Agreement (e.g., applicable RTOs) or (b) the performance of a material portion of Services that do not have a time period specified is hindered or delayed for more than seven days, then Client, at its sole discretion, may terminate any portion of the applicable Service Agreement so affected, the applicable Service Agreement (and any related Service Agreement) or the applicable Statement of Work (and any other Statement of Work), as of the termination date specified in the notice with the payment of 50 percent of any termination charges.

Notwithstanding the foregoing, if the performance of all or a portion of the Services is prevented, hindered or delayed for more than 20 days, then Client may exercise its termination right pursuant to this Section without cost or penalty and without payment of any termination charges. Client's right to terminate pursuant to this Section with respect to a particular event will expire 60 days following Service Provider's resumption of the affected Services.

CHAPTER 38

DON'T EVEN THINK ABOUT CRASHING MY PARTY

I do not support a client retaining a step-in right during the delivery term. Just as I do not want a third party coming in and automatically adjusting my prices via a benchmarking provision, I do not want the client or a third party coming in and taking over the delivery reins, even in the most egregious circumstances. Frankly, I would prefer that the client terminate the agreement and allow each party to exit stage left.

So, what exactly is a step-in right? Well, it is exactly what it sounds like. In a set of contractually stipulated circumstances, the client retains the right to step in, or designate a third party to do so on its behalf, and either supervise or perform the affected services from whatever location they are being delivered. The circumstances that trigger the step-in right may include a materially adverse disruption of service delivery (including from a force majeure event) that is not cured in 15 days; a repeated failure to achieve the minimum service level targets that materially affects the client's receipt of a service; a critical failure; or a directive by a legal or governmental authority to step in. And with the exception of a force majeure event or a government-mandated step-in order (which I have never seen and cannot even fathom under what authority such an order would be issued) resulting from the acts or omissions of the service provider, clients typically expect the service provider to be responsible for any costs and expenses incurred in the client's exercise of this right.

Even though the step-in period is typically limited to no more than 45 or 60 days and even though the client's agent, who may be a service provider competitor, executes a nondisclosure agreement and complies with the service provider's security and other policies, that is not enough, in my opinion, to warrant this extreme action. As I have already discussed, the client is likely to have a termination right that accrues during an extended disruption resulting from a force majeure event. In addition, the client also has a termination right related to repeat service level defaults, especially for a repeated failure of the service provider to achieve the minimum service level targets.

Given those rights found elsewhere in the agreement, this type of step-in provision is not legitimate and is nothing more than a belt-and-suspenders approach to address an on-going performance deficiency. From my perspective, it rises to the level of a quasi-termination right in that it allows a third-party vendor to enter the current service provider's domain, supervise or perform the services on the client's behalf, and gain exposure and access to the other service provider's facilities and intellectual property. Once the third party vendor has done this, it can still seek to lobby the client to exercise its termination right either during the step-in period or after it ends because, typically, stepping in does not affect the client's ability to terminate. I would say that when faced with these circumstances, the client can work with the service provider through the informal and formal dispute resolution processes to address any performance issues or extended service disruptions. I feel confident that the service provider will work diligently to address the performance issues (as it is probably writing a healthy service credit check each month) or to resume service as quickly as possible.

If these conversations are not productive, if the client has lost all faith in the delivery capabilities of the service provider, or has a viable alternative, then I would encourage the client to pull the termination trigger, take advantage of any termination assistance services, and make a transition to the services of a new vendor. But as I have discussed, this should be an option of last resort because termination does not yield rainbows and lollipops for either party.

It is clear that I am not a proponent of a step-in provision, but in the interest of full disclosure, I will provide a sample provision for your review. It is as follows:

Step-In Rights
In the event (A) of a materially adverse disruption to a Service (including a disruption arising out of a Force Majeure Event) that is not cured

within 15 days, (B) of repeated Performance Standard failures of Minimum Service Levels which adversely affect the Service Recipients' receipt of a Service, (C) of a Critical Failure, or (D) client is directed, or required, by Law or Governmental Authority to step in, client may step in and supervise or perform, or designate a Client Agent to step in and supervise or perform, Service Provider's performance of impacted Services that are provided from within dedicated client environments at Service Provider Service Locations or from client locations, for a period lasting no longer than 60 days from the step-in date.

Service Provider will be liable for client's costs and expenses incurred as a result of client exercising its rights under this provision except if the disruption arises out of a Force Majeure Event or if the step-in right is directed by law or governmental authority as a result of the acts or omissions of the service provider.

Client's exercise of its rights under this Section will not constitute a waiver by Client of any rights it may have (including Client's rights to terminate this Master Agreement or the applicable Service Agreement) before, on or after the Step-In Date. Service Provider will cooperate with Client or such Client Agent in respect of such step-in, including by providing access to Software, Equipment and Service Locations and any other assistance and information requested by Client or the Client Agent, and by providing Client or such Client Agent space at the Service Provider Service Location; provided, however, that provision of such information, access and use to a Client Agent will be subject to such Client Agent (1) executing a non-disclosure agreement with Client that is at least as restrictive as the confidentiality provisions set forth in this Master Agreement, and (2) complying with Service Provider's security policies to the same extent such policies are applicable to Client under the Agreement.

And if you are going to allow the client to step in, then you ought to have clear boundaries on when the client needs to exit. I have provided a sample step-out provision for review as follows:

Step-Out

If the Client exercised its step-in rights, the Client may elect to cease exercising its right to step-in at any time by giving notice to Service Provider, provided that the Client must step out within 60 days following the Step-In Date.

Within three business days after the Step-In Date, Service Provider will develop a plan to demonstrate to Client how it will resume the proper performance of the applicable Services ("**Step-Out Plan**"), and will submit such Step-Out Plan to Client for approval. The Step-Out Plan and delivery of the Services, except to the extent Client is performing any Services, will remain Service Provider's responsibility. Once Client has notified Service Provider of a Step-Out Date, Service Provider will devote all resources identified in the Step-Out Plan to implement the Step-Out Plan such that delivery of the affected Services by Service Provider is restored to the Performance Standards, and that the affected Services are delivered in accordance with all other provisions of the Agreement, from the Step-Out Date.

During any step-in period, the Parties will meet at least weekly to discuss progress toward remedying the event which gave rise to exercise of the step-in right, including deciding whether or not Service Provider can resume performance of the affected Services. By exercising its right to step-in Client will not, and will not be deemed to, assume any obligation to resolve the event giving rise to its right to step-in or relieve Service Provider of any obligation or liability in relation to such event or relieve Service Provider of any of its other obligations or liabilities under the Agreement, other than Service Provider's obligation to perform the impacted Services in accordance with applicable Service Levels in the event that Client or a Client Agent is performing such Services pursuant to this Section and the failure to meet a Service Level is due to the act or omission of Client or a Client Agent.

CHAPTER 39

DO WE NEED A REFEREE?

Although I do not want to focus on the consequences of failure, a dispute is likely to arise during the delivery term of an outsourcing engagement. The typical term of an outsourcing engagement is five years or longer, and no one gets along perfectly for five years. Even though we know a dispute will occur, it is hoped that it can be resolved through an informal dispute resolution process. If that process fails, then a formal dispute resolution process should be available as well. Ultimately, the hope is that the parties can resolve any disputes through their respective hierarchies, optimally before they seek external intervention by a court.

Clearly, different options can be used for the informal dispute resolution process. For the process to be effective, it must be clear as to how a dispute begins, what parties are responsible for resolving the dispute, and what the timeline is for good faith discussions at each hierarchical level before the dispute escalates further or before the parties can seek intervention through arbitration or a court of competent jurisdiction. I am a strong proponent of an expeditious, informal escalation process. It should take no more than 30 days for the dispute to navigate through the hierarchical levels, because one or both of the parties will be working under duress, and having a dispute hanging over the delivery environment is not in either party's best interests.

To initiate the dispute resolution process, either party may do so by providing notice of the dispute to the other party. Such notice should clearly articulate the nature of the dispute and the relief sought. Within a contractually stipulated timeline—optimally no more than 5 days after the notice is received—the parties (initially, the representatives may be a contract or project manager) should meet and attempt to resolve the dispute in good faith. If the initial parties are unable to do so within, say, 5 days of the initial notification, the dispute should be escalated to the next level (maybe a more senior delivery executive and the executive's client peer, or the management committee responsible for overseeing the project) in the respective hierarchy of each party to try to resolve the dispute. If the designated representatives conclude in good faith that the amicable resolution of the dispute through continued negotiation is unlikely, then either the client or service provider may start legal proceedings to resolve the dispute. Unless some exigent circumstance applies, optimally no more than 30 days should pass before the parties can seek external intervention from a court of competent jurisdiction or from arbitration, depending on what venue may be specified in the formal dispute resolution process in the agreement.

In addition to the dispute resolution process just discussed, the agreement does, of course, contain a provision that specifies the governing law, jurisdiction, and venue where any such claims are filed. Finally, one provision that is always in the dispute resolution provisions is that of continued performance. It states that each party will continue performing its obligations under the agreement while a dispute is being resolved. Given this obligation to continue performance, a quick and efficient dispute resolution process is a necessity. Parties should not wait around for a contractually stipulated time period to elapse before they can escalate the dispute or pursue other alternatives. I have seen many agreements use a "go-slowly approach" under the mantra that more time to discuss a dispute yields an agreement. In my experience, extended time periods have a detrimental impact on the relationship between the parties and, typically, make one party work under duress for a long time. Given the detrimental impact a "go-slowly approach" may have from both a relationship and delivery perspective, I recommend a dispute process with a short time frame between the various escalation levels, say 3 to 5 days. This can be bypassed as necessary to maintain forward momentum in resolving the dispute.

CHAPTER 40

TERMINATION RIGHTS—BE CAREFUL WHAT YOU ASK FOR AND MAINTAIN TRIGGER CONTROL

Another provision in an outsourcing agreement that receives a tremendous amount of scrutiny and is clearly focused on the consequences of failure is termination. Termination is an extreme measure that can be exercised by either party in a variety of circumstances, the overwhelming majority of which result from a contractual breach or performance deficiency. Although prudence dictates that termination rights be in the agreement, an objective, steady, and reserved hand should be on the trigger because termination comes with extreme and what can be uncomfortable consequences for both the service provider and the client. Unlike in a management consulting or systems integration agreement, where the termination rights might be more balanced, the service provider has extremely limited termination rights under an outsourcing engagement. These rights are limited because of the mission-critical services outsourced and the detrimental impact on the client's business if the service provider's termination rights were broader. The service provider typically can terminate the agreement only as a result of nonpayment by the client. And do not get any ideas that you can terminate the day after the current monthly invoice is due. The termination right typically does not accrue for disputed fees until the disputed fees cap is crossed and does not drop below that threshold in a certain number of days, or, for undisputed fees, until the client has been given ample—and I mean ample—opportunity to make the payment.

Termination comes in two flavors—termination for cause and termination for convenience. The primary differences between the two depend on the following:

the underlying action which triggers the termination event; whether the client pays a termination fee; the extent and the visibility of the termination event and its impact on the service provider's reputation in the marketplace, specifically, on its ability to successfully capture similar opportunities in the future; and, of course, the relationship between the parties. Termination for cause typically results when the service provider materially breaches the terms of the agreement or has a significant deficiency in performance that calls into question the ability of the client to receive the full benefit of the services. In this instance, the client can exit the agreement without paying a termination fee.

In termination for convenience, the client may terminate the agreement for its convenience but only after providing advance notice and by paying a termination fee. In addition to paying a termination-for-convenience fee, the agreement may specify that the client cannot exercise this right until a stipulated time period, anywhere from 12 to 36 months, from the signing of the agreement. The termination fees themselves may have many components, including deferred margin or break fees that are not always well received or deemed legitimate by clients or their counsel. I believe such fees are legitimate as it is likely the service provider has made significant investments in the opportunity in exchange for a long-term transaction. These fees decline over the term of the agreement; and they may be discounted if the client exercises its termination for-convenience right after certain events occur, including a benchmarking condition, a force majeure event, or a change of control of either party.

As for the fees themselves, an example of the typical components and their amounts over the term of the agreement are as follows:

Demobilization out-of-pocket costs: These are the incremental cash costs that the service provider incurs as a result of the early termination. This category includes, for example, severance/redundancy costs, loaded cost of bench time when redeploying resources, subcontractor termination fees, lease termination fees, and other entity wind down costs.

Unrecovered investments and balance sheet items: These consist of investments made prior to termination that we were counting on the full contract to recover. All company-wide investments should be included regardless of internal funding source. This category includes, for example, unamortized transition costs, unamortized hardware and other hard assets, unamortized software/IP license fees, unamortized sales incentive, any other capital balances as of the effective termination date.

Deferred margin to-date: This is the early years margin discount compared to the margin planned for the full length of the contract. This is calculated as: (Expected Revenue to date of termination * margin percent approved for the full term of the contract) minus (Expected margin to date of termination).

Break Fee penalty: This is to recover a fair and reasonable proportion of the service provider's initial investment in securing a long term deal which may include, business development expenses and opportunity cost of not pursuing other opportunities to reflect the difference between the time period originally agreed to for a Long Term Transaction and the actual duration of the relationship. The break fee shall be structured to ramp down over time and be calculated as follows:

Year 2 termination–Break fee = 2 months of average monthly fees for that year (i.e. annual fee divided by twelve)

Year 3 termination–Break fee = 1.5 months of average monthly fees

Years 4 through n-1 (where n is final year) termination–Break fee = 1 month of average monthly fees

Final year (year n) termination = $0

For a termination for convenience, one key variable can affect the amount of the termination fee that the client is subject to, and that is the required notice period. As you see in the previous breakdown, a component of a termination-for-convenience fee is the demobilization and out-of-pocket costs of redeploying or terminating staff dedicated to the engagement. This component may also include other wind-down costs incurred by the service provider. If the client can agree on a longer notice period before the termination becomes effective, it may give the service provider the ability to significantly mitigate these costs. Generally, the notification period may range from 30 days to 6 months depending upon the scope of services being provided. Given that robots don't require any time to demobilize, don't require severance, and can be immediately transitioned to the client or re-deployed to other service provider engagements, a lengthy notification period before the effective date of the termination may no longer be required. Of course, the appropriate notice period will have to be determined based upon the actual composition (robots versus humans) of the service provider workforce. In addition, the deployment of automation may also impact the amount of termination fees, especially if the client previously paid for the cost of developing, configuring, and implementing the robots. If these costs have not been recovered by the service provider as of the termination date, then it is legitimate for them to be included in the termination fee schedule. Also, given the client's immediate ability to assume responsibility for the robots or contract with a successor service provider to configure and implement replacement robots, the requirement for and duration of any termination assistance services may be limited.

Finally, a longer notification period would be required only for the managed service component of an outsourcing engagement. The notification period for a project conducted in conjunction with the services would not have such a lengthy notification period before the termination would be effective.

Another point regarding the termination-for-convenience fee structure is identifying those circumstances where the service provider is willing to offer the client a discount for the termination fees. Such discount, of course, varies according to the event that caused the client to exercise its termination right. Examples include the client exercising its termination for convenience resulting from a benchmarking condition that the parties cannot resolve, a force majeure event, or a change in control of either party. Although there is no set standard, I am a proponent of a 50 percent reduction in the termination fees in the areas I have previously identified.

As I have discussed before, clients may also seek the right to insource or repatriate a component of the services when the delivery term begins. Although clients typically seek unfettered rights in this area, I believe that there must be some limitation on their ability to insource or repatriate. I believe that an annual and cumulative maximum limitation should exist on the number of services that a client can repatriate before a de facto termination for convenience has occurred and a termination fee applies. It is reasonable for a client to have the ability to repatriate a de minimis number of services. However, some limitation must exist, because its lack undermines the integrity of the solution and price developed by the service provider. The ability to insource with no restrictions has become a common request in the applications outsourcing world. Clients make multiple application bundle awards and may seek to "lift and shift" applications across bundles to other providers during delivery. A sample termination-for-convenience provision that addresses this repatriation right is as follows:

Termination by Client for Convenience and Repatriation

1. At any time (a) after the third Contract Year or (b) upon a Change of Control of Client, Client may terminate this Agreement or any SOW (as the case may be) by providing notice to Supplier of such termination in Client's discretion upon (i) 100 days notice to Supplier in respect of termination of the Agreement and (ii) 90 days notice to Supplier in respect of a SOW; provided that upon the exercise of this termination right, Client will pay to Supplier: (a) for the termination of any SOW, charges incurred through the effective date of termination plus a pro-rated portion for Deliverables in progress: and Wind Down Costs incurred by Supplier exclusively in respect of the Services prior to the date of termination; and the then relevant Termination Charges set out in the SOW and (b) for the termination of this Agreement as a whole, the sum of all charges incurred through the effective date of termination plus a pro rate portion for all Deliverables in progress, all Wind Down Costs incurred by Supplier prior to the date of termination for all SOWs, and the then relevant Termination Charges set out in the SOW.

2. Client may terminate any Project for convenience upon providing Supplier with 30 days' prior written notice. Upon any such termination, Client shall only be liable for any charges incurred though the effective date of termination plus a pro-rated portion for Deliverables in progress and Wind Down Costs incurred by Supplier prior to the date of termination. Termination Charges

may also be payable in respect of a termination of a Project (and its related SOW). Immediately upon receipt of notice of termination, Supplier shall take commercially reasonable measures to reduce any costs for which Client would be liable.

3. If Client terminates this Agreement, or a SOW, or a Project, in accordance with clauses 1 and 2 hereof, all applicable Fees related to such terminated Agreement, SOW or Project (as the case may be) will be eliminated as of the effective date of termination of the Agreement, or such SOW or Project (subject to the applicability of Transition Assistance Services).

4. In addition, at any time after the Effective Date, Client may repatriate Services within a SOW provided that (1) such repatriated Services shall not exceed in any year 5 percent of the Services performed by Supplier under such SOW, calculated based on the Fees (excluding Pass-Through Expenses) in the year prior to repatriation; and (b) such repatriated Services shall not exceed a cumulative maximum of 20 percent of the Services under such SOW in the aggregate during the Term of this Agreement, calculated based on the total Fees payable (excluding Pass-through expenses) under such SOW as of the effective date of such SOW. The Parties shall agree on an equitable adjustment to the pricing and other related terms for the remaining Services taking into consideration the interdependencies within the SOW. Notwithstanding the foregoing, any such repatriation is subject to Client's payment of Wind-Down Costs and a *prorated* portion of the Termination Charges payable under the affected SOW, subject to a 35 percent discount on such Termination Charges.

5. The Parties agree that the Termination Charges relevant to a SOW will be set out in the SOW, and, with respect to SOWs for Managed Services (i.e. outsourcing services SOWs), the Termination Charges should not be greater than: (i) if termination occurs in the last two years of a SOW Term, one month's Fees otherwise payable under

such SOW; and (ii) if termination occurs prior to the last two years of a SOW Term, two months' Fees otherwise payable under such SOW.

6.   The Parties agree that the Termination Charges relevant to a SOW for a Change of Control of Client will be set out in the SOW, and, with respect to SOWs for Managed Services (i.e. outsourcing services SOWs), the Termination Charges for such termination should not be greater than: (i) if termination occurs in the last two years of a SOW Term, three month's Fees otherwise payable under such SOW; and (ii) if termination occurs prior to the last two years of a SOW Term, four months' Fees otherwise payable under such SOW.

For termination for cause, we should first differentiate between a material and nonmaterial contract breach. A material breach is a party's failure to perform that strikes so deeply at the foundation of the contract and is so substantial that it would allow the aggrieved party to terminate the agreement and pursue any appropriate legal recourse. In contrast, a nonmaterial breach is a minor deviation from the terms of the contract; it is a minor performance failure that is not significant enough when evaluated in light of the entire agreement to trigger a termination right and destroy the value of the contract. Termination for cause yields a no-cost termination right; if a material breach occurs, the client could exercise this termination right and exit the agreement without paying any termination fees.

As you can probably imagine, a client typically has a termination right for a material breach committed by its outsourcing service provider that cannot be cured within a contractually stipulated cure period, typically, anywhere from 30 to 60 days. In addition, the scope of the termination right varies according to where the breach or material performance deficiency occurs. Under this construct, a material breach at the master agreement level allows for terminating the master agreement itself as well as all outstanding service agreements executed under it. A material breach of a service agreement, however, gives rise to a more limited termination right for the agreement itself and, possibly, for any related service agreements. It is important to have a definition that is as objective as possible for the term "related service agreements." Therefore, a material breach of a service agreement for application outsourcing services may result in the termination of that service agreement and any other application outsourcing service agreements, but the master agreement and any nonapplication outsourcing service agreements would remain intact.

While service providers would prefer to limit the scope of the termination right where there has been a material breach of a service agreement, clients prefer the ability to have a broad no-cost termination right that extends beyond the boundary of the service agreement under which the breach occurred. The client perspective is that there may be a breach which is so material in nature that it brings into question the ability of the service provider to deliver any services for which it is obligated under the master agreement or makes the client question if it wishes to maintain an on-going business relationship with the service provider as a result of the breach. It is important to find the appropriate balance as to scope of the termination right resulting from a material breach as it would render a no-cost termination event for the client across all of the impacted service agreements.

A client may also seek a termination-for-cause right for minor breaches of its duties or obligations under the agreement if these breaches, within the prior 12-month period, rise to the level of a material breach when evaluated overall. This concept is reasonable and may be legitimate, depending on the nature and recurrence of the minor breaches. It is, however, extremely subjective and may result in a dispute about the number of minor breaches required and the degree of their severity before a material breach is deemed to have occurred. I prefer that the provision state that for it to be triggered, the service provider must breach the same obligation a certain number of times in a rolling 12-month period. Although this may spark robust debate about the number of breaches required to trigger the termination right, at least the trigger is objective and measurable.

Clients also typically seek an immediate no-cost termination right triggered by a change in control of the service provider or by the insolvency or a material adverse change in the financial condition of the service provider. Although such a request is not necessarily unreasonable, as either situation could have an impact on the delivery of the services, I am not a proponent of such a black-and-white termination trigger in these circumstances. I would prefer including a measurement term immediately after the triggering event to determine if any degradation of the services has occurred. If yes, then an immediate no-cost termination right may be legitimate; however, if the service provider continues to deliver the services and to meet the service levels, I do not believe that a de facto termination right should be offered. Other areas where a client may seek an immediate termination right include a breach of the confidentiality provisions or failing to comply with the client's IT and security policies. While establishing termination rights in these instances may be legitimate, careful restraint should be utilized before squeezing the termination trigger as doing so will not result in sunshine, rainbows and lollipops for either party.

A sample no-cost termination-for-cause provision at both the master agreement and statement of work or service agreement levels, which includes the recurring minor breach and service provider insolvency concept, is as follows:

Termination by Client

Client may terminate any service agreement (to which the following termination events relate) by providing notice to Supplier of such termination in each of the circumstances set out below:

> Supplier commits a material breach of the applicable service agreement or a material breach of this Agreement as it relates to the service agreement, and fails to cure such breach within 30 days of receipt by Supplier of notice of such breach;

> Supplier commits a material breach under this Master Agreement that is not capable of being cured within 30 days but is capable of being cured within 60 days and fails to (a) proceed promptly and diligently to correct the breach, (b) develop within 30 days following notice of breach from client a complete plan for curing the breach, and (c) cure the breach within 60 days of notice thereof;

> Supplier commits a material breach under this Master Agreement that is not subject to cure with due diligence within 60 days of notice thereof;

> if Supplier commits a breach of the same obligation set out in this Agreement or the applicable service agreement due to the same cause four times in any rolling 12 month period;

if Supplier commits a material breach of this Agreement or the applicable service agreement and such breach is not capable of being cured;

if a Supplier Insolvency Event occurs.

Client may terminate the Master Agreement by providing notice to Supplier of such termination in each of the circumstances set out below:

if Supplier commits a material breach of this Agreement and fails to cure such breach within 30 days of receipt by Supplier of notice of such breach;

If Supplier commits a material breach under this Master Agreement that is not capable of being cured within 30 days but is capable of being cured within 60 days and fails to (a) proceed promptly and diligently to correct the breach, (b) develop within 30 days following notice of breach from client a complete plan for curing the breach, and (c) cure the breach within 60 days of notice thereof;

if Supplier commits repeated breaches of the same obligation under this Agreement which are the result of the same cause and which breaches cumulatively constitute a material breach of this Agreement, and fails to cure such breaches within 30 days of receipt of notice of such breaches by Supplier;

if a termination right set out in any provision of this Agreement that provides for a specific termination right of the Agreement on the part of Client occurs;

if there is a Change of Control of Supplier to a Client Competitor; or

if a Supplier Insolvency Event occurs.

Another no-cost termination right that a client typically seeks is related to multiple service level defaults which indicate a chronic performance deficiency. We will have a robust discussion of service levels in an upcoming Chapter. It is safe to assume, however, that in an outsourcing agreement, some of the service provider's fees are at risk, a set of critical service levels and key performance indicators are measured during service delivery, and the client accrues service level credits if targets are not achieved. A number of actions may trigger a service level default and a variety of options determine the amount of the service level credit itself. Despite these variables, this type of termination right is typically triggered when a recurring critical miss of the same critical service level occurs or when an excessive number of critical misses occurs such that the at-risk amount in a series of months exceeds a contractually stipulated threshold.

Although such a provision may seem reasonable, it is critical to pay close attention to the termination trigger. In particular, it is important to determine the number of service levels measured monthly and confirm that any termination trigger should accrue only if consecutive misses occur on the *same* critical service level or if the service level credits accrued in consecutive months cross over a significant threshold such that the overall integrity and quality of the services are in question. I recently negotiated an agreement in which the client sought a termination right for four critical misses of *any* service level during a contract year, with 20 critical service levels measured monthly. This approach would have given the service provider a 1.6 percent error threshold over the year. Clearly, that yields a very thin margin of error and one to which I would not agree. A sample provision that addresses a more reasonable termination right related to service-level defaults is as follows:

Termination for Multiple Performance Standard Defaults

In the event Service Provider, with respect to any Service Agreement, (A) experiences three or more consecutive Critical Measurement Defaults with respect to the same Critical Measurement; (B) experiences four or more Critical Deliverable Defaults with respect to the same Critical Measurement within a rolling six-month period; or (C) incurs more than 75 percent of the applicable At-Risk Amount with respect to such Service Agreement for any two or more months within a rolling six-month period, then Client may, by giving notice to Service Provider within 180 days from the last day of the calendar month in which the last default described above occurs, terminate this Master Agreement or the applicable Service Agreement, in whole or in part, as of a date specified in the notice of termination, without cost or penalty and without payment of any termination charges by Client.

Before I discuss the service provider's ability to terminate an outsourcing agreement, I should briefly discuss the client's ability to partially terminate a service agreement. I am not opposed to a partial termination right as long as the charges associated with the affected service are adjusted accordingly. Three scenarios with regard to the termination of a service agreement are as follows:

1.   If an entire service agreement is terminated, all charges for the service agreement cease.

2.   If a partial termination eliminates a service altogether, all charges for that service cease.

3.   If a partial termination reduces the volume of a service but does not eliminate the service, the charges are adjusted in accordance with the charging methodology in the agreement.

As I mentioned previously, the service provider typically has a very limited termination right under an outsourcing agreement and is usually limited to nonpayment or the misappropriation of the service provider's confidential information. For nonpayment, the termination trigger accrues only after the client has been given notice of the nonpayment and ample time to make payment. A few examples of supplier termination provisions are as follows:

Termination by Supplier

•   **Supplier may terminate any SOW by providing notice to Client of such termination if Client:** (a) fails to pay undisputed Fees invoiced by Supplier in accordance with such SOW (or the applicable Pricing Exhibit), or fails to pay disputed Fees relative to such SOW in excess of the Disputed Fees Cap, and fails to cure such non-payment within 30 days of receipt by Client of notice of the failure to make such payment, which notice shall be provided to the Client individuals identified in the agreement and specifically to the Client senior executive designated in the applicable SOW and shall indicate that failure to pay such amount will result in a termination of the SOW on a specific termination date; (b) continued material breach after receipt of Supplier's written notice of a breach of Supplier's Confidential Information; and (c) ongoing material misappropriation of Supplier's intellectual property after receipt of Supplier's written notice of a misappropriation of Supplier's Confidential Information.

- Supplier may not terminate any SOW pursuant to this Section if Client has cured the non-payment that gave rise to the termination right on or prior to the specific termination date in Supplier's notice of termination.

- Due to the devastating impact any termination of this Agreement would have on Client's business, Client's failure to perform its responsibilities set forth in this Agreement (other than as provided in Section 1 above) shall not be deemed to be grounds for termination by Supplier. SUPPLIER ACKNOWLEDGES THAT CLIENT WOULD NOT BE WILLING TO ENTER INTO THIS AGREEMENT WITHOUT ASSURANCE THAT IT MAY NOT BE TERMINATED BY SUPPLIER AND THAT SUPPLIER MAY NOT SUSPEND PERFORMANCE EXCEPT, AND ONLY TO THE EXTENT, SUPPLIER TERMINATES PURSUANT TO SECTION 1 above. Client's failure to perform any of its responsibilities set forth in this Agreement (other than as provided above in Section 1) shall not be deemed to be grounds for termination by Supplier.

- Upon a Termination by Supplier of a SOW under this Section, Client shall pay Supplier all applicable termination fees.

Although this example extends to the misappropriation of a supplier's confidential information, the following example is limited to nonpayment:

Termination By Service Provider

No Right to Terminate Master Agreement

Service Provider will have no right to terminate this Master Agreement.

Termination of a Service Agreement

With respect to a Service Agreement, in the event that Client fails to pay Service Provider undisputed Charges or disputed Charges in excess of four months' Charges and fails to make such payment within 20 days following receipt of notice from Service Provider of the failure to make such payment (which notice will expressly reference this Section and Service Provider's rights hereunder), Service Provider will provide a second notice to Client. If Client fails to make such payment within 25 days of Client's receipt of the second notice, Service Provider may, by giving notice to Client, terminate the applicable Service Agreement as of the date specified in such notice of termination. In addition to providing such notice of non-payment in accordance with this section, Service Provider will also provide notice, through the approved methods described in this agreement to Client's Chief Information Officer, Chief Financial Officer and General Counsel.

Service Provider will have no other right to terminate a Service Agreement.

Agreement on termination provisions is clearly focused on the consequences of failure. Although there are legitimate reasons why a client would terminate an outsourcing agreement for its convenience, the more common scenario is a termination for cause for a breach of the agreement or for a performance deficiency. The best advice I can give in these instances is to focus on the following key principles.

1.   Termination-for-cause provisions that may be triggered by a material breach should allow for a reasonable cure period ranging from 30 to 60 days.

2. If a series of recurring breaches of the same obligation triggers a termination right, the parties should agree on an objective threshold and measurement period.

3. The parties should agree on an initial moratorium period when the client cannot terminate the agreement for its convenience.

4. Clearly articulate the scope of any termination fees so there are no surprises in a termination event.

5. Identify which instances the client is entitled to a discount on the termination fees after exercising its termination-for-convenience rights under the agreement.

6. Attempt to limit termination rights to those circumstances that yield a clear, detrimental effect on service delivery.

7. When developing a termination right related to critical service level defaults, make sure that the termination trigger threshold has a reasonable scope. It is a fact of life that service providers miss service level targets and that clients accrue service level credits. If a termination right is available to the client in these circumstances, it should have a limited scope.

8. Always be mindful of the client's ability to insource or repatriate services. A reasonable limitation needs to be placed on its ability to do so during the agreement term. Otherwise, this capability yields a de facto termination-for-convenience right.

9. Remember that termination is not desirable for either party, and any such rights should be exercised with the appropriate level of restraint.

With these key principles in mind, I am now terminating this Chapter for my convenience.

CHAPTER 41

SO YOU HAVE TERMINATED ME ... NOW WHAT?

Let's assume that the client has exercised its termination rights. Exactly what will happen now? Typically, when you are fired from a job, you pack up your personal belongings and hit the road. Unfortunately, it is not so easy to sever the cord in an outsourcing engagement, given the nature of the services provided. When you look at the entire process in retrospect, it seems like a vicious cycle. The client selects the service provider based on its value proposition and ability to deliver the services in a timely, quality, and cost-effective manner. The transition plan is put into motion and service delivery begins shortly thereafter. For whatever reason, either for cause or for its convenience, the client has decided to terminate the service provider. Instead of packing up its pencils and calling it a wrap, the service provider is contractually bound—through the termination or transition assistance services provisions in the agreement—to continue to provide the services during the termination period, without degradation, and to assist in the transition to the newly selected vendor. Nothing like being fired and having to wait around and help the new guy successfully transition into your old job, right?

If the client decides to terminate all or a portion of the services, it provides notice to the service provider of the effective date of that termination. When that notice is tendered, the termination assistance period typically begins, and the service provider is obligated to provide termination assistance services as defined in the agreement. Although there is no general rule, the termination assistance period could begin upon notice of the termination or, at the client's discretion, within the six months before the terminated service agreement expires and continues from the termination date for up to 12 months or longer, depending upon the scope, complexity, and anticipated transition process of the outsourced service. As we have discussed, the extent of automation deployed may limit the requirement for a lengthy termination assistance period given the client's ability to assume immediate control of the robots or contract with a successor service provider to configure and implement replacement robots. Given that robots learn quickly, a transition or knowledge transfer period is not required.

During the termination assistance period, the service provider works with the client to develop a termination plan that facilitates an orderly transition to the new vendor. During the transition period, the service provider may assign leases to the client or sell equipment to the client that was dedicated to the delivery of the services at the time of termination. For charges during the termination assistance period, the expectation is generally that the service provider continues to be compensated according to the fee construct in the applicable service agreement as the service provider is still responsible for service delivery during that period.

If the termination assistance services cannot be accommodated by existing service provider resources without affecting service quality, the client typically can direct the service provider to divert existing resources to the termination assistance activities, irrespective of any service quality effect, or can direct the service provider to dedicate additional resources in accordance with a set of predetermined time and materials rates in the agreement. In addition to the obligations just mentioned, the existing service provider is typically obligated to assist the client in issuing a request for proposal (RFP) for the terminated services. That assistance should have a reasonable scope but may include information that assists prospective bidders in preparing a bid for the terminated services. So not only are you, as a service provider, losing a revenue stream but are also likely to be required to assist in the procurement process for a new vendor. A sample provision that identifies the scope of transition services offered and addresses the impact these transition services may have on the day-to-day delivery of the services is as follows:

Termination Assistance Services

Upon Client's request, Supplier will provide Termination Assistance Services during the Termination Assistance Period. In addition, the quality and level of performance of the regular Services during the Termination Assistance Period will not be degraded. Without limiting the generality of the foregoing, during the Termination Assistance Period, (a) Supplier will perform the regular Services with at least the same degree of accuracy, quality, completeness, timeliness, responsiveness and cost-effectiveness as it provided and was required to provide the same or similar Services during the Term and (b) Supplier will continue to provide the regular Services (and any replacements thereof or substitutions therefor), unless Client explicitly requests the discontinuation (or a partial, phased elimination) of such Services during the Termination Assistance Period.

Supplier will provide Termination Assistance Services to Client or its designee regardless of the reason for the expiration or termination of the Agreement, including the partial termination of the Agreement or the Services, or the repatriation of Services.

As part of the Termination Assistance Services, Supplier will, unless otherwise requested by Client:

1.   In a timely manner transfer the control and responsibility for all information technology functions, Software, Hardware, Equipment, Systems and Services previously performed by or for Supplier to Client or Client's designees by the execution of any documents reasonably necessary to effect such transfers;

2.   Provide any and all reasonable assistance requested by Client to allow:

    (a)   the Systems and processes associated with the Services to continue to operate effectively and efficiently;

    (b)   the Services to continue without interruption or adverse effect; and

    (c)   the orderly transfer of the Services to Client and/or its designees.

(d) Perform services to assist in implementing the termination plan;

(e) Train personnel designated by Client in the use of any Hardware, Equipment, Software, materials or processes to be transferred and the processes set out in the Operations Manual;

(f) Inventory and transfer control and responsibility for all Software, Equipment, Client Data and Hardware used to provide the Services, provide machine readable and printed listings of source code for Software and assist in its re-configuration;

(g) Analyze and report on the space required for the Client Data and the Software needed to provide the Services;

(h) Assist in the execution of a parallel operation, data migration and testing process until the termination to Client or Client's designee has been successfully completed;

(i) Co-operate and assist Client and its agents as reasonably required;

(j) Provide other technical assistance as requested by Client.

Supplier will provide all Termination Assistance Services at no with the supplier personnel then-assigned to provide the services provided that if 5 percent or more of such personnel are requested by client to provide such services, then supplier will not be responsible for the service levels. Alternatively, client may request that supplier provide the termination assistance services using personnel not then-assigned to provide the services at the rates that shall not exceed supplier's then-current commercial rates for such additional personnel.

CHAPTER 42

MIRROR, MIRROR ON THE WALL, WHO IS YOUR MOST FAVORED CUSTOMER OF ALL?

Another provision that makes its way into most contractual templates developed by a client's counsel or third-party advisor is the most-favored-customer provision. The effect of a provision of this type is that it obligates the service provider to provide the services to the client at rates that are at least as favorable as those offered to other service provider customers for similar services in similar volumes. If this is not the case, the client expects its fees to be reduced prospectively and to receive a credit for any overpayment in the prior period.

I am not a proponent of a most-favored-customer clause for a variety of reasons. First, I would say that each outsourcing engagement, irrespective of the service or function outsourced, is different in its solution and its risk—timing, scope, contract type and structure, service levels, terms and conditions, economic climate, and geography—in delivery. In addition, I see no distinct difference in this provision versus a benchmarking provision that allows a "benchmarking condition" to occur that the service provider must respond to or face a potential termination for convenience by the client. Moreover, as I stated in our discussion on benchmarking, price is a key benefit of the bargain. I have negotiated multiple billions of dollars of outsourcing engagements, and each one was competitive. The competitive nature of that multivendor selection process should negate the need for this provision.

Finally, trying to identify an apples-to-apples—or substantially similar— engagement is extremely challenging for the aforementioned reasons. Even the largest third-party advisory firms have acknowledged the difficulty in doing so. Even if all of the previous statements were untrue, I would say that most large Tier 1 service providers, certainly the ones that have employed me, do not even have the ability to monitor and comply with this type of provision, given the typical level of decentralization in the sales and negotiation process. Under these circumstances, my preference is that the client should rely on its contractual rights in the benchmarking provisions of the agreement to give it an ongoing level of comfort that the charges it is subject to are in line with what similar customers are paying for similar services in the marketplace. If the client does not want to initiate a benchmarking exercise, it can ask for a discount and threaten to take its business elsewhere if its discount request is not addressed to its satisfaction.

I have included a sample most-favored-customer provision for your review as follows:

Most Favored Customer

Supplier represents, warrants and covenants to Client that it will make all Services provided from time to time under a SOW or a Change Order, both individually and in the aggregate, available to Client at rates (including variable and unit charges, charges resulting from a Change Order, or other incremental charges), which are at least as favourable as those made available by any Supplier Group Member, either individually or in the aggregate, to any of its other customers purchasing any one or more substantially similar services in substantially similar volumes. A customer of the Supplier Group will be considered similar if it has an annual account size in the range of at least 75 percent and no more than 125 percent of the size of Client's annual charges for Services under this Agreement.

If Client is entitled to lower rates as a result of clause (1) hereof, the Fees otherwise paid or payable by Client pursuant to the applicable SOW or Change Order in respect of the applicable Services will be reduced for future services to the amount payable by such other customer and any overpayment during such period resulting from such reduction will be refunded to, or credited against, payment obligations of Client.

Upon request by Client but no more than once in each Contract Year, the Chief Executive Officer or the Chief Financial Officer of Supplier will provide a written certificate to Client attesting to Supplier's compliance with this Section.

CHAPTER 43

OUTSOURCING IS NOT: 'WE WORK, YOU WATCH, AND YOU WIN'

As I have discussed previously, outsourcing a bundle of applications, oversight for key infrastructure, or a business process requires that the parties collaborate to successfully achieve an ultimate outcome that fulfills the client's values, that achieves the business case that was the catalyst for the decision to outsource, and that is consistent with the goals and objectives of the agreement. Despite popular belief, outsourcing is not like building a ship. The service provider does not go off and unilaterally complete the transition phase, run the service, and casually meet the client at sea trials. As I have discussed, you cannot outsource responsibility. To that end, it is critical that the agreement contain a list of dependencies upon which the service provider's ability to deliver is conditioned.

In addition to the inability of the parties to properly set expectations and manage scope, significant contributors to disputes that arise during the delivery term are the failure to identify a set of dependencies upon which the service provider's performance will be conditioned, and the failure to immediately escalate any related client compliance deficiencies. Given that dynamic, it is critical that the parties agree on a discrete list of client (broadly defined to include client agents and other vendors) performance obligations in each statement of work that must be strictly adhered to during the delivery term. Beyond identifying the dependencies, it is just as critical that the service provider immediately raise its hand when the client fails to perform. I have seen far too many instances when the service provider, most likely fearing that an escalation will have a detrimental impact on the client relationship or feeling overly confident that it can "fix" it, tries to fill the client gap.

It attempts to do so by bringing in additional resources, by waiting to see what will happen, by developing a temporary solution as a result of another client vendor's lack of compliance, or by struggling to meet service levels or other milestones, irrespective of client deficiencies. I assure you that each time this dynamic occurs, service quality is impacted and a dispute is imminent. So, identify dependencies and immediately escalate if the client is not in strict compliance.

When I speak of the service provider's delivery being conditioned on those dependencies, I mean it in a broad sense. Its delivery obligations, including service levels, as well as any liability for its failure to perform, is abated or delayed until the client or its agent complies. Many clients or their counsel avoid a dependencies provision in the agreement because they say that this concept is addressed in the savings clause provisions, which I discussed in Chapter 21. The concepts are similar and both require the service provider to use commercially reasonable efforts to meet its obligations, despite the deficiency. The typical savings clause, however, places more stringent requirements on the service provider and assent from the client to obtain relief for any service delivery failure that arises from the deficiency.

Identifying a set of client dependencies is a provision that I believe to be reasonable in operation, and pushback from clients and their counsel is not legitimate. This perspective is grounded in the position that outsourcing services are not delivered in a vacuum; the parties must work together to achieve success. The scope and complexity of a typical outsourcing engagement, combined with the ever-present multivendor ecosystem, dictates that even the best outsourcing service provider must rely on the client and the other vendors in its ecosystem to meet its service levels and achieve delivery success. What is not legitimate is the following approach: not allowing the vendor to be excused from performance where the client or its agents fail to meet any dependencies that the service provider must rely on to achieve timely, quality, and cost effective delivery. In this situation, the service provider is taking responsibility for a risk outside of its control which is not advisable under any circumstance.

A sample provision that addresses this concept is as follows:

Client Dependencies

If Client, its Affiliates or their agents fail to complete any Client Dependency on or prior to the applicable Client Dependency Deadline Date, then, (a) any obligation of Supplier under this Agreement or a SOW that is dependent on a Client Dependency will be extended by the number of Business Days that the day on which Client actually performs such Client Dependency following the Client Dependency Deadline Date, provided that Client will reimburse Supplier for any increased costs of changing the timelines agreed to in a SOW and (b) Supplier's performance of any other obligation under this Agreement that is dependent on performance of a Client Dependency shall be excused until such Client Dependency has been performed. In the event that Supplier becomes aware of a failed Client Dependency, Supplier (i) will notify Client in writing promptly of any such failure ("**Client Deficiency Notice**") and will promptly escalate the Client Deficiency Notice to the Steering Committee and (ii) continue to use commercially reasonable efforts to meet the original deadline set out for such obligation. If Supplier fails to promptly notify Client of any such failure of which it is aware (generally at the next regularly scheduled project status meeting) and escalate the Client Deficiency Notice to the Steering Committee, Supplier will be precluded from subsequently citing Client's failure as a reason for Supplier's own subsequent failure to perform, nor will Supplier be entitled to claim additional costs for any such Client deficiency.

The remedy set out in this Section is Supplier's sole remedy in the event of a failure on the part of Client, its Affiliates or their agents to complete any one or more Client Dependencies on or prior to the applicable Client Dependency Deadline Date unless in its Client Deficiency Notice Supplier indicates to Client: (i) the approximate additional actual costs (plus or minus ten percent) Supplier may incur (including costs relating to Supplier Personnel); or (ii) the impact on Supplier's ability to meet applicable Service Levels or such other obligations under this Agreement, as a result of Client's failure to complete the Client Dependency on time (in which case, unless Client objects to such additional costs or inability to meet applicable Service Levels or such other obligations—in which case the matter will be escalated through Dispute Resolution—Supplier will be entitled to charge such additional costs (identified in the Client Deficiency Notice) actually incurred by Supplier if and to the extent the Client deficiency continues, or Supplier will not be responsible for any Service Level Credits or meeting any obligations under this Agreement directly and solely related to such failure to meet Service Levels or fulfill its obligations, as applicable).

Beyond a narrowly tailored statement of work free of ambiguity and clear about roles and responsibilities, the next-best piece of advice I would give to any outsourcing service provider is to clearly articulate any client or client agent dependencies upon which its delivery is conditioned. Failure to do so yields an expedited trip to the governance and dispute resolution provisions of the agreement.

CHAPTER 44

BE CURRENT OR BE GONE

In addition to being mindful of clients seeking to have service providers bring all of their existing applications in line with their current standards and policies (see Chapter 22), another related area is the requirement that the service provider maintain all software that it is financially responsible for under the agreement, either on the current generally available release or within a stipulated number of major releases. I find this to be another provision not directly correlated to the delivery of the services or the ability of the service provider to meet the service levels. Just because I am not writing this book on the most current general release of Microsoft Word does not undermine the book's integrity or quality. The same thinking holds true about proprietary or commercially licensed software that the service provider uses to perform the services.

Although there may be some benefit in working on a current version of software, I would say that the standard should be no more aggressive than "within two major releases of the then-current release." This provision seems benign, but I have been party to disputes predicated on the client's claim that the service provider was not using the current release of a licensed software package and that its failure to upgrade was inhibiting the client's ability to receive the full benefit of the services for which the client had contracted.

All I can say is that this requirement is often embedded in an attachment or exhibit, and overlooked by the service provider. If the client is a strong proponent of the four corners rule, it could force its service provider to upgrade its software, irrespective of any effect on the delivery of the services or achievement of the service levels.

CHAPTER 45

YOU MAY BE THE SERVICE PROVIDER BUT I STILL CONTROL YOU

One issue that always arises in the managed service environment is the ability of the client to reprioritize or re-task the service provider team as needed to focus on high-priority projects or to address another client initiative. Assuming that the managed service team deployed is capable of performing the requested services, the client should be allowed to reprioritize the team as it deems appropriate. However, it should be allowed do so only as long as it gives the service provider relief from service levels or other delivery obligations during the period when the team is reprioritized on the client-directed initiatives. If the client is not willing to agree to the relief provision, then it should not have the reprioritization right. An example of a work prioritization provision is as follows:

Work Prioritization

Client may identify new or additional work activities (including work that would otherwise be treated as a New Service) to be performed by Supplier personnel already performing the Services (by executing a Change Order), or reprioritize or reset the schedule for existing Projects and Services to be performed by such personnel. Unless otherwise agreed, Client will not incur additional charges to the extent such work activities can be performed (a) by Supplier personnel then assigned to performing Services within the same level of activity such Supplier Personnel are then performing for Client (provided that such additional work activities will not place Supplier at risk of failing to meet Service Levels or its other obligations under this Agreement, and is within the reasonable competency of such Supplier Personnel), and (b) without additional Hardware and Software.

CHAPTER 46

HOW WILL YOU MEASURE ME?
LET ME COUNT THE WAYS

Legal terms and conditions affect price. However, no single factor dictates price in an outsourcing engagement more than the service level targets that the client seeks to achieve and that the service provider is measured against during the delivery term. Like acceptance criteria, I firmly believe that service levels must be objective, measurable, and verifiable.

Although there are industry standards for some components of a service level structure—the percentage of fees the service provider places at risk—there are so many moving parts in a service level scheme that identifying a market-relevant, standard, service level scheme is not possible. However, there are factors to be discussed that will help you navigate through the service level maze. The deployment of automation will certainly impact the service level targets against which the service provider will be measured and held accountable for achieving over the term. The key questions to be answered are as follows:

1. If all human error is eliminated with the deployment of the robots, then is it legitimate to expect that all service levels associated with the workload being processed by the robot be set at 100 percent?

2. If the expected targets are not initially set at 100 percent, will the deployment of the robots automatically yield continuous improvement over the term?

The answer to both questions depends upon the level of human intervention in the transaction processing and remediation process for exceptions. Even if the robots are responsible for 100 percent of the transaction processing and the number of exceptions is limited, it is not legitimate to hold the service provider responsible for any client obligations or third-party intervention or handling time required to process or remediate any exception cases.

Assuming compliance and change management are properly managed, the robots are performing flawlessly, and the amount of exception processing and human intervention is limited, there is no legitimate reason why service level targets could not be set close to 100 percent. If perfection is achievable for certain components of the service, why it is necessary for the service provider to place fees at risk tied to the achievement of the service level targets? The answer to this question will certainly evolve as automation and other emerging technologies are more routinely deployed and the parties focus on innovation and agility in the service delivery model.

While a robust service level methodology with service level targets and fees at risk is a staple in a legacy outsourcing agreement, the level of attention it receives is not consistent with the client's interest to foster innovation over the delivery term. A service level methodology can be utilized as either a carrot or a stick. The stick manifests itself in a penalty structure under which service level credits are extracted for poor performance. Conversely, the carrot reflects an incentive structure that is intended to motivate the proper behavior, to objectively measure service levels that have a legitimate impact on the underlying business operations, and to hold the service provider accountable for risks within its control.

Unfortunately, many clients and their counsel prefer the stick which requires service providers to focus solely on meeting and achieving the service level targets stated in the agreement. Under this construct, there is no extra credit or incentive for implementing innovation into the delivery model. Under a more incentive-based approach, the service provider and the client can work collaboratively to evolve the service levels based upon changing market and business conditions and drive more innovation and cost savings into the delivery model.

Ultimately, it may be this type of approach which will result in the elimination of a traditional "fees at risk" service level methodology from the outsourcing agreement of the future. To the extent the parties have trust in each other, they can set aside the effort and cost associated with achieving the service levels and administering the methodology and focus on an agile delivery model where innovation drives behavior. I am not suggesting service provider performance will not be measured; rather, the parties will have the ability to quickly adapt service levels with changing business and market conditions and quickly remediate and fine-tune performance issues without the constraints of the service level methodology.

As long as we are living in the legacy environment the key areas to be addressed are as follows:

1. How were the service levels established? Were they being achieved by the client prior to the decision to outsource? Were they being achieved by the previous service provider before its services were completed? Are they purely aspirational? If the service levels were being achieved by the client prior to the decision to outsource, does the client have historical data that reflect the achievement of the service levels?

2. Is there an objective description for each service level, including a definition of what is being measured, the expected and minimum targets, and the time period during which the service level is measured? What is the algorithm used to measure performance against the service level? Are there both critical and key measurements? Will there be any exclusion for client or third-party incident handling time? What tools are used to measure the service level? Which service levels are subject to service level credits?

3. Depending upon the answer to No. 2, is there a baseline period during which the expected service level and minimum targets are established? Alternatively, is a presumptive service level construct used to gauge the legitimacy of the stated service levels during the first six months of delivery?

4.   Are the service levels subject to any continuous or annual improvement adjustments?

5.   What percentage of the service provider's monthly fees is placed "at-risk" and subject to service level credits?

6.   What at-risk pool allocation is the client allowed to apportion across the service levels each month?

7.   How are newly introduced service levels measured and how are targets established? How are service levels promoted from key to critical? How frequently can service levels be changed and is any notice period required before doing so?

8.   How is a service level default calculated and paid? What happens if there are multiple service level defaults?

9.   Are there low volume provisions for those service levels with limited incidents over the measurement period?

10.   Can the service provider earn back a service level credit accrued by the client in a prior period?

11.   Does the client accrue any form of a termination right with multiple critical service level defaults occurring annually?

Given the number of moving parts in a service level scheme, we will carefully analyze each component. First, the client identifies the service level array against which it intends to measure the service provider's performance over the delivery term. In addition, the parties will agree upon the at-risk percentage, which is defined as the percent of the service provider's monthly fees that it places at risk and are subject to service level credits. The parties will also agree upon the pool percentage that the client will allocate across the critical service levels to calculate the service level credit that it will accrue in the event of a default.

Service levels are established to measure the service provider's performance over the delivery term. Service levels are classified in two different categories, critical measurements and key measurements. For each measurement, the client may choose to identify a minimum and expected service level or, alternatively, only an expected service level. Think of the minimum as being exactly as it sounds—the basic level of performance required for that service component. The same holds true for the expected service level, because it reflects the level of service that the client anticipates receiving for that service component.

Critical measurements are areas of particular importance to the client. As such, if the service provider fails to meet the minimum or expected service level associated with a critical measurement, it is subject to a service level credit. By contrast, key measurements are measured and monitored, but are not subject to service level credits. For each identified service level, the client identifies the following: a minimum and expected service level target; the calculation that measures actual performance; the time period when the service level is measured; the tool or system used to manage the data and to make the measurement; and any other information that may apply to calculating performance (e.g., exclusions from the calculation methodology while the incident is pending or being handled by a third party). An example of a critical measurement is as follows:

RETENTION RATE OF KEY SERVICE PROVIDER PERSONNEL

SERVICE LEVEL TYPE	CRITICAL MEASUREMENT
At-Risk Pool Allocation	10%
Expected Service Level	No More Than 1
Minimum Service Level	No More Than 2
Measurement Period	Rolling 12 Months
Service Level Description	Measures the retention rate of Service Provider Personnel filling Key Service Provider Positions
Subject to Annual Improvement	No

Calculation	Number of Service Provider Personnel filling Key Service Provider Positions that cease providing Services to client during the Measurement Period. Calculation will exclude Service Provider Personnel filling Key Service Provider Positions that cease providing Services to client during the Measurement Period whose release was planned and agreed by client
Measurement Tool	To be determined by the Parties during the development of the Policies and Procedures Manual
Other	None

The service level array is straightforward. No market-relevant standard exists for the number of critical versus key measures that should be measured during the performance period. My only advice about designating a service level as critical or key is to make sure that all critical service levels are objective, measurable, and verifiable. It is common in both application and infrastructure outsourcing engagements that multiple service levels center on measuring response times for and restoration times related to issues, service requests, incidents, or problems that have varying levels of impact on daily business operations. An example of a response time critical service level is as follows:

SEVERITY LEVEL 1 AND SEVERITY LEVEL 2 INCIDENT RESPONSE TIMES

SERVICE LEVEL TYPE	CRITICAL MEASUREMENT
At-Risk Pool Allocation	25%
Expected Service Level	100%
Minimum Service Level	100%
Measurement Period	Monthly
Service Level Description	Measures the percentage of Severity Level 1 and Severity Level 2 ADM Incidents that are Responded to within 15 minutes
Subject to Annual Improvement	No

HOW WILL YOU MEASURE ME? LET ME COUNT THE WAYS

Calculation	Number of Severity Level 1 and Severity Level 2 ADM Incidents assigned to Service Provider to which a Response is required during the applicable Measurement Period for which Service Provider provides a Response within 15 minutes from the time the Service Provider is assigned the Incident ticket, ***divided by*** number of Severity Level 1 and Severity Level 2 ADM Incidents assigned to Service Provider to which a Response is required during such Measurement Period, with the result expressed as a percentage to two decimal places.
Measurement Tool	Client's Incident Management Tool
Other	Performance against this Service Level will be measured according to the initial Severity Level assigned by the Service Desk.
	Response time does not include any period of time that an Incident record has a status code of Pending.

One service level continually cited by clients as a critical measure is customer satisfaction. Although I would never dismiss customer satisfaction as an important measure, I would never agree to designate it as a critical service level because it is purely subjective. Most people do not respond to customer satisfaction surveys and those who do are people who are unhappy with the service. Therefore, a service provider is agreeing to roll the dice on its ability to achieve the minimum or expected target, which is frequently set at 90 percent or greater. Consider the following questions that are representative of those found in a typical customer satisfaction survey and that require a response on a 5-point scale, ranging from "Exceeds Expectations" to "Doesn't Meet Expectations." I believe the subjectivity of these questions is obvious and provides legitimacy to my concern. Sample questions are as follows:

Please tell us how well the vendor:

1. Effectively focuses IT efforts on the activities that return the greatest value.

2. Understands your business goals and objectives.

3. Understands your expectations of IT service delivery.

4. Understands your IT development and supports priorities and needs.

5.   Ensures you have the information to effectively manage your IT costs.

6.   Works with you to identify opportunities to use IT to enable business value.

7.   Works with you to identify and assess alternative technology solutions.

8.   Understands your department's business processes and technology requirements.

9.   Delivers high-quality solutions that effectively satisfy your business requirements.

I am not sure about you, but I am unwilling to place my fees at risk based on how a subset of the client user community rates my services on what is a clearly a highly subjective basis. I understand that mitigating factors can be implemented, such as requiring a minimum response rate, agreeing to incur a service level credit only when the minimum target (versus expected) is not achieved, limiting the allocation of the at-risk pool that can be placed against this service level, or exempting customer satisfaction service level defaults from the termination trigger calculation. But I also know that the risk associated with a recurring default of a customer satisfaction service level can be substantial and has multiple implications throughout the agreement. If these exceptions are not agreed on, the service provider is subject to the financial penalty when it misses the minimum or expected target as well as to a potential client termination trigger if multiple minimum or critical misses occur annually. As the level of automation increases and service provider personnel can direct their attention from transaction processing to user happiness and satisfaction, clients may expect that customer satisfaction be promoted to a critical service level and that more fees at risk be tied to its achievement. I strongly recommend that you do not fall into this trap. Irrespective of how much time is spent on keeping users satisfied, the subjective nature of this measure remains unchanged. Given these potential circumstances, I strongly advise that customer satisfaction be a non-promotable key measure over the agreement term.

HOW WILL YOU MEASURE ME? LET ME COUNT THE WAYS

Consider a managed service application outsourcing engagement with average monthly fees of $400,000, 12 percent of fees at risk, and 25 percent allocated to the customer satisfaction service level. In this scenario, a monthly credit of

$12,000 ($400,000 x 12% x 25%) results if a default occurs. Although that amount may be insignificant, a recurring monthly credit over a five-year delivery term—$720,000 at a minimum before including the impact of any recurring service level default multiplier—could be detrimental to the service provider's financial health. In addition to the financial penalty, a termination right is likely triggered after multiple consecutive service level defaults and the service provider would be working under duress for most of the delivery term. These are not desirable circumstances and should be avoided at all costs.

I have had the unfortunate experience of attempting to seek relief from multiple clients when the service provider had agreed to designate customer satisfaction as a critical service level, because it was confident of its ability to manage the survey process and keep the client "happy." All I can say is that in both instances, the client refused to provide relief either in the form of reducing the service level targets or moving the service level to a non-credit-bearing key measure. Given that experience, I strongly advise strictly adhering to the principle that all service levels must be objective. There can be no exceptions to this rule.

In evaluating the service levels, it is absolutely critical to review the targets. My first order of business with a client is to understand how the service level targets were established. Are they currently being achieved by the client or an existing service provider in its management of the operation or process, or are they purely aspirational? If it is the former, I always ask to see at least six months of historical data that reflect that the service levels are currently being achieved. If data exist, then I would agree to be subject to service level credits based upon the targets supported by the historical data starting on the date the service begins or after the conclusion of a limited burn-in period (generally a two to three-month period during which the service provider is not subject to service level credits). If the underlying processes are completely automated and compliance and change management are being effectively managed, the requirement for a burn-in period may be unnecessary as the robots will assume immediate control upon execution of the agreement.

However, if the service levels are purely aspirational, I require a six-month baseline period (if the execution of the underlying process is completely automated, it may be reasonable to limit the term of the baseline period) when actual performance is measured but the service provider is not subject to service level credits. When the six-month baseline period ends, the parties review the service provider's actual performance during that period. Such performance during this period establishes the service levels (take six months of data, throw out the high and the low, and take the average of the remaining four months) prospectively. Although this approach seems reasonable as applied, clients and third-party advisors may believe that the service provider will sandbag its performance during the baseline period to try to have desirable and more reasonable service level targets over the delivery term.

To address the sandbagging concern, another market-relevant option is using a presumptive service level construct. Under that construct, the parties agree to establish the service level targets at the stated level and gauge the service provider's performance over the presumptive service level measurement period, typically six months. After the measurement period expires, the parties review the measurement trends and performance levels achieved during the period from which the actual targets are established. During the presumptive level measurement period, the service provider is not subject to service level credits, unless it is unable to achieve an interim minimum performance standard established by the parties.

The net result of this process is that if the service measurements reflect that the service provider consistently met the presumptive service level, then that level is established as the final service level for that component of the service. If the measurements reflect that the service provider consistently exceeded the presumptive service level, the parties negotiate in good faith to establish the final service level for that component of the service. And if the measurements reflect that the service provide was unable to consistently meet the presumptive service level target, the service provider conducts an analysis to determine the cause of that failure and what level could be achieved using commercially reasonable efforts. From that analysis, the parties agree upon the final service level for that component of the service. An example of a presumptive service level provision is as follows:

HOW WILL YOU MEASURE ME? LET ME COUNT THE WAYS

Presumptive Service Levels

As of the applicable Service Agreement Effective Date, certain Service Levels may be designated in the applicable Service Agreement as "Presumptive" ("**Presumptive Service Levels**"). Service Provider will begin measuring its performance against such Presumptive Service Levels on the Service Commencement Date. Service Provider will continue such service measurements for six months (the "**Presumptive Service Level Measurement Period**"). Service Provider will use commercially reasonable efforts, consistent with the applicable staffing levels, to meet the Presumptive Service Levels during the Presumptive Service Level Measurement Period, but Service Level Credits will not be assessed for any failure to meet such Presumptive Service Levels during such period. After the level of service has been measured for the specified number of months, Client and Service Provider will review the measurement trends and the levels of service quality that were attained or attainable during the Presumptive Service Level Measurement Period and will set the final Service Levels for such Presumptive Service Levels as follows:

If the service measurements demonstrate that Service Provider has consistently met a particular Presumptive Service Level, such Presumptive Service Level will be established as the final Service Level for such Service.

If the service measurements demonstrate that Service Provider has consistently exceeded a particular Presumptive Service Level, the Parties will negotiate in good faith to establish a final Service Level for such Service consistent with the results achieved.

In all other circumstances, if the service measurements demonstrate that Service Provider has not consistently met a particular Presumptive Service Level, Service Provider will conduct an analysis to determine: (i) the cause of the failure to meet the Presumptive Service Levels; (ii) whether it is possible for Service Provider, using commercially reasonable efforts, to meet the Presumptive Service Level without making material changes to the Agreement; (iii) the Service Level Service Provider could meet using commercially reasonable efforts, but without making material changes to the Agreement; and (iv) the changes that would have to be made to permit Service Provider to meet the higher Presumptive Service Level. If the Parties agree that the analysis demonstrates that the Presumptive Service Level is capable of being met, that Presumptive Service Level will be established as the final Service Level for such Service. Service Provider will then expeditiously take any remedial action necessary to begin meeting the established Service Level. If the Parties agree that the analysis demonstrates that the failure to meet the Presumptive Service Level is not attributable to Service Provider's failure to competently perform its obligations under the Agreement and that it is not possible for Service Provider, using commercially reasonable efforts, to meet such Presumptive Service Level, Client will at its option, either (i) set the applicable Service Level for such Service at the highest level the Parties agree that Service Provider could meet using commercially reasonable efforts, or (ii) authorize Service Provider to make some or all of the changes identified as necessary to meet a higher Service Level and correspondingly revise the applicable Service Agreement.

With respect to each Critical Service Level that is designated a Presumptive Service Level, the Parties will establish an interim performance standard to be applied during the Presumptive Service Level Measurement Period (which will not be lower than 90 percent of the proposed Presumptive Service Level). If Service Provider fails to meet the interim performance standard during any month during such Presumptive Service Level Measurement Period, Service Provider will incur a Service Level Credit equal to 50 percent of the credit Service Provider would otherwise have incurred for a Minimum Service Level Default of such Critical Service Level. Service Provider will not incur a second Service Level Credit with respect to the same Critical Service Level during the two months immediately following the assessment of such Service Level Credit, provided that in the event of such a Service Level failure, Service Provider will use commercially reasonable efforts to identify and correct the root cause of the performance problem during the two months immediately following such failure. Following the completion of the Presumptive Service Level Measurement Period and the establishment of final Service Levels as described above, the interim performance standards will have no further force or effect. Client will not have any termination rights based on failure to meet a Service Level as a result of Service Provider's failure to meet Presumptive Service Levels. A Presumptive Service Level will cease to be a Presumptive Service Level once the process described above is complete.

In some recent negotiations, I have seen an approach to service levels that is not legitimate and is likely to yield a service provider working under duress and an unhappy client. It can be summed up as follows: The client acknowledges that the service level targets are purely aspirational but directs the service provider, with limited due diligence, to propose a team and managed service price that the service provider believes would be sufficient to meet the desired service levels, irrespective of the extreme uncertainty the service provider may encounter in the delivery process. Under this construct, the service provider is subject to service level credits at the stated levels on Day 1 of delivery. Although the client may provide historical incident data for the service provider under this construct, no data will be provided which supports achievement against the service level targets the client has identified. This supporting data is not provided because it does not exist as the service level targets are a pipe dream. For example, a service provider could be subject to a 90 percent target for a service level that the client or its existing vendor has struggled to historically maintain at a 75 percent achievement level. When this construct was described by a client's counsel in a recent negotiation, he acknowledged the risk but stated that his client was focused on partnering with a vendor that was willing to, nonetheless, "step up."

In these instances, I would say that the service provider should consider taking its proposed fees to the blackjack table, because the odds of success are a coin flip, at best. Although I can certainly understand why a client desires service levels hovering in the 100 percent range, this approach is not legitimate in a price sensitive and highly competitive selection process and seems to do nothing but set false expectations for both parties to the transaction.

Let's assume that we have agreed on the service level array and corresponding targets, and are in Year 2 of a five-year term. The next client expectation is that the quality of the services will improve annually and that the service level targets for certain service levels, both expected and minimum, will follow suit.

Although asking for an annual improvement expectation is a legitimate request, any such increase should be reasonable and should not result in unattainable targets. A typical approach to calculating an annual improvement adjustment in expected service levels is to look at the average of the highest measurement period results in the most recent year and reset the service level accordingly. For minimum service levels, a typical approach is to take the existing minimum service level and adjust it upward by a percentage of the difference between the current minimum service level and 100 percent. An example of a provision that embodies both adjustment mechanisms is as follows:

Expected Service Levels—Annual Improvement Adjustment

The Parties agree that certain Expected Service Levels designated in the applicable Service Agreement will be modified at the end of each Service Agreement Year, as follows: (a) the Expected Service Level associated with each Critical Measurement and Key Measurement will be reset to the average of the four highest actual Measurement Period results (e.g., 99.6 is higher than 99.4 percent) that are at or above the Expected Service Level applicable to the immediately-prior Service Agreement Year, provided that (b) if Service Provider met or exceeded the applicable Expected Service Level fewer than four times during the immediately-prior Service Agreement Year, then the Expected Service Level will be reset by taking the four highest actual Measurement Period results, replacing each such actual result that is below the Expected Service Level with the Expected Service Level, and dividing the sum of the resulting four numbers by four.

Sample Calculation: If the Expected Service Level being adjusted was 99.60%, and there were three actual results that were higher and none equal (e.g., 99.90%, 99.80%, and 99.70%), the target would be adjusted to [(99.90% + 99.80% + 99.70% + 99.60%) / 4] = 99.75%.

In no event will any single increase in an Expected Service Level pursuant exceed 10 percent of the difference between 100 percent and the then-current Expected Service Level. For example, if the Expected Service Level being adjusted were 99.60%, the maximum increase for that reset would be 10% of 0.4%, or 0.04%, and the Expected Service Level would be reset to 99.64%.

Minimum Service Levels—Annual Improvement Adjustment

The Parties agree that the Minimum Service Levels associated with certain Critical Measurements and Key Measurements designated in the applicable Service Agreement will be reset at the end of each Service Agreement Year by adding to the Minimum Service Level being adjusted a sum equal to five percent of the difference between 100 percent and the then-current Minimum Service Level. In the event the adjustment of a Minimum Service Level would increase such that the Minimum Service Level for a Critical Measurement or Key Measurement would exceed the applicable Expected Service Level, then the Minimum Service Level will be set to an amount equal to the Expected Service Level.

Sample Calculation: If the Minimum Service Level being adjusted was 99.40%, the target would be adjusted to 99.40% + [(100% 99.40%) * 5%] = 99.43%.

Let's assume that the parties agree that annual improvement adjustments are legitimate, given the initial service level targets, and that the adjustment mechanism is reasonable. Then, the next issue to be addressed is the process for additions, modifications, or deletions to the service levels or modifications to the at-risk pool allocation for any critical measurement. Typically, clients seek broad rights to add or delete service levels, to change service levels from key measurements to critical measurements (or vice versa) with a minimal notice period, or to change the at-risk pool allocation. Given that a service provider must have time to adequately prepare for the introduction of a new service level and that the parties need to agree on the measurement methodology, I would say that reasonable restrictions are needed on the frequency (no more than once a quarter or twice a year), notice period (anywhere from 45 to 60 days), and number of changes (no more than three per change notification), that may made to the service level scheme during the delivery term.

Irrespective of where these adjustment terms end up, the same general principle holds true that any new service levels must be objective, measurable, and verifiable. Assuming that any new service levels meets this standard, then the parties need to agree on the expected and minimum targets for the newly introduced or promoted service level. If the parties cannot agree and if the service provider can measure its performance against the service level for a reasonable number of prior measurement periods (assume six is a good sample), they can use the average of all service measurements over that prior period to establish the expected service level, with the minimum service level set at the second-lowest measurement in that period. If a measurement does not exist for the preceding six-month period, the parties can agree on the targets using industry standards for similar service levels. Or, they can engage the services of a mutually agreed on third-party advisor to help establish the new service level. Alternatively, they could treat the client-proposed service level as presumptive and follow the process defined previously.

Now that we know our service levels and the associated targets, I should discuss the percentage of the service provider's fees at risk and size of the pool that the client can allocate for the critical measurements. The concept of fees at risk is straightforward. The service provider agrees to place a certain percentage of its monthly managed service fees at risk and subject to service level credits that the client accrues in the event of a service level default. Similarly, the agreement may also stipulate that the service provider place a similar percentage of its project fees at risk for projects completed in conjunction with the managed service scope. In addition, and as I have discussed, a similar percentage of transition fees may also be placed at risk that would trigger a credit when a critical transition deliverable or critical transition milestone was not achieved. The service level array typically contains service levels that apply to both the managed service (nondiscretionary services) component as well as the project (discretionary) component of the service offering.

For the percentage of fees at risk, the market-relevant standard hovers in the 12 percent to 15 percent range, depending upon the opportunity. Some clients and their counsel have sought to move the market by suggesting that 18 percent of fees at risk is appropriate. My perspective is that there is no right answer on this issue. Like liability provisions, it is important to evaluate the percentage of fees at risk in light of the following: the aggressiveness of and historical basis for the service level targets; the number and composition of the critical and key measures; the existence of any earn-back provisions; the impact of multiple service level defaults on the financial viability of the opportunity; and the overall terms and conditions in the agreement. The key here is that the percentage of fees at risk can't be viewed in isolation, because it is so tightly interconnected with the overall service level scheme and the overall agreement.

In addition to the at-risk amount, the agreement stipulates an at-risk pool that the client may allocate among the critical measurements identified in the agreement. Just think of it like this. In the example referenced previously, assume the client has $400,000 in monthly managed services fees and 12 percent of its fees, or $48,000, per month at risk. The client has an at-risk pool that typically ranges anywhere from 200 percent to 300 percent that it can allocate across the service levels in a manner that reflects its determination of the critical nature of each service level. Just see it as the client having 250 percentage points that it can allocate across the service levels—the roulette wheel—from which it can recover up to $48,000 per month if it places its bets against those service levels that yield a default in the measurement period.

In addition, the market-relevant standard is to place a limitation on the portion of the allocation pool that can be allocated against a single service level. I believe this limit should be no less than 30 percent and no more than 50 percent, and should vary depending upon the overall service level scheme. Irrespective of the number of service level defaults in a month, the general rule is that the client can never recover more than the fees at risk, or in this example, $48,000.

Now that we know the size of the stack of chips the client is holding, we can look at what instances trigger the payment of service level credits and what, if any, penalties may result for multiple critical misses of the same service level, up to and including the accrual of a termination right. It is pretty much a given that the service provider accrues multiple service level credits during the delivery term. Most service level schemes include escalation penalties for multiple critical misses and termination-for-cause triggers for multiple critical service level misses measured on a rolling 12-month basis. Therefore, it is important for the credit scheme to have reasonable thresholds in these areas. No service provider is perfect, and it is in the best interests of both parties that the service provider not work under duress with a termination right hanging over its head for what seems to be a reasonable number of service level credits accrued annually. Consider the following provision:

> If vendor misses, in any combination, a monthly Critical Service Level as set forth in the Service Level exhibit and/or the customer satisfaction level set forth in Section X of this agreement five times in a 12-month period, Client may terminate this agreement for cause.

Although you might find that five misses over a 12-month period is reasonable, imagine the implications when measuring 20 critical service levels plus one customer satisfaction level per month. With around 252 measuring points per year, that leaves a margin of error of 1.9 percent before a termination right would be triggered. Thus, be mindful of the number of monthly measuring points and the threshold for error before such a right is triggered. A more reasonable termination right triggered by multiple performance standard defaults is as follows:

Termination for Multiple Performance Standard Defaults

In the event Service Provider, with respect to any Service Agreement, (a) experiences three or more consecutive Critical Measurement Defaults with respect to the same Critical Measurement; (b) experiences four or more Critical Deliverable Defaults with respect to the same Critical Measurement within a rolling six-month period; or (c) incurs more than 75 percent of the applicable At-Risk Amount with respect to such Service Agreement for any two or more months within a rolling six-month period, then Client may, by giving notice to Service Provider within 180 days from the last day of the calendar month in which the last default described above occurs, terminate this Master Agreement or the applicable Service Agreement, in whole or in part, as of a date specified in the notice of termination, without cost or penalty and without payment of any termination charges by Client.

Although there are myriad options, some more lenient than others, it would be reasonable to expect a service level credit to be accrued in the following instances:

1. Whenever the service provider's level of performance for a particular service level fails to meet the particular service level.

2. While option No. 1 reflects no tolerance for error (you miss, you pay), the following instances do not reflect the accrual of a service level credit until multiple or consecutive misses of the same critical service level occur:

- The service provider's level of performance against the applicable critical measurements meets the applicable minimum service levels, but (a) fails to meet the expected service level for such critical measurement during the applicable measurement period and (b) such failure is the fourth (or subsequent) failure to meet an expected service level for the same critical measurement within any rolling 12-month period.
- The service provider's level of performance against a critical measurement (a) fails to meet the expected service level for such critical measurement during the applicable measurement period and (b) such failure is the third (or subsequent) consecutive failure to meet the expected service level for such service level.

3. The following reflect other instances that yield a service level credit:

- The service provider's level of performance against a critical measurement fails to meet the applicable minimum service level during the applicable measurement period.
- The service provider's level of performance against a critical measurement during the applicable measurement period is below the minimum service level by more than two times the difference between the expected service level and the minimum service level.
- The service provider fails to report on its performance against a critical measurement or key measurement.
- The service provider fails to measure its performance against a critical measurement or key measurement.

In the typical agreement, many instances may result in the accrual of a service level credit. The bottom line is that all service level credits that occur in a month are accumulated and paid to the client as long as the total at-risk amount is not exceeded. While multiple service level defaults may occur in a month, only one service level default and corresponding credit accrue if multiple critical measurement defaults are from the same root cause event. It is common to find a multiplier effect in a consecutive service level default for the same service level. To determine how much a service level default costs, let's take a look at a sample calculation:

> For each Critical Service Level Failure, Vendor shall pay to Customer a Service Level Credit that will be computed in accordance with the following formula:
>
> Service Level Credit = **A x B**
>
> > Where:
> > **A** = At-Risk Amount; and
> > **B** = At-Risk Pool Allocation
>
> For example, where Vendor fails to meet the Minimum Service Level for a Critical Measurement assume that (i) the monthly charges for the applicable measurement period under a Service Agreement to which the failed Critical Service Level relates is $1,000,000; and (ii) the At-Risk Allocation Percentage for such Service Level Failure is 25 percent; and the At-Risk percentage is 12 percent. The Performance Credit due to Customer for such Critical Service Level Failure would be computed as follows:
>
> > $120,000 X 25% = $30,000
> > **A** = the At-Risk Amount (12% of $1,000,000 = $120,000),
> > Multiplied by
> > **B** = 25% (the At-Risk Pool Allocation)
> > = $30,000 (the amount of the Service Level Credit)
>
> If more than one Critical Service Level Failure has occurred in a single month, the sum of the corresponding Performance Credits shall be

credited to Customer, except that in no event shall the aggregate amount of Performance Credits credited to Customer with respect to Critical Service Level Failures occurring in a single month exceed, in total, the At Risk Amount for such month.

As I have mentioned before, you are likely to encounter a multiplier effect in a consecutive service level default for the same service level. Clearly, these provisions can become punitive, but then again, the circumstances that they apply to are extreme, namely, the consecutive failure of the same critical service level. Because these provisions typically do not take effect until the third or fourth consecutive miss of the same service level, I do not object to including them as they seem to be commensurate with service quality. Even under this multiplier construct, the at-risk amount cannot be exceeded in any one month, so the net effect is that you reach the at-risk threshold more expeditiously. Most important, if you miss the same service level four months in a row, it may be time to consider another profession.

The key to any form of multiplier or penalty escalators is to make sure that despite the critical misses, the at-risk amount and at-risk pool allocation remain unchanged. By doing so, your risk remains the same, but, as I have discussed, you may arrive at the maximum at-risk amount much more expeditiously. A few examples of a multiplier construct are as follows:

- If a Critical Service Level Failure recurs in three (3) or more consecutive measurement periods, the amount of the applicable Performance Credit shall be doubled for such third measurement period and remain doubled for such subsequent measurement periods. For the avoidance of doubt, (i) the Performance Credit shall only be doubled one time, and (ii) such doubled amount shall be payable for all successive, consecutive Critical Service Level Failures for the subject Service Level. Upon correction of performance on a Critical Service Level, the amount of the applicable Performance Credit will revert to its original weight.

- With respect to Critical Measurement Defaults, the amount of the applicable Service Level Credit payable to Client for the applicable

Critical Measurement Default will increase by 25 percent upon the fourth and each subsequent Critical Measurement Default, up to a maximum of three increments, or a multiplier of 1.75. For example, the Service Level Credit applicable to the (a) fourth subsequent consecutive Critical Measurement Default would be calculated by multiplying the credit payable for the third consecutive Critical Measurement Default by 1.25; (b) fifth subsequent consecutive Critical Measurement Default would be calculated by multiplying the credit payable for the fourth consecutive Critical Measurement Default by 1.50; (c) sixth subsequent consecutive Critical Measurement Default would be calculated by multiplying the credit payable for the fifth consecutive Critical Measurement Default by 1.75; and (d) seventh and subsequent consecutive Critical Measurement Defaults would be calculated by multiplying the credit payable for the sixth consecutive Critical Measurement Default by 1.75. Notwithstanding the foregoing, the At-Risk Pool will remain at 250 percent and the At-Risk Percentage will remain at 12 percent for the applicable Service Agreement.

Two issues remain to be mindful of when evaluating a service level scheme: low volume and earn-back credit provisions. Low volume provisions are exactly what they sound like. They allow for an adjustment mechanism to normalize low volume-affected critical service levels measured on a percentage basis, with fewer than 20 items measured by the service level, and when the service level is not 100 percent. Examples of service levels that may be subject to low volume provisions include the number of projects delivered on time, the number of projects delivered in accordance with the approved budget, or the number of approved changes implemented on time, all of which are expressed as a percentage. If the service level meets these criteria, the following formula applies:

Service Level = $(Y-1)/Y*100\%$
(Where Y is the total number of items in the Service Level measurement period).

For example purposes only, the following sample calculations illustrate how the above algorithm would function to determine the Service

Level (i.e. Changes Implemented within Schedule with a Service Level of 98 percent) in order to achieve this Service Level, in each case given a different number of total items occurring during the corresponding Measurement Period:

If the number of items is 17, the Service Level is 94%, $(17–1)/17*100\% = 94\%$

If the number of items is 10, the Service Level is 90% $(101)/10*100\% = 90\%$

If the number of items is 5, the Service Level is 80% $(5–1)/5* 100\% = 80\%$

If the number of items is 2, the Service Level is 50% $(2–1)/2 * 100\% = 50\%$

If the number of items is 1, the Service Level is 0% $(1–0)/1 * 100\% = 0\%$

The final component of the overall service level construct that I should discuss is the ability of the service provider to "earn back" service level credits accrued by the client in a prior period. Generally, a service provider can earn back such a credit if the service provider can meet or exceed the expected service level for measurement periods immediately after the measurement period (anywhere from three to four periods is reasonable) when the service level default generating the service level credit occurred. Although some clients and their counsel may reject an earn-back provision, I would say that it is a reasonable and legitimate component of a service level scheme.

Finally, the typical service level construct provides for the reporting requirements that the service provider must fulfill during the delivery term. Typically, the service provider is required to report its performance against the service levels no earlier than the 5th and no later than the 10th of the month. In addition to providing a report on performance, the service provider is required to describe any service level defaults and articulate a plan for corrective action. The service provider may also be required to identify any issues related to the prior period defaults that were caused or exacerbated by the acts or omissions of the client or any other vendor in the client's ecosystem, and conduct a root cause analysis as may be necessary.

Overall, service level schemes can be complex and have a significant number of moving parts. Given their importance, these schemes should be given plenty of attention during the negotiation process.

CHAPTER 47

I WANT A VOLUME DISCOUNT

In addition to seeking competitive rates for the services outsourced, clients seek a volume discount for all service agreements executed under a master service agreement. Generally, I am not a fan of discounting my services, especially when I have probably been hard-pressed by the client to do so during the selection process. If you are going to offer an additional discount tied to volume, you should set aggressive thresholds where the volume discount takes effect. In discounting, I follow the general rule that if you are going to give something, then you should be getting something in return—and that something should be something more than I would get in the ordinary course of business. I typically agree to offer the client a volume discount but only in exchange for its achieving volume targets that exceed its historical annual run rates. If you commit volume to my organization, I will reward you accordingly.

For the discount itself, I suggest a simple structure. Be mindful of the scope of the discount—is it limited to all service agreements executed under the master agreement or does it extend beyond the master agreement to all agreements executed during the measurement term? Once you determine the breadth of the discount, you need to look at which components of fees are included in the calculation. I would suggest calculating the volume discount based on total professional fees (excluding expenses, pass-through items, and disputed fees) paid by the client in a calendar year. I would also recommend calculating the volume discount incrementally and applying the discount earned as a credit toward professional fees in the following period instead of as a cash rebate. This way, I am ensuring a pipeline of future opportunities that the discount can be applied to instead of allowing the client to abscond with the cash and direct it to another service provider. An example of a volume discount structure is as follows:

TOTAL ANNUAL LABOR FEES	DISCOUNT PERCENTAGE	MAXIMUM REBATE PER TIER
0 – $2,500,000	0%	$0
$2,500,000 – $5,000,000	2.5%	$62,500
$5,000,000 – $10,000,000	5%	$250,000
$10,000,000+	10%	10% of fees in excess of $10,000,000

Given this incremental structure, the volume discount applies only to the incremental portion of the labor fee volume above the identified thresholds. For example, if total annual labor fees are $6,000,000, then the client receives a 0 percent discount on the first $2,500,000, a 2.5 percent discount on the next $2,500,000, and a 5 percent discount on the next $1,000,000, for a total of $112,500 that would be applied as a credit against professional fees in the following period. You may also want to include limitations on how much of the previously accrued volume discount can be applied to any single opportunity in the subsequent period.

SECTION 4

CHANGE IS IN THE AIR

CHAPTER 48

LET'S CHANGE THE WORLD

As I have discussed in great detail, the terms and conditions in an outsourcing agreement can be complex, and the implications for both parties can be significant. The introduction of automation and the "digitize or die" approach adds additional layers of complexity given the pace of change and the hybrid composition of the service provider workforce. I have always been fond of the quote, "In chaos comes opportunity" and I am a strong proponent of embracing the digital revolution when negotiating the outsourcing agreement of the future.

Despite the focus on innovation, I believe that the current sales cycle and procurement approach are inefficient across time, quality, and cost parameters and an industry shift is inevitable. Let's review the current environment:

1. The costs of third-party advisors and external legal counsel are prohibitive. Given the open-ended time and materials billing construct by which they are engaged, there is no incentive to change. In addition, clients may be naïve about market-relevant terms and conditions, and competitive pricing. They may blindly follow the lead of their legal counsel and advisors who may have a dual agenda in not only closing the transaction but also in moving the market standard.

2. The time associated with deal-shaping, downward pricing pressure, multiple down selections, decision gates, and checkpoints, and contentious and parallel negotiations with multiple vendors is unnecessarily long, resulting in a delay in commencing service

delivery and achieving the savings contained in the business case. In many instances, the solution driven by the third-party advisor—dropping the crate at the end of the driveway versus white-glove treatment—is not commensurate with the solution contemplated by the client. To that end, the terms and conditions are not based on collaboration and partnership, and the pricing evaluation is grounded in the notion that the service is nothing more than a commodity.

3. The contract templates developed by counsel are not balanced, are heavily skewed in favor of the client, are not commensurate with the market, and do not yield an acceptable level of risk and reward for both parties to the transaction. As I have discussed, industry standards exist for each substantive term and condition but are generally ignored as a starting point. This approach is not consistent with the long-term relationship contemplated by the parties because too much emphasis is placed on the consequences of failure versus collaborating for success.

4. Assuming an agreement is ultimately executed by the parties, the result is suboptimal. Relationships have been damaged, the best-suited vendor has not necessarily been selected, collaboration and innovation have become afterthoughts, and timely, quality, and cost-effective delivery has been compromised.

5. Ultimately, continuing with the status quo undermines the integrity of the business case and detrimentally affects any expected return on investment.

Given the current state of the outsourcing industry, I firmly believe that a change must occur, and it should embody the following structure:

Fixed-price or value-based advisory, legal, and negotiation costs.

• Expedited procurement life cycles—focus on existing preferred vendors and efficiency.

- Balanced and market-relevant contractual templates as starting points.
- An interest-based and principled negotiation process grounded in legitimacy.
- Focus on collaboration versus allocating blame and the consequences of failure.
- A contract that can flex, based on growth and advances in technology, and can govern future opportunities across the consulting life cycle.

If the industry can have the foresight to execute against the aforementioned structure, the anticipated value to be achieved is significant and will yield:

- Efficiency—a better, faster, and cheaper approach to procuring outsourcing services.
- Achieving the value proposition associated with the outsourced service.
- Significant reduction in procurement costs.
- Expedited time to service commencement and return on investment.
- Timely, quality, and cost-effective delivery.
- Trusted advisor relationships with service providers.

CHAPTER 49

RULES OF THE ROAD

As I thought about the content for the conclusion of this book, I considered a number of options. I could provide a detailed summary and recap of everything I discussed, filled with inspirational quotes and anecdotes. But I wanted to give you something practical that you could use long after you flipped past the last page of this book. In that spirit, I have decided to provide you with a list of my rules of the road—a set of guiding principles you can use to successfully negotiate terms and conditions that govern the delivery of outsourcing services. These rules apply regardless of the geography and industry in which you are engaged and the nature of the services provided. Although I do not *guarantee* success because I do not believe in that word, I do say that adhering to these principles leaves you well positioned for the successful negotiation and delivery of your outsourcing engagement in a timely, quality, and cost-effective manner.

They are as follows:

1. In chaos comes opportunity.

2. Focus on putting your best foot forward and agree that industry-standard terms are the starting and departure points from a negotiation perspective. Don't start on opposite ends of the spectrum. Instead, temper and fine-tune these standards to yield an acceptable level of risk and reward for the parties that is commensurate with the buyer values and delivery model. For the golfers out there, just liken it to surrounding the hole and then determining the line and pace necessary to sink the putt.

3. When negotiating terms and conditions, remember that you should never absorb a particular risk if you are not best able to control the events that may lead to its occurrence.

4. Focus on those components of the agreement that are most critical and that support the timely, quality, and cost-effective delivery of the services. These are the following: a narrowly tailored statement of work; absolute clarity on the roles and responsibilities of the parties; objective, measurable, and verifiable acceptance criteria and service levels; a well-documented governance process with mutual incentives to escalate issues early and often; any key assumptions and dependencies upon which the service provider's delivery is conditioned, especially in a multivendor delivery environment; and a change order process that is understood and strictly followed.

5. Irrespective of the service and the expertise of the service provider, you cannot outsource responsibility. The client and its respective IT and other supporting organizations still own the delivery and the service, and they must collaborate and work in partnership with their service provider to achieve success.

6. The current negotiation process for outsourcing agreements is inefficient from a time, quality, or cost perspective.

7. The overwhelming focus of the negotiation process is on the consequences of failure and the allocation of blame if there is a performance deficiency.

8. There is no value in having each party take an extreme position, then each agreeing to minor concessions over an extended period of time, and ultimately compromising, reaching a point where they both knew they would end up anyway—the market-relevant standard on that particular issue.

9. Caving in to a position after months of saying "no" is extremely frustrating, and erodes trust and credibility.

10.   Constantly asserting what other vendors may have or have agreed to lacks context and is irrelevant. Focus on market relevancy and let's stop playing games.

11.   There is no purpose in unnecessarily extending the sales cycle, creating tension among the parties, and detrimentally impacting a relationship that has yet to officially begin.

12.   Prudence dictates that the parties prepare for the consequences of failure; failing to do so would be negligent, to say the least. But a focus on partnership and collaboration is much more aligned with the mission, vision, and the trusted advisor relationships every IT service provider strives to achieve with its clients.

13.   A trusted advisor relationship with a client gives you credit in the bank, a seat at the table, the luxury of being considered for opportunities that may not fit exactly in your sweet spot, a first look at new opportunities, and insight into the client's agenda and priorities. This relationship, however, is by no means a guarantee of success.

14.   Trust matters, but it's the deal that counts.

15.   Don't be overly confident in relationships. The bottom line is that a 5 percent gap in price is an acceptable variance that would justify making an award to a higher-price vendor based on a best-value evaluation process. Don't hold out hope for the white knight; he is not coming.

16.   It is critical that you help procurement understand your value proposition. It is imperative to include procurement in your power map and manage those relationships in a manner consistent with other key stakeholders that may influence the buying decision.

17.   Make sure that the client is paying premium prices for premium services and that the prices they are paying for commodity services are competitive with those of other vendors in the marketplace.

18. If you decide to give additional incentives, concessions, or discounts, then make sure you are getting something in return—a volume commitment, preferred vendor status, access to the Csuite or to certain procurements historically reserved for other competitors, exclusive marketing rights to a particular entity or region, more favorable payment terms, changes in roles, responsibilities, or scope, or the elimination of high-risk terms and conditions. But make sure you get something in return and consider all possible options if you pursue this course of action.

19. When you have given all that you want to give and believe your rates are competitive in relation to those of other vendors in the market for similar services and reflect the level of risk in delivery, then remain calm, hold your ground, focus on your value proposition, make it clear that low price does not equal best value, consider your options and alternatives, and be prepared to say "no."

20. When negotiating a master agreement, it is critical to focus not only on the initial opportunity but also to develop a sustainable agreement with a rate structure and governing terms that can cross over the full consulting lifecycle.

21. Make sure that business leadership understands the legal issues, so they can retain control of the negotiation and bring the attorneys to the table only when absolutely necessary. Similarly, when they have been invited to the party, the attorneys need to understand the nature of the services contemplated in the transaction and the amount of risk in delivery. If you follow this approach, their level of competitive arousal can be kept in check, and reaching agreement on key terms and conditions can be achieved.

22. Temper your approach based on the amount of risk in delivery.

23. Temper your approach based on the geographic region where you are engaged.

24. Temper your approach based on the individual sitting across from you at the negotiation table.

25. In the words of Senator George Mitchell, always be mindful that "conflicts are created, conducted, and sustained by human beings and can be resolved by human beings."

26. In addition to the aforementioned four core principles, it is important to remember that every negotiation that you are engaged in has seven elements. Your ability to identify these elements, identify their connectivity, and, most important, understand how they evolve during a negotiation is the most important key to success.

27. If you are going to leave the negotiation table, then make sure you are truly prepared to leave the table and accept any consequences that come with that action.

28. Approach every negotiation as the New York Giants did for Super Bowl XLVI: Humble enough to prepare, confident enough to perform.

29. Keep in mind that the primary reason projects fail is *scope creep*, or deviations from the agreed-on scope in the statement of work. According to the Standish Group, only 37 percent of IT projects are completed successfully; 42 percent go over budget, are not completed on time, or do not deliver what they are supposed to; and 21 percent flat out fail. One of the primary reasons identified as contributing to this dynamic is a failure by the parties to properly define scope.

30. A clear set of assumptions regarding a variety of intervening factors and dependencies upon which the timely and quality delivery by the service provider is conditioned is an absolute necessity when negotiating an outsourcing agreement.

31. No matter what the circumstances, immediately escalate and seek relief for any performance deficiency caused by the client or a third party.

32. For an effective governance process, the parties must be willing to exercise their rights under the process immediately upon recognizing that a dispute exists.

33. An efficient change order process is when both parties to the transaction are clear that there will be no deviations in scope unless a written change order has been executed by the parties. No exceptions to this rule are allowed, regardless of the exigency of the circumstances.

34. For each of the stipulated milestones or critical deliverables in an outsourcing engagement, a set of objective, measurable, and verifiable acceptance criteria must be identified.

35. Do not play pin the tail on the donkey with mission-critical applications needed to run the client's business. Focus on legitimate service levels, not aspirations or pipe dreams.

36. Like executing a statement of work for the entire outsourced service, a discrete transition plan must be drafted that clearly articulates the transition phases, the transition timeline, any transition milestones or deliverables, as well as any critical deliverables that must be accepted by the client before transition is completed and the run phase of the engagement can begin. In addition, the transition plan should clearly articulate the roles and responsibilities of the parties as well as the specific activities, quality gates, and corresponding acceptance criteria that must be met before the service provider can navigate through the transition phases.

37. Carefully review the activities that must be completed before the service provider can move from one transition phase to the next. As with any acceptance criteria, make sure that they are objective, measurable, and verifiable. If not, the service provider could remain in the transition phases much longer than anticipated.

38.   Do not accept the approach taken by third-party advisors that transition is the service provider's responsibility, with limited input from the client.

39.   For a sweeps provision, carefully manage the size of the broom. Better yet, keep it the size of a handheld dustpan capable of sweeping in no more than a de minimis number (no more than 5 percent) of additional delivery obligations to the service provider.

40.   Managed service fees should be adjusted when there have been material changes in the volume of tickets or incidents supported, or in the number of service recipients.

41.   Although it may be legitimate for a client to have the ability to insource or resource an application or some portion of the outsourced services, there must be a threshold identified that, once crossed, requires that the client continue to pay at that threshold or renegotiate the base charges for the remaining scope of the outsourced service. If such a threshold did not exist, a client could continue to remove scope from a service provider with no consequences, in essence, a no-cost termination for convenience.

42.   For every software and non-software deliverable, as well as for any milestone, there must be a set of objective, measurable, and verifiable acceptance criteria—capabilities, functions, specifications, descriptions, or standards against which the deliverable is reviewed and tested.

43.   Define a reasonable time window when the client can test the deliverables and milestones to determine if they conform to the acceptance criteria.

44.   If the client does not respond after a reasonable time window has elapsed, acceptance should be deemed to have occurred.

45.   Determine what, if any, actions taken by the client with regard to the deliverables trigger acceptance.

46.   Identify the process that must be strictly adhered to by the parties when a deliverable is accepted, rejected, and repaired and retendered, and the remedies available to the client if the service provider cannot achieve acceptance after multiple delivery attempts have occurred.

47.   The bottom line is that the multivendor delivery environments are here to stay, and service providers and clients need to determine how to find the appropriate balance among cooperation and quality delivery and allowing its vendors to maintain the integrity of their intellectual property that gives them a competitive advantage in the marketplace.

48.   Cooperation provisions also reinforce the absolute requirement that statements of work are clear and concise about the roles and responsibilities of the parties. If there are discrete handoffs between different vendors, those lines of demarcation must be clearly drawn, especially when the clock is running, service levels are being measured, and service level defaults that may have a significant financial impact are likely.

49.   The service provider is responsible for complying with laws that apply to its business and to the provision of the services. The client is responsible for all laws that apply to its business. If the client has outsourced a service that requires the service provider to comply with any laws that apply to the outsourced service, then the client provides the service provider with a compliance directive that directs the service provider on how a particular law or regulation should be implemented on the client's behalf.

50.   With regard to changes in laws, the general rule is that each party is responsible for the cost of remaining in compliance with laws that apply to its business.

51.   Although conducting a background check on service provider staff meets a legitimate client interest, the scope, recurrence, and cost of such checks should be tempered by the scope of the services provided, the data that the service provider team has access to, and the industry where the client resides.

52.   There is no standard for the number of key personnel. Given the importance of these roles and the restrictions placed on these individuals, the roles and individuals should be carefully selected in a manner that is consistent with the nature, complexity, and scope of the services provided.

53.   Unique nuances are associated with an outsourcing engagement. The service provider truly steps into the shoes of the client during delivery. Therefore, the parties must prepare for the following: how the service provider makes its IP available for the client to receive the benefit of the services; how the service provider shares its IP with other vendors in the client ecosystem; and how service provider IP that becomes such an intricate part of the services will survive a post-termination or post service agreement expiration event.

54.   Seek pre-approval in each service agreement for a list of potential locations for service delivery. Under this construct, the service provider still must notify the client about a potential move but retains the flexibility to provide its services from any pre-approved location.

55.   When seeking relief under a savings clause, do so without delay and be mindful of the following questions: (1) When did the service provider first identify that the client or third party failed to meet its performance obligations? (2) Once the service provider realized that the client's deficiency would cause its nonperformance, did the service provider immediately notify the client? In writing? (3)

Irrespective of its nonperformance, did the service provider take measures to mitigate the impact of the nonperformance?

56. Be mindful of the state of the applications that are transitioned in an applications management outsourcing engagement as well as any client architectural standards at the time of contract execution. Make sure that the client does not expect and that the contract is clear that the service provider will not bring the applications into conformance with the client's IT policies or architectural standards before exiting transition.

57. Follow a "no surprises" approach to successful client and contract management, and maintain an open channel where both the client and service provider proactively address potential problems before they turn into formal disputes.

58. When the delivery of services begins, it is advisable to execute a change order so that both parties can become accustomed to the rigor of this process. Even if it is a no-cost change order of little consequence, this instills discipline in the parties because it highlights the importance of formally documenting any changes in or deviations from the original statement of work.

59. The following principle should apply to unilateral changes in client policies that impact service delivery: If you change, you pay.

60. Don't let your blood pressure get too high about audits and insurance. Let the subject matter experts hash out the details and a reasonableness standard should apply.

61. The tax provision in an outsourcing agreement should have one objective: Neither party pays a dollar more in taxes than necessary.

62. Despite all the attention it receives, the benchmarking provision is seldom exercised by clients because it is expensive, time consuming for both parties, and, frankly, not necessary for a client to rely on to seek changes to the agreement, whether it be terms and conditions or price. So relax on this issue and maintain a reasonableness standard.

63. Do not agree to any form of an auto-adjustment provision. It is not legitimate for a third party to introduce a report that automatically resets price, which is a key component of the bargain.

64. For personal data, avoid handling it at all costs. If you must, agree on specific data-handling protocols and require least privileged access.

65. In the spirit of the four corners rule and to avoid disputes that lack substance, strive for an agreement that is clear about the performance obligations of the parties and that has objective, measurable, and verifiable acceptance criteria and performance standards.

66. In establishing the overall scope of an indemnity provision, take the following approach:

Questions:
- Is the "action/omission/event" for which an indemnity is requested by the client within the service provider's control?
- Are the "general" or "broad" indemnities requested by the client covered by one or more of the specific indemnities requested?

Core Principle:
Indemnities, which are excluded from the liability cap, must be reasonable and limited in a service contract; otherwise, the liability cap is, in essence, meaningless.

67. Remember the following: "Just because you have always done it that way does not mean it's not incredibly stupid."

68. And while you're at it, live less out of habit and more out of intent.

69. It is legitimate and time well spent for the parties to focus on what should happen if a catastrophic event occurs that impedes the ability of the parties to perform their obligations under the agreement.

70. Do not allow the client or a third party to step in and take over the delivery reins, even in the most egregious circumstances. Termination is a much more desirable option.

71. For an informal dispute resolution process to be effective, it must be clear about how a dispute is initiated, who is empowered to make settlement decisions, and the timeline that must elapse for good-faith discussions at each hierarchical level before the dispute escalates further or before the parties can seek intervention through arbitration or a court of competent jurisdiction.

72. Be a strong proponent of an expedient informal dispute escalation process by allowing no more than 30 days for a dispute to navigate through the hierarchical levels. Having a dispute hanging over the delivery environment is not in either party's best interests.

73. Although prudence may dictate that termination rights are in the agreement, there should be an objective, steady, and reserved hand on the trigger, as it comes with extreme and what can be uncomfortable consequences for both the service provider and the client.

74. Develop a complete list of dependencies upon which the service provider's timely, quality, and cost-effective performance is conditioned. Failure to do so will likely lead to a dispute.

75. Outsourcing services are not delivered in a vacuum; the parties must work together to achieve success. The scope and complexity of a typical outsourcing engagement, combined with the ever-present multivendor ecosystem, dictates that even the best outsourcing services provider must rely on the client and the other vendors in its ecosystem to meet its service levels and achieve delivery success.

Given that dynamic, figure out how to play nicely in the sandbox with the other children and have the contract support it.

76. The service provider should always be excused from performance where the client or its agents fail to meet any dependency that the service provider must rely on or that its delivery is conditioned on. Period. Hard stop. Any other result is not legitimate and makes the service provider take responsibility for a risk it does not control.

77. Any agreement for outsourcing services must have a formal change order process that must be strictly adhered to for **any** change made during the delivery term.

78. When thinking about deferring the execution of a change order, ask yourself: Why bother executing a narrowly tailored statement of work with clarity on roles and responsibilities if you are not going to document any changes that are made during the delivery term?

79. Like acceptance criteria, service levels must be objective, measurable, and verifiable.

80. Customer satisfaction and other subjective service levels should be non-promotable key measures over the agreement term.

81. When evaluating client-stated service levels, try to understand how the service level targets were established. Are they currently being achieved by the client or an existing service provider or are they purely aspirational? If it is the latter, proceed with caution.

82. If the service levels are purely aspirational, you should require a six-month baseline period when actual performance is measured but the service provider is not subject to service level credits. Alternatively, a presumptive service level construct can be used.

83. If you agree to purely aspirational service level targets with limited or no due diligence process, and are subject to service level credits

Day 1 of delivery, I have a viable alternative: Fill a suitcase with the proposed fees you expect to receive under the engagement. Skip the negotiations. Head directly to the high-limit slot, or the roulette or blackjack table at the nearest casino, because the odds of success under this construct are a coin flip, at best. And if you go forward with the agreement anyway, go to the sports book and bet every penny on a performance-related termination event before Month 6.

84. When evaluating a no-cost termination right related to the recurrence of critical service level defaults annually, be mindful of the number of monthly measuring points and the threshold for error before such a right is triggered. And please do not be overconfident in your delivery capabilities.

85. Irrespective of the number of service level defaults in a given month, in no event can the client recover more than the fees at risk. No matter what.

86. Successfully selling any product or service requires brand awareness, quality products and services, and a reference base that speaks to your ability to deliver a similar solution in a timely, quality, and cost-effective manner. Do not lose sight of this in the sales process.

87. Bring references or go home. Unless you can provide references where you have delivered a similar solution, do not expect an easy road to success.

88. Avoid being commoditized. Carefully articulate your value proposition and the distinct advantages that differentiate you from the competition. Once procurement or anyone in the buying community renders the services you are providing as commodities, procurement will focus very heavily on price and migrate to the low-cost provider.

89. **Buyer beware:** remember that the bitterness of poor quality is remembered long after the sweetness of low prices is forgotten.

90. It is very difficult and costly to unseat a firmly entrenched competitor that is delivering in a timely, quality, and cost-competitive manner. It may be more prudent to focus your sales efforts elsewhere.

91. Never, under any circumstance, commingle resources from one rate card with another's. If you commingle resources, you completely undermine the integrity of the differentiated pricing structure and lose credibility and trust with the client. This is a problem from which you will not be able to recover.

92. If procurement is benchmarking your rates, make sure that you are being evaluated against similar vendors delivering similar services. Work diligently with procurement on this issue.

93. Offer volume discounts where appropriate based on a set of predefined contracting volume materiality thresholds, the duration of the engagement, or the size of the team. Offer the discount as a credit against future work (rather than as a cash rebate) to ensure a long-term pipeline with the client. In any event, keep the discounting scheme as simple as possible.

94. Provide a rate card structure that serves all contemplated delivery geographies—provide rates in local currency commensurate with the cost profile in that country or region.

95. Agree on the prevailing rate card (home location versus location where services are being delivered) for resources that will be crossing geographic boundaries for service delivery.

96. Agree upon a policy for rate increases and labor category re-slotting resulting from staff promotions during the engagement.

97. If you decide to give additional incentives, concessions, or discounts, make sure you are getting something substantive in return.

98. It is OK to tell the client "no" and to state that your offer is firm and final.

99. Make every attempt to keep your competitive arousal in check when negotiating terms and conditions and rate cards. Focus on seeking to understand the opposing party versus seeking to be understood.

100. Remember that no deal is better than a bad deal.

101. Do not get engaged in sport discounting. Remember that you are no more likely to win the deal with a nominal discount than with a mid-size discount. It takes zero negotiation skill to provide a client with what you believe to be a competitive price for your services if you intend only to discount it by 30 percent two weeks later in the negotiation process.

102. Be smart: If you agree to a price concession, it really raises the question about the integrity, and potential over-inflation, of the initial price submission. Let us not forget the following principle: If your client does not trust you, then you might as well call it a day and play golf.

103. When it comes to changing the sales and negotiation process for outsourcing services, remember the quote by John Paul DeJoria, the founder of John Paul Mitchell Systems: "Pay attention to the vital few and ignore the trivial many."

104. Do not be afraid—humans can and will peacefully co-exist with the robots.

105. Buckle up—it should be a wild ride.

With these rules in your hand, I'll look forward to seeing you in the market.

Made in the USA
Columbia, SC
11 September 2019